With My Own Eyes

With My Own Eyes

By Bo Giertz

TRANSLATED BY BROR ERICKSON

An Imprint of 1517 the Legacy Project

With My Own Eyes

© 2017 Bo Giertz

Published by:
NRP Books/New Reformation Publications
PO Box 54032
Irvine, CA 92619-4032

Publisher's Cataloging-In-Publication Data
(Prepared by The Donohue Group, Inc.)

Names: Giertz, Bo, 1905–1998. | Erickson, Bror, translator.
Title: With my own eyes / by Bo Giertz ; translated by Bror Erickson.
Other Titles: Med egna ögon. English
Description: Irvine, CA : NRP Books, [2017] | Translation of: Med egna ögon.
    Stockholm : Svenska kyrkans diakonistyrelses förlag, 1947.
Identifiers: ISBN 978-1-945978-53-1 (hardcover) | ISBN 978-1-945978-54-8
    (softcover) | ISBN 978-1-945978-52-4 (ebook)
Subjects: LCSH: Bible. Gospels—Criticism, interpretation, etc. | Bible.
    Gospels—Commentaries.
Classification: LCC BS2555 .G5413 2017 (print) | LCC BS2555 (ebook) |
    DDC 226/.06—dc23

Printed in the United States of America.

NRP Books, an imprint of New Reformation Publications is committed to packaging and promoting the finest content for fueling a new Lutheran Reformation. We promote the defense of the Christian faith, confessional Lutheran theology, vocation and civil courage.

Cover design by Peter Voth (http://www.PeterVoth.de)

Contents

Preface

"That half year cured me of my liberal theology. I could read my Bible with completely new eyes. It smelled of earth and daily life. It reflected a reality that one could still see with their own eyes. Many of the theories and arguments that the radicals regarded as irreversible all fell together like a house of cards. They were desktop productions, wisdom from the Western ivory tower that assessed the oriental environment based on its own very narrow conditions. So the result has often been just as timestamped and short-lived as the starched cuffs these authors used to wear."[1]

This is how Bo Giertz would later recall the time he spent in Palestine, the trip he would translate into *With My Own Eyes*. It was 1931. This was at the tail end of his studies in Uppsala, where he had been considering pursuing a PhD in theology under Anton Fridrichsen, who had begun advocating for a "realistic interpretation of the Bible" in contrast to the liberal interpretations that ruled the nineteenth and early twentieth centuries (though it would not be until 1936 that Fridrichsen would put this theological program to print). Giertz had started in Uppsala as a radical atheist who planned on becoming a medical doctor like his father. However, through the influence of Christian intellectuals on the campus, he became a Christian and changed his course of study to become a pastor. It was then that he came into contact with his mentor, Fridrichsen.

---

[1] Bo Giertz, quoted by Folke T. Oloffsson in "Bo Giertz teologiska väg fram till Torpa" from *Talet om korset—Guds kraft: till hundraårsminnet av Bo Giertz födelse*, ed. Rune Imberg (Göteborg: Församlingsförlaget, 2005), 120. My translation.

Giertz would ultimately drop his ambitions for a PhD after this trip to Palestine. He came to realize that he really wanted to be a parish pastor. Such was his love for the church. Still, later in life, Giertz would say that he spent his whole career trying to disseminate what he had received from Fridrichsen. This is nowhere more apparent than in *With My Own Eyes*.

When Giertz left for his trip to Palestine, Fridrichsen admonished him, "Go and see everything. Take it all in. See every place. Walk every valley. Experience and commit to memory every change in color, scent, and day so that you can see every biblical narrative against a real background."[2] This was the idea behind Fridrichsen's push for a "realistic interpretation of the Bible." He understood that these stories recorded actual events that took place in a real setting, in a particular historical background, and were not just fables and legends edited and put together by later generations with no connection to the real historical Jesus Christ. He was done with the Jesus of liberal theology that refused to take the Biblical texts and what they had to say about Jesus seriously. In his view, "the faith of early Christianity in Jesus as Lord had its roots in Jesus' own Messianic self-consciousness."[3] With this in mind, it was Fridrichsen's idea that "when it came to interpreting a text the scholar had to use not only his philological knowledge, but also his knowledge of the historical, cultural and religious environment in which the text had originated and which the text sought to elucidate."[4]

It is unfortunate that Fridrichsen was never able to produce more than the small monographs and articles he wrote as a professor. He had plans to produce commentaries on Mark and the book of Acts, but he died long before. It would be left for his student Giertz to translate this program into production, which he did in his sermons (published posthumously), his own commentaries on the New Testament, his devotional *To Live with Christ*, and perhaps most strikingly in *With My Own Eyes*.

---

[2] Algot Mattsson, *Bo Giertz: ateisten som blev biskop* (Göteborg: Tre Böcker Förlag, 1991), 64. My translation.

[3] Erik Beijer "Anton Fridrichsen as Academic Teacher in the Service of the Church," introduction to *Exegetical Writings: A Selection*, by Anton Fridrichsen, trans. Chrys C. Caragounis and Tord Fornberg (Eugene, OR: Wipf and Stock Publishers, 1994), 10.

[4] Ibid., 18.

Fridrichsen himself accompanied Giertz for a time on the trip to Palestine that inspired this book. It was cathartic for both of them, especially in regards to the liberal theology with which they were increasingly dissatisfied. When they both returned to Sweden, Fridrichsen arranged for his lifelong friend Rudolf Bultmann to come to Stockholm. Giertz records that when Fridrichsen tried to explain to Bultmann how much he had come to understand in a new manner after encountering the land and the milieu, Bultmann had no time for it: "For him, theology and Christianity were a system of thought, a philosophy, and the gospel a product of men's conceptions that theologians were supposed to analyze."[5]

Giertz writes *With My Own Eyes* using his notes and memories from the half year he spent in Palestine at a time when farmers still sorted the wheat from the chaff with a winnowing fork and the fisherman on the Sea of Galilee still plied their trade in the manner of the apostles Peter, James, and John. He combines all this with a profound understanding of the Biblical texts that was born out of a true love for God's word and an earnest desire to understand it completely. His undergrad degree in classics shows its worth as he uses extra biblical literature such as that by Josephus and Juvenal to paint the picture surrounding the gospels. As always, he writes for the sake of the readers.

Giertz was, for all his genius, a profoundly humble man who did not care for academic accolades. He wrote for the layman. This isn't to say he didn't care for academic theology. He knew it all well. But he cared for the church. He wanted to build it up. He wanted to feed the sheep that were entrusted to his care. He wanted them to hear the gospel so that in hearing they might believe and have hope. He knew what it was like to live without that hope, without the forgiveness of sins. He wanted to cure everyone he could of a life lived like that, as that half year in Palestine healed him of his liberal theology. He wanted them to understand and believe in Jesus so that they might walk in the newness of life, sharing the same hope and love of Christ that brought such joy to his own life. This is why he wrote *With My Own Eyes*.

---

[5] Mattsson, *Bo Giertz*, 65.

It was this warmhearted pastoral approach to the task of writing that first endeared me to the writings of Giertz and has caused me to find such great joy in translating them since.

With My Own Eyes has seen itself in English translation before in Britain. I first read it in that translation. At first, my plans were to somehow get that translation back into print. However, when talking with Bo Giertz's daughter Birgitta about copyright issues surrounding the book, she asked me if I wouldn't just retranslate it for the American market with updated English. So I bought an original copy of the Swedish for considerably less money than I could find any of the English translations and went to work.

It has been a blessing to me many times over as I have come to greater understanding of the Biblical texts myself. I hope that you find as much joy reading it as I have found translating it. With that in mind, I would like to thank my wife, Laura, for her patience with me as I toiled on this project, and Zion Evangelical Lutheran Church of Farmington, New Mexico, for supporting me in these efforts.

Your Brother in Christ,
Bror Erickson
Second Sunday after Pentecost, 2017

Prelude

I.

A blistering-hot wind blew in from the dry steppes filling the evening air with dust and coloring the sky with clouds of violet brown as the sun descended. The sparse grain stubble of the fields glistened orange on the dark-soiled surface while the city's high stone walls shimmered in the glowing sun.

Once again, the sweaty men adjusted their chainmail and threw insults up toward the top of the wall. The men on the wall answered with a block of stone that broke against the rock below and splintered into a cloud of chalk dust. Men on the ground turned aside as the shards clinked against their shiny armor. They laughed with contempt. They had been at it for several hours now.

Uriah was standing just a bit off to the side. His shield already had two broken arrows in it. He knew that anything could come whistling down from up there, but he only kept half an eye directed toward the city wall. He gazed out beyond, to the endless expanses where the desert began and to the long rows of hills in the west, where the sun went down like red copper in the dense haze. He held the shaft of his spear so tightly that the dark skin of his hands yellowed at his knuckles.

He did not know how long he had been standing this way. He hardly noticed that he was staring straight into the sun before he closed his eyes to see dark flecks dancing in the flickering sea of fire. His heart was in Jerusalem, and now he was replaying everything over again in his head for the hundredth time.

It had been one week since he had been given the task. As if borne on wings, he had traveled to Jerusalem through the suffocating heat of the Jordan Valley and climbed over the mountains on the other side. It was so inconceivable that he, a Hittite, would receive the honor of being envoy to the king, to return home while the others lie on the hot ground outside of Rabba. When he crested the last hill and saw the city clinging to the ridge, he stood and dried the sweat from his forehead as he smiled at the view. There was the king's palace, towering high above the cluster of small houses. And there, almost at its foot, so close that the shadow of the palace tower fell upon it in the noonday sun, was his own house, sandwiched between the walls, with its small courtyard, two low doors, and the little pool of water. And she was there too.

The king gave him a warm reception on the carpet. When he finished explaining the siege and losses, he was graciously told to go to his own house in peace and wash his feet. On the way down through the dirty alley, a servant of the king greeted him with a brown earthenware jug of wine and a delicious-smelling bowl of stew, salutations of the king, bidding his servant Uriah a joyous evening.

Uriah took the gifts in his arms. It was at that moment the evil eye met him. It made his heart sick.

Did it come from David's servant? Was there something ambiguous and meaningful behind the eyes of this dutiful and respectful mask, something at once both compassionate and impudent? Or was it one of the evil demons of the twilight that would gladly run him through with thoughts of what happened in these alleys while he was gone?

He stopped and almost dropped the wine jug in the street. Now he remembered how he had seen the king's palace tower above his own little house, overlooking, commanding, and foreboding.

He stood before the gates, the poor little wooden doors in the bare walls against the street, the gates he had longed for with all his heart and all his body. He took a deep breath and placed the king's gifts on the threshold in complete silence so as not to be heard. Then he returned quietly, as if he was afraid of being caught. He had made his decision. He would have clarity. If this was the situation, then he would not be made a fool. She would be held accountable. He would not help cover it up.

That night, he slept in the suffocating stone halls outside the castle where the gate guard stood and where mobilized men could spend the night when they gathered in Jerusalem. In the morning, he got ready to travel back through the desert with sullen silence. But then another summons came from the king. The message caused his thoughts to flare with a searing suspicion. Once again, King David was his friendly self, patronizing and laughing. His eyes twinkled but seemed to hide something behind their joviality when he asked why the long distance courier had not gone home to sleep in his own house. Uriah himself was amazed at the serenity in his voice when he answered: "The ark and Israel and Judah dwell in booths, and my lord Joab and the servants of my lord are camping in the open field. Shall I then go to my house, to eat and drink and lie with my wife?"

The king looked him in the eye, calmly and appreciatively, as only a king can do. Yet he still betrayed himself. He asked Uriah to stay for another day. He asked him to sit at the table and gave him sweet heavy wine. And Uriah drank it. In wild spite, he drank in a rush and then gave thanks and left. He imagined how the wandering eyes followed him inside the palace. In defiant triumph, he pulled his mantle about him and laid down on the stone slabs between the archways. He laid there, watching the stars wander across the heavens as he was consumed by hate for her whom he had loved more than his own life just two days before. And yet, could he really hate?

The next morning, he slept off his hangover before taking the royal letter in hand. He went on his way without many words. But that day, he was not born on wings through the hill country's oven-like heat and sun-swept paths.

Now he stood here looking into the dark dust clouds that swirled in from the desert. They swept the entire besieged city in smoke. His body felt decrepit and old. His vitality was gone, his limbs heavy and callous. His heart did nothing but ache.

Something hissed toward him, and he instinctively raised the heavy shield just in time to keep the arrow from piercing his face below the eye. He hit the arrow shaft with his lance. This was the third he carried in the shield today.

In that same moment, a whole shower of arrows sailed like a swarm of whistling birds down about them. The men closed ranks behind their shields in expectation of what would come, and in the next moment, the little gate in the corner between the long wall and the tower opened for a swarm of defenders, who rushed out screaming as they swung their swords and spears.

Uriah hurried over to his comrades and took his place like an annoyed ram. Then he rushed toward the screaming men. Another minute, and he was in the midst of the maelstrom's confusion where swords crashed against the shield wall. Suddenly, he sensed that he was surrounded. He tried to look around, and with a quick glance over his shoulder, he caught a glimpse of his comrades beating a quick retreat to camp. Then he threw himself against the attack again.

That was when the same evil pierced Uriah's heart for the second time, the same poisoned arrow that had met him in the street just outside his own house. In a moment of bitter clarity, he saw the connection. He was outwitted. The king had won the game. In a wild wrath, he tried to hack his way out. He wanted to hold the guilty responsible. But an Ammonite spear point had already pierced his armor.

*

The road to the king's hall was long.

Never had it seemed so long as it did today. At first, it was all the narrow streets with the hills and slippery mud. Then it was the gates, the courts, and the vestibules. Then it was the long series of salons and waiting rooms, arched stone chambers, and interconnecting covered walkways.

There amidst the dim shadows, Nathan was seized by the desire to see sunlight and the clear-blue autumn sky once again. He was still a man, but it would be certain death if he was to think like a man. He may as well have stood under the watch tower and asked the guard to drop one of the heavy blocks they kept for attackers upon him. But he was driven forth by an invisible hand, and his steps became ever more confident with every new threshold he crossed. Now he stood in the waiting room just outside the throne room, which would otherwise throng with shepherds seeking help, and the owners of orchards and vineyards. The walls were full of trophies, the golden shields of Hadadezer, and bronze plates from Berothai. Everything displayed the power and the successful campaigns that had followed the great king because God anointed him.

The veil was pulled aside by a slave dressed in blue, and Nathan was allowed to enter. As usual, the king was alone when he received the prophet. He looked at him questioningly. Was there some word from the Lord? Was there something not right in the land?

Yes, there was.

The prophet's answer was short and picturesque. Two men lived in the same city, the one rich and the other poor. The rich man had herds in abundance, the poor man a single lamb that he had purchased. It grew up with his sons. It ate from his table. It drank from his glass, and was like a daughter to him. Then a sojourner came to be a guest in the rich man's house. But the rich man didn't have the heart to touch his many sheep. Instead, he took the poor man's lamb and prepared it for his guest.

That was all. The prophet stood quietly and waited for the royal judgment. It came like a bolt of lightning from a dark cloud: execute the man who acted so mercilessly and provide fourfold compensation for the lamb.

Then Nathan lifted his arm, pointed at his lord the king, and said, "You are the man."

And then came a flash of thunder against which all human anger would seem pale and tranquil, a wrath that was not human, not bitter nor spiteful, but pure, calm, and full of an authority that lent a sense of naturalness to the unbelievable words, words that otherwise could not be said before this all-powerful king: The Lord says I have given you everything, and I am even willing to give you more. But you have murdered Uriah the Hittite. You have murdered him with the sword of Ammon's children. You have taken his wife for yourself. And worst of all, you have become an enemy of the Lord and despise him. For this reason, disaster shall fall upon your own house.

The lightning had discharged. The king sat quietly. He was free to scoff, to call in the bodyguards, to rid himself of this offender of his majesty. But none of this happened. The king only bowed his head and said, "I have sinned."

And Nathan answered, "So also the Lord forgives your sin; you shall not die."

The prophet continued to speak sternly and with authority above the king's bowed head. There was no refuge from this authoritative word. Yes, there was defiance and insincere righteousness. But the king could not go in that direction despite his human passion and lust. The word was great and sent for him. He was bound by this word.

All of his people were bound by it. For centuries—no one really knew how long—the Lord had ruled over this people with his promises and his deeds, his word and his law. It had begun when the command came to Abraham to leave his land and pursue an uncertain future in a strange country with nothing but the Lord's promise. He had done it. He had been faithful even to the point of sacrificing his own son. And the Lord had blessed him.

There had been an inescapable earnestness since the day when the Lord had brought the fathers out of Egypt and led them through the desert to the land he had promised them. When they crossed the Jordan, they had carried an ark with them, a testament and a law that separated them from all other people. If they tried to break loose from this God who had chosen them, he sent judges and prophets. If they tried to go against his will, they were burned by his zeal. They had tried innumerable times to worship the deities of the vineyards and wheat fields, the Baals and Ashtoreths that gave good harvests, who sustained licentiousness and turned a blind eye to false oaths and dishonest scales. But they had not been able to go their own way.

No one was able to do that, not even the king. Nathan had the last word. Without waiting for the king's permission, he had turned back and the gates opened for him. But the king remained on his throne, his head bowing deep under the Lord's hand.

II.

Two vultures swept their heavy wings over the camp. They made a beeline straight to Michmash, where the flock of birds hovered above the field of corpses. The men on the ground watched them sullenly. It was part of the plague that filled their days. They had to watch as the birds circled above the hills or sat stuffed and bloated upon the mounds of rubble. Nobody cared about it anymore. They had lost their ability to be horrified after fire broke out in Solomon's Temple and the plundering Chaldeans hunted children and women like hares in the alleys. The last king of the House of David had had his eyes gouged out after his children were slaughtered in his presence. God's temple had become a pile of stone. God's own people were sent to their ruin in Chaldean slave camps. The last of those who carried the power, glory, and fear of God in Judah lay on the ground in rags, chained together, dirty and sore. Demoralized and dejected, they waited their turn to be transported to unknown lands in the east.

Irijah, son of Shelemiah, turned his disgusted eyes from the plain where the blackened ruins of Rama rose against the blue summer sky, and with his head to the ground, he cursed the day of his birth. Deaf and embittered, the words rose from the hot earth that he almost touched with his lips. He cursed the day he received the sign of circumcision on his body and was received into the people who called upon God in vain. He praised the fortunate heathens who never heard the LORD's name and were never tempted to believe that he chose Zion to be his dwelling place or bound his name to Jerusalem. He wished that he had never heard the names of any gods other than those of Marduk and Nergal, Astart and Baal. They were good divinities that did not jealously watch over their worshipers or intervene in their people's most secret deeds. They were satisfied if one sacrificed and served them in the temple.

Ebed-Melech, the Ethiopian, stretched out his skinny arms so that the chains rattled against the stones on the ground in an attempt to silence the blasphemer's mouth. His thin lips opened to expose small teeth. He spoke fiercely, but only half as loud as the hungry normally did.

"Do you want to trade?" he said.

Irijah lifted his head from the ground for a moment and gave him a spiteful look.

"What should I trade with you, skeleton? Do we not both share the same condemnation?"

"I'll trade all the gods for whom I burned smoke in my days for your right to belong to the LORD's people."

Irijah's voice was bitterly derisive.

"More than happy to! That would be like trading an old, fat, and senile wife who wasn't at all faithful for a harem full of sixteen-year-olds. I'll trade!"

The others began to listen. They barely lifted their dirty matted heads from the ground, but their eyes came alive within their emaciated faces. Only Ebed-Melech sat up. His blue calves were like reeds and the skin on his feet looked like old cracked papyrus.

"Listen up, Irijah," he said. "You don't know what you are trading away. What would your people be without the LORD?"

"Fortunate," Irijah said quietly. Then he turned on his side. It seemed that he had been a handsome man before the siege and famine. "A thousand times more fortunate than now! If we had never been duped to believe that he lived on Mount Zion and that his temple was worth more than all other temples."

Ebed-Melech took a moment. Then he said, "You duped yourself, Irijah. Because the LORD chose Zion among all the mountains on earth, you believed that you would always have him on your side. Here is the LORD's temple. You saw. But then you broke your covenant and took back the slave upon whom you had bestowed freedom, because you believed that everything would work out in the end!"

Irijah raised his voice. In his prime, it would have sounded like thunder, but now his vocal chords betrayed him, and he sounded hoarse and shrill.

"You black idiot, do you comprehend nothing? Do you not understand that we have been duped? Had he really chosen Zion, then he would not let the Chaldeans trample in the Holy of Holies!"

"Why not?"

Irijah was speechless. All around people fixed their gaze on the little Ethiopian. He put his head in his hands as if it was too heavy for his emaciated neck.

"Does he need us?" Ebed-Melech said slowly. "He who made the mountains, and heavens, and the earth, and all that moves upon them."

Then Irijah got his voice back:

"But if no one knows him? If he has only one temple in the world and it is burned up? If he has one chosen people and they are lost?"

"They won't be lost," the Ethiopian said slowly.

"How do you know that?"

"He himself has said it."

Irijah growled contemptuously. He laid facedown and dug his nails into the earth. Those who believed the doomed prophets didn't deserve answers.

Ebed-Melech nodded slowly.

"In the first year of Nebuchadnezzar's reign, which was Jehoiakim's fourth, Jeremiah prophesied . . ."

"Don't speak of that traitor!"

". . . prophesied and said, 'Because you have not obeyed my words, I shall send and take all the northern tribes; I shall send word to my servant Nebuchadnezzar, and I will bring them against this land and these inhabitants. And I will banish the voice of mirth and gladness, the voice of the bridegroom and the voice of the bride, the grinding of millstones and the light of the lamp. And in seventy years, I will punish the king of Babylon . . ."

Irijah had stuck his dirty fingers in his ears and lay there motionless. All around, there was a bitter and dismissive silence. The Ethiopian continued:

"But after seventy years, the Chaldeans' turn will come for the sake of their fury. Now Judah has drunk the cup filled with the wine of wrath from the hand of the Lord. But when this chastisement is complete . . ."

There was a vigorous rattling of chains farther away from the men on the ground, and in the blink of an eye, a stone came flying through the air. It landed at the Ethiopian's feet. Someone screamed at him to be quiet, but he was silenced by the other voices. Someone said that Jeremiah was still right, and perhaps there would be a word from the Lord.

Ebed-Melech continued:

"The amazing thing with you Jews is that you, who have received more of the heavenly light than any other people, seem to see so little of it yourselves. It is almost thirty years since I learned to know you. It was high up in Egypt, in the town that we call Jeb, right on the border of my land. There was a group of camel drivers and mercenaries from Judah sitting there and talking. They were just as broken and dirty as such people are throughout the world. And I thought they would tell the same salacious stories as such people tell throughout the world. But they told of one of their forefathers, who was sold as a slave to Egypt and was a servant in a fine house and who would have been able to take the lady of the house as his lover, but he said no because he did not want to do that which was evil in the eyes of God. Then I became interested and wanted to know more about your people. So I came here . . ."

One could see the hostility around him softening.

"Well," someone said, half-flattered and half-anxious, "what did you think then?"

"That you were just like all other peoples . . . and yet completely different. From the world, you have learned to fight and unite, to lie and conspire like all the other people. But from heaven, something has come to you that is not found among the others. For the most part, you don't want to know about it, but heaven doesn't seem to let go of you."

"But he has certainly forgotten us now?"

Ebed-Melech shook his big childlike head.

"No! Have you not heard about the New Testament that he shall institute in coming days? Do you not know that there shall come a prophet like Moses who can restore everything again?"

Now Irijah turned. He had long since taken his fingers from his ears.

"Of all my misfortunes, I count this as my worst: having to have you come along to Chaldea. At least there we will be able to escape the damned prophet's nonsense!"

Now Ebed-Melech smiled.

"You will escape me. I shall go free. Jeremiah told me this during the siege. But in Chaldea, the Lord will come to awaken new prophets for you. He does not let go of you. Therefore you still have hope."

Irijah turned away with an air of infinite disgust. At the same time, one of the Chaldean fools let loose a loud and clanging sound that was just as merciless as the thick-limbed, swarthy guards.

The whole field stirred. What had looked like piles of dirty rags between the stones took on newfound life—the weak and drowsy life of a sleepwalker waking up from his stupor. Three or four shifted around within the long lines to witness once again the dismal spectacle of a few hundred being selected and driven away. No one knew where.

But something unusual happened today. When those being deported were marched off—rattling their chains, limping, and staggering—the trumpet blasted again. A Chaldean with a groomed beard and black eyebrows looked at his board and called out a few names. Those called were brought to the guard chamber. There, their chains were loosened. They were given a piece of cloth and a bag of bread and the injunction to go in peace wherever they wanted. And among them was the Ethiopian, Ebed-Melech.

III.

For the last time, the long line of women walked with baskets on their heads and dumped the gravel on the waste piles. The men digging in the pit had already put aside their tools and gone up to the main tent to get their day's wages. The work was finished for the day.

He began to pick out the latest finds in the cardboard boxes. He was the youngest of the coworkers here and still didn't have his tenth term at university behind him. His face had become a copper brown over the last few weeks, and the soft golden-blond stubble glistened against the sharply tanned skin on his chin. Just as he began to look through the boxes, the team leader walked up and asked what the haul was like.

"Just junk."

The young man answered sullenly. He had been standing at the sieve in the heat of the sun all afternoon, and his humor was not the most cheerful. He realized he wasn't being very polite and continued apologetically.

"A pair of bronze clumps that could have been found in a rubbish heap anywhere between Alaska and Ceylon. And then a broken scarab that I don't believe we can date. And then of course half a sack worth of shards from the worst pottery, as with all stoneware in this country."

He looked up. It almost seemed as if he wanted to ask the other man for an account.

"Do you here . . . is there really any meaning to any of this here? We have now spent five weeks here digging in this garbage pit. Every day costs us money. And have we found a single item that a decent museum would care to show?"

The other man thought for a moment.

"No, I do not believe so."

The kid looked at him with grim triumph.

"And I'll bet it is the same at three quarters of the places where they stand and sift earth here in the land in the summer."

The other nodded.

"I would believe that to be probable."

Now the youth let go all his misgivings.

"Listen," he said. "I have thought about this a lot. Is there really any point to this excavation? Is there any land in the world that is less worthwhile to dig in than this one, which just happens to be called 'the Promised Land'?"

Now the other didn't say anything. He looked half-amused. The youth became a bit more heated as he continued:

"Has this miserable people ever once done one thing that has contributed to the development of technology? Have they discovered anything themselves? Is there a single piece of artwork here? Something that is not a poor plagiarism of something that existed in Egypt and Babylon?"

The other shook his head in agreement.

"And aren't these high places and stone pillars precisely the same rubbish that one can find wherever they want, whether up toward Damascus or down toward Petra?"

Once again, the other held his peace.

"And do you not get the impression that Israelites were precisely the same tramps as all the others? Their earthenware is even worse than the Canaanites'; their tools, houses, granaries, and city walls are on-the-dot the same as all the others found in Moab, Edom, and Ammon. Is it not all simply miserable compared with the most modest of that which is dug out of the Euphrates?"

"And yet I still won't trade," the other said calmly. "If that is what you mean."

Now the young man looked at him with a bit of uncertainty.

"But of course it is another thing when you find something . . ."

"Why is that? Have you never considered that one can make incredibly great discoveries when one finds nothing?"

The young face was almost indignant.

"But one doesn't need to travel out with an expensive and grand expedition for that!"

"Yeah . . ."

He looked at the younger man kindly. "See, twelve years ago, when I came here the first time, I thought the same as you. And I have certainly been able to find a few stylish things that look good in a glass cabinet. But that which we find is not the most important thing. The most important thing, we have come to find out, is precisely what you have said: that there really isn't the tiniest bit of difference between Israel and all the other little peoples here, neither in terms of housing or gear nor, well, hardly in terms of speech and living habits either. All of them were actually small, puny nomadic tribes that came here to the coast and tried to learn a bit of culture—as well as they could—from the natives and their nice neighbors."

"But then it is pretty silly to make such a huge fuss over these Jews," the young man said irritably. "Then there is no good reason that every child should read about them and learn more about their history than they do about their own."

"What sort of logic is that?" the older man asked laughing. "A people's meaning does not depend only on how many can openers or machine guns they have invented. If there are any inventors of a people, then it must be artists. And if there are no artists? Then it may as well be prophets. And then it can be a matter of taste, whether one thinks that the world needs can openers more than prophets."

The young man was silent. They began walking toward the tents, each with their burden of cardboard boxes. The older man continued:

"And now I believe it is precisely our task here to give them something to think about at home. The more we dig, the clearer it becomes. There isn't the slightest material or economic or political reason that Israel should have a different history than any of the other small peoples around here. If Marx had been right, Israel's history would look just the same as Moab's or Aram's. It is as if to say, 'No one should have ever heard the name Israel, except maybe for some expert in cuneiform.' Neither would they have heard anything of Moab or Edom if we hadn't had the prophets."

They put the boxes down, and the older man went to the wash-basin and splashed the water. Then he stood there with a towel in his hands and said, "But now it is all connected. You see all these prophets who lived here among this strange little people and this fantastic faith in God that has guided them even when they were carried off into captivity. This faith that they would receive a Messiah that would be a light for all peoples. Of course, it could all be fabricated foolishness. Yet it is quite miraculous that this people should come back from Babylon when all the others were wiped out so that every child back home right now would know the name of a man that was born right here in this place."

He threw the dirty water out on the hot ground and filled the basin again.

"Well, boy, what should we say? As men of science, we seek a reason. Now we are absolutely certain that there is no reason among those things that would leave a mark on a city. So we have to seek a reason in something else. For example, perhaps the prophets were right?"

He looked up and laughed again.

"Shouldn't you wash? I believe dinner is ready. You can think about the rest when you stand at the sifter again tomorrow."

In the Same Place

The winter sun set behind the vast bare limestone ridge to the west, where the path coiled up on the crest. The flat valley ended in the blue shadows of the desert at dusk. Wind whistled cold and sharp across the expanse. The olive trees seemed to roll up their leaves and huddle together, small, gray, and hunched over as if they dreaded the cold night air. The sheep still grazed eagerly on the green-leafed rosettes that the autumn rains coaxed out from between the stones. They too seemed to feel the threat of the coming night. Far off in the east, far beyond the desert's endless ridges and the deep valley where the Dead Sea waters lay heavy and motionless, the mountains of Moab rose like flames of golden red. But then the shadows climbed up from the depths slowly extinguishing the glow as the dark-blue evening arched from the west and snuffed out the last red glow of the heavens.

The shepherds looked suspiciously at the small fluffy clouds being driven over the ridges by the cold wind. Was it possible that it might still rain? Would there be a storm such that even the farmers in the city would understand that it was time to take in the sheep? The shepherds really wanted a good sleet storm to pelt the houses crowded about each other on the hilltop to the southeast. A storm that would drive the icy water right up to the foot of the bedrolls that the city's farmers were just now rolling out upon their dirt floors.

It was a dog's job to be shepherd. They had said it a thousand times. It was the last thing a man should devote his life to. They spent the whole summer wandering about in the suffocating heat of the sun, climbing like goats along the rock walls that burned when anyone touched them, and sleeping like dogs between the stones as hyenas laughed their wicked laugh. You never let go of your sling and club, and always looked with suspicion at anything that lived or moved around you. There was always reason be concerned as soon as an animal disappeared behind a stone wall in any of the winding ravines . . . And then these winter nights, freezing in the cold and waiting hour after hour for the first bleak streak of dawn to touch the peaks of Nebo and Pisgah, "more than watchmen for the morning, more than watchmen for the morning," as King David said in the psalms that the pilgrims still sang when they went up over yonder hills to Jerusalem, even though they could not imagine how one could long to see the sun again . . .

In any case, King David understood it. That was something wonderful; he too had been here in the desert with sheep. He had thirsted and froze. He had fought with both lions and bears, and had come straight from the herds when he felled the Philistine. But one wonders if he had been a true shepherd, as lousy as a dog and as famished as a jackal. He was still a farmer's son, and there was quite a difference between him and a poor wretch who lived among the animals in environs of Bethlehem.

It was a great wonder that that smoky heap of stones up there was David's city, and that it was among these walls of rubble that the dynasty had its roots. An even greater wonder was what the prophet had said about this Bethlehem Ephrathah, so tiny among the clans of Judah. From her would come a prince to be a shepherd for Israel.

The shepherds nodded. Yes, it was wonderful. But, of course, he was the Messiah, the Anointed. When he came, everything would be different. It was like a glimpse of light amidst the darkness of winter, something to hope for while one froze. If only one could be there for it.

They had finished talking and gathered together by the stone walls where they sat and watched the darkness creep up from the ravines that opened like cracks in the bottom of the flat valley. Then the oldest of them rose up and let loose his long rolling call, a guttural gurgling that caused the sheep to lift their heads and scout the twilight. But then he was quiet and remained standing with his face against the last light of day.

"Look," he said. "Have you ever seen . . . ?"

The others slowly turned themselves to the west. Something appeared as a black silhouette in the evening sky's last glimmer of light. Up there on the heights moved an entourage, like tiny insects, clearly contrasted against the sky. This wasn't anything remarkable. Over these last days, one had seen enough of these wayfarers. The whole world had been on the move ever since Caesar had gotten this census in his head. People who hadn't been home for many years appeared again in order not to lose their citizenship. That latecomers were still arriving wasn't anything spectacular either. Neither was it remarkable that they seemed to be in a hurry, given how quickly darkness fell upon them. The strange thing was that she was the one riding. The man walked ahead with a long stride, dragging the donkey along after him. One could see how he had girded up his clothes and how he set the stick hard against the ground. And the woman actually sat in the saddle. There was no doubt about the matter. They had probably seen a thousand similar entourages come up over the heights over the years, but it was always him riding and she who followed with her burden on her head or her child on her back.

"She must be very sick," one of them said.

The entourage disappeared below the horizon just before the place where Rachel was buried, where the path to the city gates turned away from the route that continued to Hebron and the south. It was quiet again. So, rising slowly, the shepherds halfheartedly began driving the flocks together for the night.

*

Panting with eagerness and effort, they came up over the hill. They stumbled over the olive tree roots and crashed against the stones, but they held together, guided with the help of starlight peering through the clouds. They had learned the art of seeing in the black of night over the course of many nights spent searching for sheep that had broken through the thorn hedges or ewes that had been lost in the rocky desert.

Something different drove them tonight, something they had never before experienced the likes of. Just as their feet staggered over the stone blocks, so their thoughts tumbled about and the words stumbled from their lips when they spoke about it. It was too much all at once: the light that was clearer than day and yet not day, the glory that pierced right through them and made them feel like the vilest of sinners precisely because it was such an indescribable glory. And then he stood there and spoke with a voice that was like all the consolation of scripture, all the blessed promises taken together. He was as beautiful as the feet of he who bears good news when he comes over the mountains to proclaim the joyous message, full of the jubilee that bursts forth from the mountains when the Lord comforts his people and has compassion on the afflicted. He proclaimed to them the greatest joy of all on the earth: it was the Messiah who was born up there in the city of David. In the blink of an eye, the whole sky was filled with the praise of heavenly hosts buzzing and glittering as they sang. There was a radiance, a sound, and a glory that no words could describe.

But amidst the total incomprehension, there was one thing absolutely comprehensible. It was the sign that God had spoken of, the sign that he had given them as the seal of all of this. It was that which they were on the way to see now: the child that they would find, newly born, swaddled, and lying in a manger.

They had reached the steps that led up alongside the long stone wall. There was no longer any difficulty finding their way. Above the wall, there was a terrace with one of the many wheat fields that bordered the city. It was this field that Ruth had once gleaned, just as it was written in the scriptures and as every child in Bethlehem heard it told from their fathers. She was a Moabite, Ruth. And yet she became a mother in the line of King David! It was wonderful. The scriptures said that a circumcised male should never marry a foreign woman. But if the Messiah had been born this night from the descendants of David, then he was also of the impure and despised in the same way.

They were before the great open place outside the city's northeast corner. The adjoining houses were dark and quiet before them. Alone in one of the hollows of rock, a little flame flickered from an oil lamp.

There was something unusual about the light. The shepherds knew the grotto well. They had driven their animals in and out through the opening countless times. Normally, the rocky crag gaped with darkness, and the door in the half-hewn stone wall was usually closed. Now it stood ajar, and light was filtering out through the gap.

Not until they stepped in under the stone vault did they get an explanation. There had been people living in the cave at night, apparently poor wayfarers who were pushed out from the shelter. They had lit an oil lamp that sat in the niche of the rock. The flame was hardly more than a pale drop of brilliance on the wick, but it was bright enough for the shepherds, whose eyes were accustomed to the night watch. In just a second, they had taken in the whole scene: the pale face of the woman leaning back against the straw and looking at them with kind eyes, the man straightening up the poor bundles he had been searching through as he stood, the animals in the corner looking at the light with huge dumb eyes, and then the child, the sign that they had been promised to see. Now he lay there before their own eyes.

They stood there on the earthen floor staring awkwardly. The little one was wrapped tightly in the swaddling cloth like all other children—a little newborn boy laid to rest in the stone manger hewn deep into the rock, on the left, under the stone ceiling.

The woman kept looking at them with the same confident and kind eyes. Then they began to stutter as they spoke. It sounded so strange. They could not say it. They felt as if they would be laughingstocks. But the woman nodded slowly, as if she understood them. They felt encouraged and spoke more boldly. A few strangers came. They seemed to be familiar with the man. They told them everything they had heard that night. They were no longer shy. They had gotten their earnestness back. They read great amazement in the faces of others, amazement but not mockery. And the woman looked at them knowingly and kindly.

They felt so wonderfully at home here. The wet straw spilling on the floor, the smell of the animals and the cool night air—it was their own poor world. And in the midst of this poverty was the sight that had been promised to them. Amazed and happy, they stood at the manger with muffled voices and clumsy tenderness.

"Just like one of us," the oldest of them said.

As they went back to their animals, passing between the great trees outside the cave, they came to think about something strange. They said that this was the place where Samuel kept the sacrificial feast with Jesse and his sons. Here he had poured oil over David's head and anointed him as king. Here had been the beginning of the splendor of David's house. And here also had been born this night the one who would be the last and greatest of all the rulers on David's throne.

So they praised God and sang the song of the prophet Micah about Bethlehem Ephrathah, the song that every child in

Bethlehem knew by heart. When their forced and hoarse voices came to the place where it is written, "Therefore he shall give them up until the time when she who is in labor has given birth,"[1] They burst out in new praise. They rejoiced to have been so fortunate as to see what Isaiah had foretold: "Unto us a child has been born, unto us a son has been given." And all the more, they praised God because he who would be called "Wonderful Councilor" and "Mighty God" had come just like one of them, just as poor and forgotten as the vilest of his brothers in Israel.

---

[1] Micah 5:3 (ESV)

Out of Egypt

King Herod is dead!

A sigh of relief washed over all of Jericho. It was as if the city had woken to life again. The people stretched by going outside to enjoy themselves in the cool of the evening. It began with the slaves and eunuchs in the palace who could still feel their heads on their shoulders. Then it spread throughout the rich city to the wealthy people that King Herod had included on a list of those who should lose their lives. Then it made its way to all the simple citizens who no longer had to fear because they owned a well-managed vineyard or a house in a good location. At the same time, the joyous news reached the loiterers in the street outside the inns. They had never been safe from the king's insatiable need for men to man his grand building projects or to be sold as slaves.

They had all lived in fear when the king came down to the city, even when he was terminally ill. They cursed the day that Herod got the notion of building a winter palace down here in this valley, where nobody and nothing knew what winter meant. They were timid and always viewed the floral displays spilling over the walls with suspicion when they knew that the powerful man was hiding behind them. Yet he had never been as mad as he had been this winter. The king had been incapacitated by chills and insane with paranoia. He saw enemies and insurrectionists everywhere. He wasn't able stand on his own feet, but that didn't keep him from torturing a few young hotheads and a couple old rabbis who had torn down the gilded Roman eagles on the temple mount. He sentenced them to be burned alive. Even at the beginning of this week, he had his own firstborn son retrieved from prison and executed. That would be the last of his ill deeds. Now he was dead at last.

He was an unfathomable man, this Herod. Flatterers called him "the Great." In a certain sense, he deserved the title. He'd had no crown or land when he started out, neither birthright nor inheritance. Now he ruled over a kingdom that shined like King David's. Never had any king in Judah strewn such grand spectacles of engineering and architecture about himself. The first of these was the temple, which amazed even the fussiest of the Greeks and was named one of the world's wonders. Then there were all the other buildings of grandeur in Jerusalem: the fortress and palace, the theater, and the racetrack and stadium.

That was just the beginning, though. From the ground up, he had completely rebuilt the city of Samaria and made it into such a model modern city that it even made the Greeks of the Decapolis feel backward. In Caesarea, he acquired something that the land had never before possessed: a real harbor with a wave break that thrust the blinding-white columns of the streets straight out into the dark sea like the great white arm of a giant.

But that was not enough. In the desert below Bethlehem, he had a castle on top of one of the highest precipices. Then down within the scorching chasms of the Dead Sea, he built an eagle's nest atop Mount Masada. It was so high above the dizzying crags that no one could storm it. He had even dared to donate and build in the finest cities of ancient Greece, Sparta, and Athens. No one was ashamed of his buildings there. It was no wonder that his flatterers called him "the Great."

Yet he was the most hated of all the kings that had ever sat upon David's throne. It was said that his father was a temple slave from Ashkelon. It was certain that Herod was an impure Edomite, a barbarian and a stranger whose heart was just as indifferent to the faith of Israel as any Egyptian or Roman. He had to marry the last princess of the Maccabean dynasty, Mariamne, to make it look as if he had the right to sit on David's throne. It was said that he had loved her passionately, but his love was just as wild, just as jealous and suspicious as his lust for power. In order to make sure that no one else could have her, he had given the order that she should be cut down if he himself died an early death. He finally took her life in a fit of rage. No one knew for certain how it all happened, but one of the high officers lost his life simultaneously. There were a thousand wild rumors about Herod and his court that no one dared to share, but everyone still knew about them. Everyone knew that the king was half crazy in his fear of being driven from the throne that he had secured with so much bloodshed. When it came to securing his power, he spared no one, not even his own flesh and blood. He had eradicated Mariamne's relatives. He had strangled two of the sons she gave him after they had grown up. Yet in the midst of all this he bore a wild longing for her, a longing that he tried to drown in a whirl of pursuits and debauchery.

Now the behemoth was dead. He remained on his stolen throne to the end and never had to flee to his impregnable desert fortress. Yet he had not felt secure for a single day, nor could he ever rest his feverish head. As if chased by evil spirits, he had run about the pillared halls of his winter palace until he was laid upon his purple bed, burnt to slag by his passions, vices, and hunger-sick pursuit of power. Now he was dead. His sons had already begun conspiring for the inheritance, and the streets of Jericho gave way to the new sound of laughter.

*

The news reached the harbor of Alexandria on a ship from Tyre, and the refugee caravans struck out for the desert almost immediately. The rumor reached every small Jewish colony dotting the land of the Nile. There it became the topic of men gathered together to make small talk in the gates. Some said that, whatever else, Herod had championed the Jews among the uncircumcised. He had been in good standing with Caesar, and his word had been a shield against many treacheries. But most of them thought about the refugees. There were plenty of them here on the other side of the border. Most were poor people who didn't have any fortune to leave in the lurch. They were not tempted to stay when the ground began to burn their feet. The Egyptians had done what they could for the refugees, but it couldn't be denied that they would gladly see them disappear again.

All out of breath, one of the neighbors came to tell Joseph the carpenter all the great news. Joseph's wife gave her husband a calm smile. Joseph knew everything, and they had already begun to get themselves ready for their departure. Once again, God's hand had paved their peculiar path.

Both of them belonged to the quiet in the land, those who waited for the comfort of Israel. They lived by the word of the prophets and believed their promises. They heard them read every Sabbath in the synagogue and often spoke of them in small circles where they gathered. They knew that deliverance had to come, and they had long thought that it could not be far off. But they kept quiet and attended to their work. This is how it was among those who waited. They knew that the new day would dawn. They also knew that it was completely and wholly in God's hand. No man could stand in its way or help it along either. So they understood that the zealots were wrong when they took up arms to put an end to the foreign occupation that every real Jew felt as an affront to God's glory. They suffered as much as anyone else from seeing the idolatrous field signs that the Romans carried through the land. They turned away in disgust from all the debauchery that came from the Greek cities on the other side of the Jordan. But they had never dreamed of taking up arms to offer resistance. After brief consideration, Joseph had gone off to the census. Many of his compatriots refused, and some offered armed resistance. The quiet shook their heads at all the noise. They knew that if this happened, it must be God himself at work. Here they needed to trust the promises. Hadn't the prophet said that if they did not believe then neither would they have peace? God would intervene in due time. Then he would scatter those who had presumptuous thoughts in their hearts. Then he would throw the rulers of the age from their thrones and lift up the simple people who put their trust in his name.

Joseph trusted in the providence of God fully and firmly. Had he not led Abraham out of Ur of the Chaldeans, and the sons of Jacob to Egypt, and the twelve tribes to the Promised Land? Had not the judgment that the prophets had foretold concerning Jerusalem come true, and the grace that would occur among the remnant of Judah? So the current affliction would also have its end. The vision waited for its time as it longed for fulfilment. It would not miss its mark. If it was delayed, then the only thing to be done was to wait for it, because it certainly was coming. It would not tarry.

This had been the great instruction for Joseph: to bide his time. He had learned to be quiet. It often happened that the simple carpenter found it hard to understand, but he knew that God was at work. He had received order after order, and he had done what he was told. The only safe thing to do, it had been shown, was to take the Lord's path right away and without question.

He had thought throughout the night, then he received the order to flee. Abraham must have felt just as lonely when he left his city and his kindred or when he climbed up the mountain to sacrifice his only son. But if Joseph had tarried ever so briefly, it would have been too late. Afterward, he had heard, with a mixture of horror and comfort, how the soldiers had come and cordoned off the city. They had blocked the gates and entered the houses as if they were occupying enemy territory. There had been a lot of talk concerning this new ill deed of Herod's. Once again, everyone knew that his sick anxiety, his concern that someone else might have a better claim to his throne than he did, had driven him to spill innocent blood. Joseph had thought a lot about the peculiar ways of God. Why should all these innocents need to die? But then he thought about all the infant boys that Pharaoh let drown in the Nile and about Moses, who was still saved. Perhaps God could allow some to be lost if only he could save him upon whom the future depended. Then he looked again, long and thoughtfully, with an almost timid tenderness, at the boy playing at Mary's feet.

*

It was like a train of pilgrims on their way to the Passover feast. They had come together as small groups of travelers: poor pedestrians with big bundles and small trotting donkeys were almost lost under the burdens of worn and inexpensive household items, and now and then there was a camel that pushed on with a deceptively sleepy gate that still managed to keep pace with even the quickest of men. Songs were not absent either. As they left Egypt, they sang about the day the Lord carried his people up out of slavery with a strong hand and an outstretched arm. They sang when they saw the sea to the south—the sea that God had once pushed away with an eastern wind. They sang the song of Miriam about how God destroyed the Pharaoh and his host in the depths. And if the singing got quiet in the desert sands, it flared up again on the plains of Moab, when they stood like Moses to see the awe-inspiring glory of the Jordan Valley open before them and, off in the distance on the other side, the mountains that hid the Holy City.

Joseph fell into his thoughts again. It was such a wonderful thing to travel with this child upon these paths that Israel had taken before him. With their deliverance from Egypt, the Israelites had begun their lives as the Lord's people. At that time, they had found their God, and he had covenanted with them that they should be his people. It was a covenant that still remained and still applied to every aspect of his people's lives. The boy had been received into this covenant when Joseph had circumcised him on the eighth day after his birth. And it was written that the day would come when God would make a new covenant with the house of Israel, not like the covenant that he once made when he took them by the hand and led them out of Egypt but a new covenant that he would put into their hearts. At that time, the people's path had led from slavery to Canaan. "Out of Egypt, I called my son." He thought about God again . . . and again, he looked in wonder at the boy.

They had to rest and wait on the other side of the Jordan. Herod's heirs were still disputing over the inheritance. Then Rome sent word that it would be as Herod had determined. Archelaus, the worst of the Edomite's sons, would rule in Jerusalem. He followed in his father's footsteps in everything except willpower and agility. For many of the refugees, this meant that Judah was still closed to them.

Joseph turned to the north, where Mount Hermon's snowcapped peak rose above the mountains surrounding the Sea of Galilee. Herod Antipas ruled there. He also took after his father, but more in cunning than in ruthlessness. One could dare to live in his land. Joseph had worked there in Nazareth before the census, and it was Mary's home. So he returned to "Galilee of the Gentiles," the land beyond the settlements of Samaria and the plains of Jezreel. The spiritual dominion of Jerusalem had never held much sway there, and they did not keep statutes of the elders, at least not in the only manner the scribes considered to be right. In Judah, it was a self-evident truth that nothing good could come from Nazareth and that no prophet could ever come from Galilee. But Joseph had heard the voice of God, and he trusted the revelation, so he went where God led him, straightaway and without question.

The Voice of One Who Cries

Evening drew near.

The young, anxious rabbi looked up toward the crest of the cliff wall on the other side of valley. The desert sand still gave off a bone-white glow against the dark-blue sky, and the last of the sunlight painted a red-copper stripe on the mass of stone along the gully at the bottom of the valley. The ravine down below was otherwise covered in deep-violet shadows. It seemed as if it was just waiting for the moment when the light would fade from the edge up above.

He prodded the donkey. He wanted to get down to Jericho before the darkness descended. He watched the trail carefully as they went. To the left, the cliff wall was so close that he could touch it with his hands. To the right, the cliff fell off. They had come somewhat closer to the bottom now, but it was still nasty down there where the blocks of stone gathered amidst the dark little strand of oleander growing along the valley floor. Things could go badly if it got dark before they were out on the plains.

Like all the others, he too feared this desert, where men were never safe from robbers and lions could be gracing the thickets at the bottom of the Jordan Valley. But he had no choice, because he was traveling on behalf of the Sanhedrin. At the seventh hour, when they crested the Mount of Olives and froze in the sharp wind, their destination looked close and tempting. The entire Judean desert spread out before them like a beautiful pleated coat of the finest wool. Just beyond it was the bluish-green salt sea shimmering like turquoise, and a person could almost see the heat rising up from the valley floor. Jericho was there, at the very bottom of the mountain slopes, inviting them with her warm palm groves.

But as they rode down the endless mountain side, the white coat with its soft folds changed into a hard and burnt wasteland where the limestone descended into the vast steppes. The blinding sunlight washed it all with the same intolerable white, and it was all equally desolate. The monotony was only broken by the black rows of scattered flint fragments that twisted likes snakes on the slopes. Finally, the white surface broke, and the sand opened up into ever-deeper clefts. Now the path descended into one of those clefts and clambered gently along one side. It left just enough room for a single rider with no room to pass.

The young rabbi took a firm grip on the reins and halted his donkey. The steps swung around a corner, and the rock opened up giving the rabbi a view straight east. Between the dark rocky walls, the Jordan plains glimmered in the golden evening sun. A dark-green carpet of groves encircled Jericho. Then came the vast desert of clay, where one could sense the Jordan curling through like a gray ribbon. Off in the distance, the mountains of Moab stood silent and high, grouped together like a wall painted pink with the last rays of the evening sun.

No one knew how long he would have sat there if one of his comrades hadn't come up from behind and asked him to hurry up. He had been very contemplative. Scribe that he was, he knew that every foot of ground before him carried traces of the work of God. Over there on the horizon lay Mount Nebo, from where Moses saw the entire Promised Land in one glance. Down below, in the valley that looked like a soft groove in the rock wall, the twelve tribes had descended from Moab's heights. Even today, the stone walls of their camp could be seen, ninety furloughs long between Beth-Jesimot and Abel-Shittim. Down there, on the plains of Jericho, they had crossed over the Jordan. Gilgal had appeared there. That was where Joshua had stacked the twelve stones that he retrieved from the riverbed. There, Israel had received its first king, and there lay Jericho, shimmering in white amidst the deep green.

Shimmering white . . . The rabbi clenched his thin hand around the reins. That was the poison in the cup that had formerly flooded over with goodness and mercy. There it was, the new palace, with all of Herod's statues in their naked marble grandeur, a mockery of the Lord's law and an insult to all Jewish piety. And then, down there on the plains, they would march. Perhaps even tonight, there was some Roman centurion with his idols or maybe some Greek merchant driving his camels from Pella and Gerasa, laden with all the jewelry, cloths, and ointments that the Greek unbelievers used to turn the heads of Jewish daughters.

It wasn't any better since Herod's death either. He had been a half heathen too, yet he had still realized there were things that one could not do in Israel. Archelaus did not understand this quite so well, and the Roman procurator didn't understand anything. They had had Pontius Pilate for three years now. He was like a scourge on their back. Nothing had gotten any better in the years since he first sent his soldiers to Jerusalem. He had allowed them to carry their field signs at night and set their idols up over the temple. The young rabbi would never forget those days. He had joined the vast crowds that marched down to Caesarea on the coast and had stood in the crowd outside the procurator's palace, waiting day after day. He had lain prostrate with the others in the street. He had thrown dust and dirt over his head and torn his clothing. He could still feel the trembling thrill that went through the masses when Pilate had stood on the royal grandstand, threatening to let the soldiers loose and massacre them all if they did not dissipate in a half an hour. They had all shouted their answer. They would rather lie there in their own blood than see God's city shamed by these forbidden graven images. That time they won. The picture of Caesar was removed. But they had played with death for a whole week.

Their solidarity had not always been so good. Things were good for the turncoats: publicans who sold themselves to collect taxes for the occupier and the harlots who drank his wine and gladly received his whore allowance. There were still many who were lukewarm and cowardly. They limped on both sides, following the illustrious example of the fine old priestly families and the whole lot of Sadducees, who wanted peace in the land at any price so that, without disruption, they could continue to collect the temple tax with tranquility while enjoying the return from their olive groves and vineyards.

He clenched his hand in anger again. Of course it was true that one should not take up arms before God's hour was at hand. But that is why it was so important that everyone remained faithful to Israel's law to the very end and not give an inch when the heathen tempted and threatened. If Israel was ever united, the Romans would not be able to do anything. But now there was this hazy and cowardly spirit that compromised and turned away without seeing that the fight was precisely the same as when Antiochus Epiphanes once wanted to put an end to Israel's faith and the Maccabees rose up against him. There was still a lot of the Maccabean faith that remained. He took pride in being a Pharisee. They cared for the great inheritance of those days. His party had its roots in the powerful wave of awakening, repentance, and obedience to the law that had swept through the land at that time. When the Maccabees themselves turned from the path and increasingly became nothing more than domineering princelings who conquered heathen cities and polluted the land with foreign armies, it was the Pharisees who had preserved the path blamelessly. They knew that Israel's salvation lay in strict obedience to the law and in the relentless rejection of everything foreign. They knew that the Messiah would come to judge and that the faithful in Israel would then receive their reward for steadfastness.

The Messiah would come . . . How often had he spoken about this with his peers among the scribes. There were those who said that he would come soon. They tried to show it with the help of the prophets and all the scriptures, but the evidence wasn't certain. Only the excitable and constantly erratic people believed it. But they did not know the scriptures, and unfortunately, they were content to be less eager to keep the law than they were for showing up to run the Romans out of the land.

The Messiah would come . . . Never had the words been so full of the hidden embers and tantalizing allure as during these last few weeks. It wasn't spoken of openly, but everyone knew it. There was a dangerous and bewitching rumor going through the land. Everyone knew who it was about. Everyone heard the talk about him, and it seemed everyone had been there. There had been a great migration down through the desert and across the white roads through the Jordanian plains. It wasn't really easy to say what one should believe about this John, the son of Zachariah.

His father had been a priest of the old line. He belonged to the Abias branch and was not counted among the noble families. He was not a Sadducee by any account, but neither was he any Pharisee. Yet he belonged to those who even a Pharisee could count as the best in the land, one of the quiet and faithful who believed in the prophets, loved the temple, and tried to keep the law even if there were perhaps some comments to be made about their obedience to the law if one measured it by the true measuring stick of the scribes. There wasn't much to say about Zechariah but that he'd once had some vision in the temple when he was tending the incense of the evening sacrifice, and he was not able to speak when he came out.

What was more remarkable was his son. He was called John, and it was alleged that he had received the name through some revelation. Like Isaac and Samuel, he was born when his parents had given up hope for the fruit of life. Ever since his youth, there had been something peculiar about him. He lived out here in the desert, and he would often go missing for weeks. It was alleged that he was able live off of grasshoppers, roots, and wild honey like an Arab. It was certain that he had never tasted wine or worn normal clothing. Many said that he was crazy, but the Lord's Nazarites had been the same. They did not taste that which came from the vine either.

The young rabbi liked all this. Israel had been brought to ruin by mixing with people in Canaan, by learning their customs and worshiping their gods. This is why, already in their day, the Rechabites wanted to turn back to the way of life that the twelve tribes had when they still lived in tents. And there was a certain amount of condemnation in John's wonderful manner of living. It was an example that should waken the slumbering Judah.

But now he had suddenly begun preaching. He had stepped forth just as erratically as the prophets of old. People had spotted him all over the place throughout the plains. His message had gone through them all like a shockwave. He had spoken the unspeakable, what every scribe shied away from saying. What the rabbis spoke about in confidential discussions, what they carefully examined and weighed with reasons and counterpoints then cautiously hid away—this he cried out with a voice that resounded through the desert and over the highlands and gave echo from Dan to Beersheba: THE KINGDOM OF GOD IS NEAR!

How could he know this? There was no doubt about what he meant—that it would come now. All who heard him had attested that he preached repentance, but not merely on account of the cruelties filling the land. No, he clearly said that the ax was already laid to the root of the tree and judgment would come.

It would happen now. They had been waiting for this time of wonder for so long, and now it was to break in here and now, amidst these men who swarmed upon the upland roads. This is why he baptized.

The rabbis also baptized. If an uncircumcised man converted to God's people, then he would not only be circumcised; he would also be baptized. For both men and women, both adults and children, this baptism would wash away their old heathen existence and consecrate them to their new life under the law. But John's baptism was something more. It meant that a person left his old life in order to wait for the Messiah. He repented in order to stand ready for the coming of the Messiah.

The young rabbi felt short of breath before all of this. This John was so sure that he dared to draw all these people to him and wash them in the Jordan so that they would wait for the Messiah. How did he know that the Messiah would come? When would he come?

Here these issues came to life again, glowing like hot iron. A person couldn't touch upon them without getting burned. They glowed like coals bedded in ash throughout the land, and they could get an uprising fanned into flame like nothing else, just like laying a bundle of thorns on a fading fire. Yet the most serious consideration wasn't whether the land would be filled with wild sword-wielding enthusiasts overnight. The bigger question was if there really was a Messiah—if one would suddenly stand before his throne in the valley of Jehoshaphat.

Faced with these questions, the rabbi felt like a shaking leaf on the great tree of his people. His body felt every flicker of tense expectation in the land. So he lifted his head and his hands to praise the name of the Most High when he got word that he had been chosen by the Sanhedrin to be among those sent to try to get clarity on the issue.

Who was this peculiar John?

It was whispered . . . No, it was just as well not to say it. One should be careful with fire. But he must ask him even that. And of course, before the Messiah, Elijah would come. He could be him. There were also many who said that some of the prophets would rise again or that at least a prophet would come, a real prophet after these four hundred years of humiliating silence, this long bitter night when the Lord withheld his word and the people would have sat in darkness if it was not for the diligence and faithfulness of the scribes preserving the law that the Blessed One had given them in former times.

*

The sun had already begun to burn the Jordan Valley's wide mud flats when they left the palm forest the next morning. They had taken good advice and spent the night in Jericho. It was hardly a two-hour ride from there down to the river. They could have found their way by moonlight, but they had been warned in Jerusalem against over-nighting on the Jordan. Ever since John had begun baptizing, it was overflowing with people down there, and it seemed to be impossible to get a decent spot to camp for the night in a reasonably dry place under the tamarisks. It was even hard in Jericho, but the recommendation letters they had opened doors everywhere.

The blinding white of the upland plains now lay before them. A few lonely trees stood, gray and dusty, by the roadside, and a camel grazed patiently among the thorny bushes. Dust rose from a little group of sojourners far ahead of them. Otherwise, all was empty and quiet.

Again and again, the rabbi looked to the south, where the vapors had already begun to rise from the Salt Sea, causing the huge wall of mountains to disappear in the haze on the horizon. Sodom and Gomorra had been somewhere down there. The elders taught that from Mount Nebo, Moses saw hell open itself down by Soar. It fitted this cursed tract where everything was dead, where the water itself destroyed all life that it brushed against, and where the sun forged the stone masses until nothing could set its foot on them.

But if the Most Highly Praised had been able to accomplish this with his wrath on a couple puny nests of sin, what then would not be possible if his kingdom really was now at hand? How horrific must this day be for Rome and Alexandria and for the apostates of Israel? It was good to know that one preserved his own feet from coarse sins and kept his house immaculately, if that day was now approaching.

They encountered groups of wanderers coming up from the river. It seemed that they slept under the bare sky and had been out on strange paths. There were all types of people: honest young people from Jerusalem and Joppa, poor farmers from the hill country, and one or two of the gentry with both donkeys and servants. Everyone seemed to have something in common and talked as if they were old acquaintances. A few Syrian merchants were the only ones who hurried by with suspicious eyes and with their coats pulled up high about their faces, as though they saw something on the path that made them uncomfortable.

The rabbi looked around one more time. His observation wandered from uplands of Moab over to Gilead's forested ridges and way up to the north where the huge mountains of Galilee disappeared in the haze. With a look over his shoulders, he could see the hills of Ephraim on the other side of the valley and a glimpse of the mountains of Samaria and, to the south, the bare slopes of Judah with the Mount of Olives high on the crest. Here he had the whole history of his people before his eyes. The two milestones were Mount Nebo, from where Moses saw the Promised Land, and Bethlehem, from where the Messiah would come. They stood opposite each other on either side of the immense Jordan Valley that sank between them, the beginning and the end of all of Israel's struggles and all their labors in this land where they were carried by the Almighty's hand to be his servants and bring his light to the nations. He himself now rode in the midst of these two mile markers on this peculiar day that might mean the Lord of hosts was now carrying his people over the threshold to a new era.

They had reached the edge of the level clay plains, and the path made a steep plunge into the deep furrow the water had dug into the layers of marl. The winter floods had cut the riverbank into a labyrinth of precipitous clay mountains. As one walked between them, he could only see the white peaks contrasting against the blue sky in bold, curved shapes. They looked like people dancing in white coats. The rabbi thought of the psalmist's words concerning Israel's exodus from Egypt: "The mountains skipped like rams, the hills like lambs." Yes, it was truly fitting that the mountains danced for joy in the place where the Most Highly Praised carried his people up into this land to glorify his name over all the earth. He had done all this with his people in order to make them a light for the heathen. So it was written, and so shall it be, when the one who was to come finally came.

And think if he came now. If now they were before the other milestone . . .

They reached the bottom of the valley, where the grayish-green trees thronged along the shoreline and the scrubby bushes braided themselves together into an almost impenetrable thicket. The ground was marshy, and they watched eagerly while they walked on it because it was known that nowhere else were there so many poisonous insects as there were crawling here.

The beaches at the ford were already full of people camping in small groups, and there were more when they got to the other shore and asked for directions. First, they were pointed upstream and then to a path along a small trickle that came down from the plains. It soon widened itself into a flat valley overgrown with poplars whose small silver-green leaves glittered in the wind.

At once, the rabbi saw that they were in front. A very large crowd of people were gathered in the trees, and they could hear a voice speaking. It was not strong and powerful, as the rabbis had imagined that a prophet ought to speak, but calm and educational. They heard someone ask a question; otherwise, everyone was quiet.

They left the donkeys with a servant and slowly elbowed forward. It was difficult because everyone looked straight ahead, but when the people finally noticed who was coming, they made way. Finally, the rabbi caught a glimpse of the man who spoke. The speaker was standing between two aspens that towered above the crowd sitting in front of him.

His first thoughts went to the words of scripture. Was it not written that King Amaziah's servants who were sent to inquire of Baal-Zebul, the god in Akron, turned back unsuccessfully because they had encountered a man who wore a coat of camel hair and that was girded with a leather belt about his loins? And had not the troubled king immediately said: "It is Elijah the Tishbite."

He must have looked like this. A brown coat bleached by the desert sun and scuffed by the thorns of the wilderness, pulled together by a leather belt just like one of the fathers of that era when Israel lived in tents. And then this face! Angular, marked by fasting and deprivation, burnt by the heat of the rocks and by the night frost on the heights. Yes, it was true enough that this man lived off of grasshoppers and wild honey. And perhaps it was also true that the voice of the Most High came to him. Elijah the Tishbite must have looked like this when he came again from Mount Horeb, where he encountered the Lord in the calm whisper after the storm and the earthquake.

The rabbi took in a wider view. To his surprise, he saw that there was a pair of legionnaires standing before John, apparently a pair of soldiers from the border patrol. The Baptist was speaking to them firmly and curtly. It was a simple and clear thing he told them: they should not extort food and wine from the farmers but pay properly for themselves, nor should they rattle their swords and extort money where they are quartered but settle for a soldier's pay. This is what they had to do while they waited.

Then there was someone that a person might take for a publican if it wasn't so ridiculous to find such a person among those who confessed their sins. He too wanted to get advice and to know the way. John's answer struck like a bolt of lightning to the chest of the young rabbi.

"You have the tariff," he said. "You know what is prescribed. Take what is right and no more . . ."

He was a publican, he who stood there asking questions! A Roman tax tenant! And he could continue doing it! He could then stand there and dig in bundles, whether or not they contained pig skins or had been borne by an unclean woman!

The rabbi crossed his eyebrows. Could this be the Lord's word to his people?

The whole scene touched him strangely. Here they came, one after another, wanting to know the way. There were people of all stripes, people who were never known to come to the scribes with their concerns. And one could tell they were serious. They wanted answers. They never challenged—perhaps they asked for better clarification, but they seemed to submit when they received the answer.

But the answer? John never cited any of Israel's great teachers. He never said where he learned his interpretation of the law. His answers betrayed the opposite! He did not know and did not care about the exposition of the law that the scribes gave. His answers weren't very profound and were completely unlearned: People should share their food and give away their coats if they saw another man freezing. Was this the kind of wisdom that passed for a great teaching in Israel?

And yet there was something about this that would be good for him to take back with him to Jerusalem. No one disputed here.

No one got upset and argued. That which was said was said clearly and with authority, and it applied. It was so strange. In Jerusalem, in the schools of the rabbis, where they had the law in all its glory and knowledge of it in full measure—there, it was if it never applied. Everything became controversial, everything was twisted and turned. None of the great teachers recognized the authority of the others. This is why it was so hard for a noble Pharisee to get people to bow before the truth, and many laughed at it altogether. Here, they bowed, even those who laughed in Jerusalem.

But what was it they bowed to? The delegation had to get clarity on this point. If nothing else, they had their assignment to fall back on.

He looked at his comrades. Apparently they were thinking along the same lines. They had all come to stand in front. Because they were priests and Levites, people had turned aside respectfully. Now John also noticed that there was something peculiar happening and looked at the newcomers inquisitively.

Yes, they wanted to talk to him—but alone. He nodded. He was evidently accustomed to this.

A little farther off, there was a large hut built of rushes. He pointed them there with his hand and asked them to sit down in the shade of its wall. They sat in a circle on the ground. He looked at them questioningly.

The oldest of the priests clarified who they were with a couple words. He said something polite and courteous about the interest with which one followed the remarkable events that had come to pass around Jericho and about the sincere desire, shared by all, that everything that happened would be blessed by he who is to be greatly praised in eternity.

"Amen," said the others. John looked at them searchingly. Then the oldest of the priests went straight to the matter and asked straight out, "Great things demand great words. Tell us the truth, God be praised. Who are you? Are you the Messiah?"

The rabbi held his breath and stared into John's face. It was completely calm. The question didn't seem to surprise him in the least. He answered naturally and quickly, with such a loud voice that the people also heard what followed. The camp wondered if they would be allowed to know what this solemn embassy was about.

"No, I am not the Messiah."

The rabbi drew another breath. He felt a wonderful relief blended with a touch of disappointment.

The old priest had apparently determined not to walk gingerly today. He asked again, just as carelessly and straight to the point, "Who are you then? Are you Elijah?"

And the answer came just as matter-of-factly and calmly as before:

"No, I am not him."

Again, the rabbit took a breath. Not him either! The Tishbite's mantel did not cover the Tishbite himself. The feeling of disappointment grew a bit stronger. But he was still overcome with relief.

The old man continued just as unremittingly:

"Are you, then, the Prophet?"

"No," came the answer just as firmly and without a hint of hesitation.

The old man's face betrayed an easy puzzlement. It was obvious that his storehouse of possible options was running out.

"Who are you then?" he asked. "Tell us so we can give an answer to those who sent us here. What do you say about yourself?"

The tension barely grabbed hold of the rabbi's heart before the Baptist had answered.

"I am the voice of one who cries in the wilderness, 'Prepare the way of the Lord.' Just as Isaiah said."

The tone of his voice was completely ordinary. One could see that all this was obvious to him. But what did he mean? He was right; Isaiah had talked about the voice that would cry in the desert to prepare the way of the Lord and pave a smooth road for him in the desert. But what did this mean now? These words about the desert had a particular resonance for him today, as he had just traveled over those dusty paths. Again, the rabbi felt a strange fascination grip his heart when he thought about what had been written in the same place: "The Lord's glory shall be revealed, and all flesh shall see it together. For so has the Lord's mouth spoken."

Could it be that God would send a forerunner before his Anointed? Was it with divine authority that this voice cried in the desert? Was it the Almighty who bid his people to repent and called the pious to be baptized as if they were proselytes and not Abraham's children? Did he really want his people to yet again pass through the Jordan and come up out of its bed renewed to observe their entrance into the Promised Land? Were they before the milestone? Was the kingdom of heaven so near?

Apparently, the others were not so concerned about the Baptist's answer. They looked at him askance, and their spokesmen questioned him a bit more sharply than before:

"Why, then, do you baptize if you are not the Messiah, nor Elijah, nor even the Prophet?"

John looked at him with a long clear gaze, half-searching, half-challenging.

"I baptize with water," he said, "a baptism of repentance. But among you stands one who you do not know. He was before me, and he comes after me. His sandal I am not worthy to untie."

And then he began to speak about this mightier one, who would baptize in the Holy Spirit and fire and who would have his winnowing fork in hand and would purge his floor to gather the wheat into the barn but burn the chaff in a fire that would never be extinguished.

Now it was the rabbi's turn to look searchingly at the Baptist. Perhaps he had underestimated that man's knowledge. This was a deeper wisdom than he expected to find just now. But he only understood it partially. Who was he who would come? Was it still the Messiah? Would he baptize in the Holy Spirit? It must be the Spirit the Lord had promised through the prophet Joel. He would be poured out upon all flesh before the great and terrible day of the Lord. And the baptism in fire? It must be the judgment of wrath over the unbelievers. The strangest thing was that the Baptist spoke the whole time as if this applied to them all. He shall baptize you, he had said. You? All? Without distinction? But what, then, did it serve that they bore the yoke of the law for so many years if they would now be like publicans and legionnaires?

The others had apparently heard enough. They rose at the sign of the old man and took their leave with reserve. They were clear now. He was not the Messiah. His right to baptize was such and such. And they themselves did not need any part of his baptism of repentance.

Could the Baptist read thoughts? Just as they took their leave, he said, "Do not think you can say to yourselves, 'Abraham is our father.' See these stones? God can awaken children of Abraham from them if he wants."

There was only one answer to this: to slowly walk away with dignity and without looking at him.

After all, they were men with a mission, and they had received the answer to their commission. But they still stayed half a day down there at the Jordan. Without engaging in discussions, they questioned people. They hadn't misconstrued anything. Even if many of the people didn't want to question it and believed that it probably still was the Baptist who was the Messiah, "but secretly," most confirmed that he spoke about one who was greater than himself and who would come after him. It was also obvious that he meant for all people to repent now. He made no distinction whether for scribes or priests. He had even called some Pharisees a brood of vipers and asked the Pharisees who had warned them to escape the wrath to come. And so he had told them to repent. There were many witnesses to that.

With all of this clear, the delegation turned back over the desert after the sun had already descended upon the ridge on the Mount of Olives. The crowd was indignant, and the men talked to each other in hushed voices. Still, the young rabbi rode a little behind the others, quietly and pensively. He was not yet finished with the day's impression.

As they approached Jericho, he saw a wonderful vision. Golden clouds tossed up against the deep-blue sky were illuminated for a moment in the last rays of the sun, and then they lost their glow as they fell into the dark. It was a picture that didn't really belong to the season. One of the farmers stood outside his house and tossed a little pile of grain. Either it hadn't been done very well this summer or he hadn't worked it in the oppressive heat when the oxen finished trampling on the threshing floor. Now he set the winnowing fork's flat wooden tines into the soft pile and let the golden seed spin above his head so that the evening wind took the wheat and carried off the glittering golden flakes. It was a friendly sight that belonged with the beautiful season when the grapes began to mature and the trees bore their fruit. But this evening, the young rabbi thought about something altogether different. He could not escape the Baptist's words. He who comes will have his winnowing fork in hand. He will purge his floor. And then the chaff will be burned up in the fire that never dies.

When they trotted into Jericho between palms and sycamore trees, where their donkeys suddenly danced upon light feet and pushed their way ahead of the small donkeys at the well, the young rabbi came riding in far behind the others, very quiet, very serious.

Galilee of the Heathen

He stood for a moment on the heights above Nazareth. It had been just two hours since he left Cana. Here on the ridge, he was given one last glimpse of his hometown on the hill beyond the plains at the foot of the great mountains. Once he descended into the depths down below, it would disappear from his view. But for how long?

What did they think at home? Was his mom crying? Surely she didn't think he was considering buying a sword and starting a fight with Pontius Pilate. Certainly he had thought about that before, but Judas of Gamala had cured the people of that thought once and for all with his unsuccessful uprising.

Nathanael turned and looked back at the proud Sepphoris he had just left. On top of its hill, it looked so close that he thought that he could touch the battlements of the fortress. It was now Galilee's second-greatest city, with palaces and banks, bazaars and numerous synagogues. But his father had told him what it looked like when Quirinius had his census and Judas staged his uprising. When Varus had successfully chastised the leaders of the uprising, he withdrew his legions and left the whole city a pile of sooty stones and charred beams. People could smell the stench of burnt flesh and scorched wool rags a long way off, and for many weeks, there was a stink that rose from the countless crosses the Romans had nailed the followers of Judas to. The skies were covered with whirling clouds of ravens and carrion birds, and all those spared the cross were driven down to Acko, where they loaded onto Roman slave ships. No one heard from them again. It was the most dreadful scourge that had passed over the area in many lifetimes. And all this because a few madmen didn't want to take part in the great census that Caesar had decreed!

Now Sepphoris had been rebuilt from the ground up, and Herod Antipas kept his happy court there without inquiring about what the scribes said when they came wandering from Jerusalem to speak in the synagogues. It seemed to Nathanael that he felt an air of happy frivolity as he walked through the streets. There were luxuries everywhere, transparent fabrics, makeup and jewelry, mirrors and cushions and inlaid tables of the strangest wood. There were strange loudly dressed people everywhere, colorful Greek prostitutes, eunuchs, and mercenaries. And then there was the traffic! In this part of the country, where all the eastern roads converged, people were accustomed to movement in the streets. But today, he had already encountered an endless train of dusty legionnaires, tall, light-skinned men from Gaul or Germania on the way to the border posts beyond Damascus, and a similarly endless train of Syrian camels on the way to Gaza or Egypt. He had heard at least eight different languages and seen blacks, Egyptians, and people of mixed race. And he had not yet come to the largest route, which crossed the great plains at his feet like a large white band and ran up to the pass at Megiddo—the great sea route that came from Damascus and ended at Caesarea by the sea.

Nathanael had begun to make the climb down the steep slope to Nazareth. His eyes swept over the landscape to the south. Nazareth was the last town in Galilee. Then it was just a long steep descent through the narrow valley before one stood at the wide plain of Jezreel and Megiddo, which began in the east, where the road rose up out of the Jordan Valley before Mount Gilboa, and ended over by the sea in the west, where Mount Carmel sat like a crouching lion looking down at the brown sails outside of Acko.

There again beyond the plain were bluish mountains. There was the border of Samaria, where one was already beyond the borders of the kingdom, among strangers and enemies.

He actually had more sympathy for Judas of Gamala than he wanted to let on. Of course, it was insanity to start a war with Rome. It was also an act of unbelief, for when the day came, God himself would vindicate his afflicted. No force in the world could bring this day about. But still, it was said of Galileans that they placed honor above mammon. This is what separated them from the people in Judah. It was easier to live when one knew that his compatriots hadn't sold their souls for the Roman embrace. The fight was hard and the temptation dangerous. On the one side of the sea were the polished Greeks with their wisdom, their theaters and houses of fornication. On the other side, by the sea, there was Tyre and Sidon with their gods of lust, who taught their worshipers their own debauchery. The seaward side was full of all that had washed up on the shore—vain people and loose morals—and from Damascus came all the enticements of the East. Wherever one turned, there was a reminder that within less than a day's journey, one had all that this wicked world could offer in the form of luxury and refined goods. Nathanael had always thought that this was a point of honor for Galileans: that they more often grasped swords than reached out for all this glittering misery.

Now, as he descended the hills into the valley of Nazareth in the brisk winter weather, he felt kinship with his honor-loving and combative countrymen. The song of clashing swords had been sung on these slopes. The whole landscape was filled with the echo of weaponry pounding amidst the cries of battle. Barak had broken through and struck Sisera on Mount Tabor to the east, pursuing his nine hundred chariots to the river Kishon. On the heights of Mount Moreh beyond Tabor, the Midianites had made their camp, and there they had been slain by the Lord's sword and the sword of Gideon. Mount Gilboa appeared just beyond there—that was where Saul and Jonathan fell in battle with the Philistines, and a little farther to the west appeared Megiddo, where the pious King Josiah fell in battle with Pharaoh Necho. And there on the horizon was Mount Carmel, the mountain where Elijah slaughtered the prophets of Baal and of the Lord's revilers until the river Kishon was red with blood.

No one could pass over these heights without their chests expanding and their wills receiving a new sense of importance and power. It was great to belong to the Lord's people. One ought rather to praise than belittle these farmers and fishermen who would rather let themselves be cut down than compromise with the foreigners' lasciviousness and worship their idols.

Nathanael had to laugh at himself. Now he was almost ready to buy himself a sword and go to war against the Romans. And yet he had learned since childhood that the Lord alone should be exalted on that day. For that reason one should not put his trust in princes, nor in the horse and sword, but alone in him who said, "I shall do it."

Yes, he would do it. But when?

Like so many others, Nathanael had absorbed the words of the prophet: "Oh that you would rend the heavens and come down" And, like many others, for this reason his blood also had burned ever since the first rumors of the new prophet had reached him. So he, like so many others, was unable to stay at his work but instead bundled some bread and olives and went on his way. He had to hear him for himself. He had to know if it was true that the Messiah would come.

He didn't stay in Nazareth. It was a poor little village of the usual type, inhabited by farmers and a few craftsmen. The small square houses with their flat roofs and the high-walled courtyards imbedded with olive trees and vineyards were like those in the rest of Galilee. He only rested a moment in the plaza in front of the well, where the women came with clay jars on their heads as in all the other villages. He ate a few olives and rested in the shade of a wall. Some carpenters were working on a house next door. The masons had already finished their work; the white roughhewn stone blocks were stacked up to the roof line. Now they were putting up the narrow rafters and binding them with wooden slats. The grass that would cover them was already prepared in large heaps. Nathanael saw that the men looked at him and laughed. When he took his bundle and went away they yelled something pejorative at him. Even the women looked at one another as if to say, "Yeah, there goes another one."

He did not concern himself with them. The people in Nazareth did not have a good reputation. If they made fun of him now, this was something to be proud of. He was happy there were already so many drawn south to John, who had become a spectacle in the land.

He continued across the empty threshing floor just outside the city and down the steep valley, with the cliffs to his left, before coming out onto the plain. The air was hot and heavy. An endless line of camels strode in a cloud of dust that filled the nostrils and caused the eyes to sting. It would be better when he reached the great sea route. The Romans had paved this with hard basalt from Tiberias so that they would be able to get around there with their heavy wagons.

Nathanael rested at the crossroads before he continued toward Jordan. In the shade of the poplars, he talked with a Jew from Damascus who had been in Rome. The man told of Caesar's palace, which was as high as a mountain with thousands of windows and gardens on the roof. He spoke about the amphitheater, where all the people in Jerusalem could be seated and where wild animals were fed living people. He talked about life among the nobles, who changed wives as casually as a person might exchange donkeys in Galilee and who would usually tickle their throats with a feather when they began to feel full in order to empty their stomachs before starting the next course. In this manner, they could eat up to fifty courses, the simplest of which cost more than a wedding in Damascus. On the road outside of Rome, the land was full of graves, stately marble tombs with beautiful wood, and on them one could read that the dead had been cremated and had said farewell to all joy. And didn't the Sadducees say pretty much the same thing? But in Rome, he had heard the scribes in the synagogue say that those dead bones would receive life again . . .

So he spoke until the heat became too heavy, and he clasped his hands behind his neck and stretched out to sleep with the donkey bound by one foot and his leather pouch tucked well inside his coat.

After the lunch break, Nathanael took company with some merchants heading south with heavy-laden camels. They came from Magdala with salted sardines and were going to Caesarea. They complained about tolls. Three times they had already been stopped to pay for road maintenance, and each time, they had been ordered to pay extra taxes for their luxuries. Naturally, the publicans had sought to overcharge them, but they kept careful track of the tariffs and suffered no fools. When they followed the black rocks east toward Megiddo, Nathanael went in the opposite direction, toward Jordan, but he found company with an old farmer from Jezreel, who had been at his son's in Nain. He complained about poverty and taxes. When he had come in the evening to his son-in-law's place, there wasn't a loaf of bread to be found in the whole house. They never dared bake more than they had immediate need for. And it was the same with the neighbors: there was no bread to loan. There was a tax on each bunch of grapes, sheaf of grain, on each and every sheep and oxen too. There would certainly be a tax on any source of water. And when one had to get the money from his scarce granary for the tax, one had almost nothing to pay because Herod acquired cheap grain from Egypt. So one starved himself though one lived in a land that the Almighty had blessed with wells, wine, and oil without end. And all this because of Herod and his senseless waste. He washed himself in wine and gave more meat in a day to one of his washed-up drinking buddies than a poor farmer could taste in half a year.

The old man nodded knowingly. He knew how everything went. His son-in-law had a brother who lived in Tiberias, just below the castle, and he could tell . . .

Nathanael had heard all this a thousand times before. He had seen it today with his own eyes. Everywhere lay the small villages on the hills, hardly a thousand feet from each other. Every square swarmed with children, and in all the small gardens, women and half-grown boys worked. Though the land was full of greenery and though the small narrow fields crept like green bands up every mountain, it was hard to find bread and olives enough for so many mouths. It was a crime of Herod's that he vied with the Romans when it came to fleecing his own people. But there wasn't much to do about all this. There were more important things in the offing.

Carefully, he began to ask the old man what they heard about the prophet who baptized at the Jordan. The old man gave him a quick, half-suspicious look.

"Are you on your way there?" he asked.

When Nathanael answered that it was so, it was as if the old man's heart had opened. He came so close that their shoulders bumped together as they walked. It was as if he were afraid that those passing by would hear something. He turned his face to Nathanael and come so close that it was known that the old man ate garlic and bad olives. So he spoke carefully, in spurts, and yet with great earnest:

John was a great prophet sent from heaven. The whole land went out to hear him. They came in palanquins from Jerusalem and on camels from Bosra. Great rich noblemen confessed that they had sinned, usurers pay back their interest rates, the poor were forgiven their leases, and soldiers became like lambs. Could anything like this happen if the Blessed had not visited his people? Could anyone speak such a word of truth if he wasn't a prophet?

But had he heard what John said?

The old man looked around quickly and then stuck his bearded chin back in close: John had said that the Messiah was near!

Nathanael nodded. He had heard it.

The old man continued, saying that now it would be over for the bravado of the oppressors. Now the oppressor's rod would be broken just as in the days of Midian. Now Herod could wallow in his shamelessness as much as he wants. It would not last long . . .

Again, he cozied up to Nathanael. Had he heard that? John had told Herod straight to his face that he lived in incest because he took his brother's wife. He told him that he had plundered the poor of the land for his wine and oil, and that the prayers of the poor rose up from his land like smoke from Soar . . . so now it could not last long.

Again, the old man winked. His steps became easy, he stopped and whispered, he slapped his knees and started again.

Still, when he compelled Nathanael to be a guest at his house and they sat on the dirt floor tearing the chewy bread and dipping his fingers in sour milk, Nathanael turned again to the great and beautiful thought: it would not tarry long now.

A Baptism of Repentance

"Do you have a wife?"

The others looked at him tentatively. He had agile hands and strong arms, he was tan but not weather beaten. It fit together. His hands were used to carving and polishing. They could glide smoothly over a yoke or cut a checkered pattern into a coffin lid. One could lay whatever beam a man wanted on his shoulders, and his arms were used to lifting. It looked as if he worked outside a lot, but not in all weather. He was not a farmer, not a fisherman, and not some craftsman of the type that worked in the street outside his house in the shade of his awning. It fit that he was a carpenter. They could tell he was from Nazareth right away because of his accent. They also understood that he belonged to those who waited for the redemption of Israel. They were drawn to him and spoke openly and without reservation to him about everything, even the children at home. But why was he not married? He had to be thirty. By that age, every other man would have been married for a long time already. To see sons grow up in his house and see his name preserved in Israel—that was what a person lived for. If a man died childless, the man had lived in vain. Only odd and strange men did that. But this carpenter from Nazareth seemed healthy and normal.

"Are you widowed?" one of them asked.

The stranger shook his head and only answered with a word of scripture: that no one ruled over his path. A man cannot guide his steps. Everyone's path is staked out.

He had a tranquil manner that was very firm and almost authoritative. It showed that he thought a lot about this. And who were they that they should censure him? So once again, they began to talk about home, about the poverty that threatened the rich districts at their lake, about the Greek naysayers over on the other side, about Herod's dissolute life and what the Baptist had said today.

They sat on a bed of black gravel mixed with clay that the Jordan had washed up on the beach. The big tamarisks dragged their branches in the water. All the leaves and branches were gray because the muddy waters of the spring flood had climbed high up on the trunks and given them a coating of sludge and mud. The tree crowns were filled with nests of the half-decomposed reeds and dead scrubby branches that floated in the river. They had made a fire of the gray driftwood and dry reeds in the night camp. Now they sat and looked at the river's swift but quiet waters. They rolled on by without a sound, all gray and muddy. For those who were used to the white foamy brooks and springs on the sun-washed slopes of Galilee, there was something strange about this quiet opaque water flowing through the overhanging branches as it slowly ate away at the gray clay of the riverbanks.

Neither did they know what they should think about this strange weather. It had been oppressively hot yesterday. Today it had been cold, and powerful thunderclouds towered up in the west, standing like a blue-gray wall behind the mountains, higher, bolder, and more frightening than the Judean cliffs. They gathered their coats tighter around them, conversations grew quiet, and they made themselves comfortable on the bed of reeds to wait for the hour the Baptist determined.

*

The evening was cool, and there were not many who came down to the place of baptism. Those who stepped up onto the beach shivered as they shook the water off of themselves and wrapped up in their coats again. Only the Baptist stayed in the gray river. He seemed to be as insensitive to cold as he was to heat.

The river's quiet waters made a sharp bend just beyond the place of baptism, and the stream swept across to the other side, where a large tree had been undermined and fell over. People saw naked tree roots everywhere. The roots had lost their grip on the clay but not the trunk they had supported, and the trunk had begun to lean. It was as if the forest itself spoke of impending doom and inevitable catastrophe to come.

"And you?" said the Baptist.

It was a middle-aged man who stepped out into the shallows. His answer was drowned out by the water splashing around his feet.

"I have taken eighteen pieces of Eljakim's inheritance . . . I have poured water from Eliasar's well. I switched my dead kid for his. I have uttered curses over . . ."

Nothing more was heard. He came up to the Baptist and knelt down in the water, and the Baptist let the water from his full hands pour over him. Then the man climbed out onto the muddy beach and withdrew with the others.

Only one remained. He had waited till the end. When the Baptist saw him come, he met him with a tentative look.

"And you?" he said.

The other one didn't say anything. The Baptist was standing completely still, with his arms hanging down, and looked at him steadily. The cold severity left his face. A great sense of wonder appeared and radiated from his eyes.

"You . . ." he said. "I need to be baptized by you . . . and you come to me!"

He raised his hands to deter him.

The other one made a small movement with his hands, and the Baptist's arms fell again.

"Do it now," he said, "in order to fulfill all righteousness."

The Baptist obeyed. He did it silently and calmly, as a mere instrument for something that must be done. Immediately, the baptized man stepped up out of the cold river, brushed the water off of him, and then almost imperceptibly lifted his face and hands in prayer. A clear ray of light broke in over the treetops through the gray stormy evening. The Baptist lifted his face to look up. His big eyes fixed as they followed something that seemed to descend upon the baptized man, then rested upon the figure on the beach. At the same time, the Baptist's face took on a tense and vigilant expression, as if he was listening to something. Without moving, he stood in the water and listened intently with a dumb struck visage of awe and merriment.

Then the other one took his clothes and wrapped them around him, fastened his belt, and said good-bye.

The Baptists remained standing until the other had disappeared into the bushes. Then he came up out of the water and fell on his knees to pray before the heavenly majesty. Quietly, he bent to the earth, deeper and deeper until his forehead touched the riverbank where the other had just stood.

*

That same evening, a fierce storm raged within the rock cliffs of the valley. The storm clouds rose ever higher and hung like a harsh threat over the rocky paths. The naked red escarpment that towered up to the heavens behind Jericho seemed to sag under the burden of so many clouds.

Where the valley opened up like a crack in the rocky bluffs, the darkness swept in, and the storm howled through the cliffs. A farmer gathering thorns on the hillside struggled in vain to keep the bundle together. He finally let go of it, and it rolled in front of him. A lone wanderer hiked up the mountain. The storm ripped into the white coat that was bound tightly around him. He looked exceedingly small against the giant desert mountains and the black thunderclouds, a single man ascending into the wasteland to meet powers that seemed impossible to defy.

The farmer shouted for him to turn back. Nights in the Judean desert held only the storm and danger, nothing but wild animals and deadly precipices. There would be nothing to eat.

The stranger turned and answered. It was not easy to hear his voice amidst the storm, but it sounded like a word from scripture—something like, "A man does not live by bread alone."

The farmer nodded and waved with one hand while he held his head scarf tight with the other. It was just one of those outlandish men of God, one of the men from the Jordan. They had to go their own way. No one could understand them. But he still praised the Almighty that there were such people in Israel again. Perhaps the spirit of Elijah hadn't died yet.

And he went back to rolling his bundle in the storm.

Follow Me

Thick vegetation along the shoreline almost hid the ragged outcroppings of basalt. The vines entangled themselves over the hard stone, and the men on the path walked through waist-high waves of flowers. The entire hillside was blue above them. The lake was just as clear as the cloudless sky, deep blue with splashes of satin-like silver. The mountains on the other side were also a faded blue but mottled with shades of light green and a touch of pink where they were steepest. Mount Hermon, capped with glittering snow, towered over the whole picture. Its white crown seemed to float in the blue haze. When looked at through the palm trees that were laden and orange with half-ripe dates and the pink blossoms of apple trees, the surreal image reminded one of a dream. The sun glittered on everything and the air was filled with the songs of birds, the scent of flowers and black soil.

Simon didn't have much of an eye for all this beauty. He stood out on the stone jetty, peering into the shallow water, his bronze body tensed from head to toe with a firm grip on his net. He waited a moment for the sparkling bustle out there to come closer. Suddenly, his whole body erupted with a smooth motion. The heavy net swiftly swinging over his head like a sling before he released it over the water. As if by magic, the clumsy-looking sack unfurled into an airy bell-shaped net and fell upon the water. In the next moment mirror-like pieces of shiny lead whipped from the edge of the net. A ring of sizzling foam formed as the net sank to the bottom. In the very same moment, Simon was out in the water and Andrew came running along the shoreline. Carefully, they pulled the dragline, letting the lead weights scrape the bottom. Then they lifted the whole mess of wet mesh out of the water. It looked like a heavy sack again, but this time, it was full of swarming fish. The men watching on the shore clapped their hands. It was a fine cast.

The brothers laughed at each other and emptied the catch into a clay pot. Then they hung the net on a stake to dry. Andrew went back to his fishing hole and picked up his net. Carefully he waded out to one of the black rocks and climbed up to get a better vantage of the shallow water.

Their father had never liked it when they fished this way. It did not pay off well. But it was the most fun, and so the two brothers made a sport of it, just like they had ten years ago when they were half-grown boys. And just like back then, they now had a crowd of spectators on the shore. No one could pass by without stopping a moment and watching the splendid scene play out.

Andrew made an unsuccessful cast. When he came back onto the shore, he looked up from the wet net to notice a new spectator standing on the beach. He must have been watching for a while before they noticed.

Andrew was surprised to see who it was: Jesus, the carpenter from Nazareth whom they had met with the Baptist on the Jordan. Andrew brought his hand up to his forehead and greeted him cheerfully. Then he called to his brother, who tossed his net aside immediately and came up. They exchanged the usual greetings and wished each other peace and blessing. It was customarily sonorous and dignified, but the words carried the meaning they had learned at the Jordan. They didn't have anything more to say. Jesus anticipated their questions and spoke calmly, merely bidding them, "Come and follow me."

"Where?" Simon asked. Just then, he felt a little embarrassed by his question. There was something about Jesus's whole demeanor that told him it was not a question of going with him to Capernaum or Nazareth, but to get up and go. Go wherever he went, always with him, just as the disciples of a rabbi followed their teacher. He continued with a hint of challenge, perhaps even a dare:

"I will make you into fishers of men."

Simon couldn't grasp it. This was something completely new, an enigma, something that laid outside the base of his experience. But there were two things he understood with unusual clarity and with a sharpness that cut right through every objection. First was that this man was to be trusted. There was no one he would rather ask for counsel or who he would rather obey. Why was it so with this man? Simon did not know. It lay in the fullness of his being. Something emanated from him that gave no place for suspicion nor objections. This was the other thing that Simon immediately understood: this man had the right to take him with him. If Simon stepped off the path and ran away now, not only would he be a coward, but somehow, he would be false. This was something he despised.

Jesus didn't wait for their answer. He calmly turned and walked away. Neither of the two waited for the other to decide either. They got up and followed him almost simultaneously. They left their nets on the shore.

They looked at each other and nodded before they had gone too far. Bumblebees buzzed in a sea of flowers all around them as a flock of pelicans lit upon the lake like an arrangement of cut flowers. The Master went north to Capernaum. The Master . . . yes, now he was their master, from whom they would learn. A wonderful master, a man of the people, not like some scribe. His forehead was not white in between the black locks of hair, and neither were his hands soft and white. His form didn't take the leaning posture that characterized long years of study. He was like the common people and yet different from them all. Simon couldn't explain it.

The Master stood as a boat pulled into shore. There were five men in it. Simon recognized the old Zebedee at once. He had two laborers with him, and his two sons, James and John. They were busy cleaning the big dragnets used for fishing on the open sea.

Jesus went up to the boat. Simon watched as they greeted one another and listened to the Master say something. He saw the puzzled faces of the servants. Then Jesus turned and came back to them. James and John let go of the nets, climbed out of the boat and followed after him.

Now they were four. They continued toward Capernaum with few words.

With Power and Authority

Simon could hardly see anything when he first came in. The sun was shining bright outside the synagogue, and it took some time for a person to adjust to the dim light inside. At first, he could only see the rows of pillars, the woman's gallery, and the half-round window over the gable wall. The people were just a dark mass as they tried to find places to stand.

As the service progressed, he began to see a bit clearer. Colors began to appear on the woodwork up front where the Torah scrolls were kept in carved cabinets and the reader would step up behind the railing. The coats and faces took on color and life, and all sorts began to emerge from the formless mass.

As usual, the singing of the psalm surged shrill and sharp as it alternated half verse by half verse. They confessed the faith of Israel. A man chanted the prayers, and the people answered with amen. It smelled of mint from the twigs on the floor. Dust danced in the sunlight that poured in from the gable window, and the women could be seen behind the squares of lattice work in the gallery. Everything was normal, but then came the great surprise Simon had anticipated. It was an anticipation that secretly filled him with excitement.

As so many times before, the old wool weaver read the scriptures melodically and with solemnity. Now the trustee turned and, according to custom, asked if anyone had a word of exhortation. Nobody really expected there to be any exposition of the law today because there weren't any wandering rabbi's sitting up front. It was only for the sake of good order that Jairus waited a moment to conclude the service.

It was then that it happened. Someone moved up from the front pillars to exchange a few words with synagogue's trustee, and then Simon's master stood in the place of the law teacher up front in the chancel.

From that moment, it was dead quiet in the synagogue. No one scraped their feet. No one sighed as they shifted position. No one shuffled on the stone benches around the walls.

Simon listened breathlessly. He drank in each and every one of these words that flowed forth like a calm but irresistible stream. There was something new in every statement, something obvious and irrefutable, but something simultaneously so new and bold that it took one's breath. This word never took refuge in the authority of the scribes. It never hid behind what others said. There was never any "possibly" or "perhaps," just an indescribably firm and authoritative "I say to you." Here was one who spoke with God's commission, a herald that cried out the great King's message. And the message was incredible. The kingdom of God was near. The time was full; all would be fulfilled. God's dominion would be established. Everyone was now called to repentance in God's name. It was the same power, the same sensation of the new age's imminent proximity, that they had experienced at the Jordan. But here, there was something even more. Repent, the Baptist had said, the ax is laid to the root of the tree. The Master also called for repentance. But he said, "Believe the gospel."

What he meant by that was not so easy to clarify for oneself. But no one could miss that it was a joyous message. In all these powerful words, there was something that shined and glimmered with great joy. When the Baptist spoke, one expected that fire would fall from heaven—bursts of wrath and judgment. When the Master spoke, it brought to mind the words of the prophet about the dew of heaven dripping from above and righteousness pouring down.

It wasn't until the Master finished that Simon noticed he was standing with his mouth open as he listened. Embarrassed, he shut it and shifted. A sigh of relief went throughout the synagogue, as if an electric shock released its grip. At the same time, a murmur of hushed questions was heard: What was this? It was a new teaching with power and authority.

Once again, Jairus stepped forward to conclude the service. He had just opened his mouth when there was a howl throughout the crowd. Everyone turned. The women pressed their terrified faces against the lattice work. Simon stood on his toes and grabbed a shoulder in front of him to see. Then he realized it was one of the possessed men, one of those crazy wretches who suddenly began to speak with a voice different than his own. They often carried four or five different spirits within them, spirits that wielded power over them. Sometimes they fell down helpless, sometimes as stiff as a board or contorted by cramps. Often they were nastily perceptive and would bluntly say what others did and thought.

The man with the spirit forced his way to one of the pillars. His face was distorted, and his mouth opened to show his missing teeth. He fought intensely to get free from the men who tried to hold him. The whole time, he roared furiously and madly:

"Go away! What do you have to do with us, Jesus of Nazareth!? Have you come to destroy us? I know who you are: the Holy One of God!"

He made another overpowering attempt to get free and dragged the other two along. The whole synagogue was one big tangle of excited people pushing and shoving. Simon didn't see anything else, but he heard the Master's voice above the commotion. It was even more commanding than he had heard before.

"Be quiet, and come out of him!"

There was a thud. Something fell to the ground. People ran away and pushed again. A ring formed in the midst of the stone floor, and Simon got a glimpse of the possessed man. He fell backward and lifted his body in an arch as he bellowed. The next minute, he was quiet. He sank to the floor. His eyes closed as he went completely limp and motionless. The men lifted him up. He looked around as if he wondered where he was. Someone took him under his arms, and he walked toward the exit. Complete calm had taken him over, and he left uninjured.

It became very still and silent. The ruler of the synagogue started up a song of praise, and the song restored calm. Only on the steps, as one stepped out into the flaming sunlight, was the spell broken and everyone gave vent to their amazement. What was that? What scribe can speak in such a manner? Such things had never been seen before.

The Master withdrew and went straight down to the shoreline at the lake. All four followed on his heels. They agreed to go to Simon and Andrew's place. But just here, on the beach, Simon remembered that he ought to mention that his mother-in-law was sick with a fever. It was not easy to welcome the Master when she lay there with the chills in the house's only room.

He thought a moment. The events at the synagogue, had caused him to wonder if the Master ought not come precisely for the sake of the sick woman. So he spoke with Andrew. Yes—one could try. They didn't need to demand anything, but . . . and so they went up to the Master and spoke with him about her. He just nodded.

They went through the gate and over the garden. In the dim light of the house, the young men stood at the door, a little doubtful. They saw the Master go over to the sick woman where she lay on her bed pad in the corner. He leaned over her and said something, then took her by the hand and lifted her up. She straightened her clothes, shook out her bedroll, and rolled it up. Then she went over to the shelf above the hearth to get the clay pot and bowls and began to prepare dinner for them.

The men followed her with amazed eyes. Her hands didn't shake, and she walked with complete calm and purpose. They looked at each other again, their eyes large with amazement. What was this?

Everyone Is Looking for You

The sun had gone down, and the Sabbath was over.

The city came to life all at once. As long as the last ray of light lingered above the temple and the white colonnades of Hippo, the Greek city high up on the mountain across the lake, the streets of Capernaum lay empty and deserted. Only a Tyrian smith, a man who asked after neither God nor the Sabbath, passed along the tall walls that shaded all the quiet streets without windows, their doors boarded up.

There was a complete change just as the last ray of light was extinguished. The doors flew open, and children ran out and danced around for the joy of being able to move again. The women rushed to the well with their water jars. The men stretched after all the sitting and breathed deep in the cool evening air. The smoke began to billow out through the roofs, filling the streets with the acrid smell of burning dung, the long awaited sign that there would soon be hot food in the houses, ready to eat.

The blind sandal maker was among the first to come out into the streets. He felt around with his stick and ran his hands along the rough basalt blocks in the wall. But this evening, he didn't stop at the bench under the big palm tree on the shoreline. He groped along to the northern part of the city. He walked slowly, counting the familiar doors in the wall and continually bumping into other people. Some people snapped at him, others laughed and helped him across the alley. There was trampling, shuffling, and murmuring around him that he wasn't used to, not even when the Sabbath was over. When he had fifty steps left, he didn't go any farther. There were people all around him; everywhere he turned, he touched clothing and naked skin. It was then that he first understood he was not the only one who had decided to seek out Simon's house this evening.

The mother with sick child was the first to come. She lived in the vicinity, and if she had dared, she would have taken the feverish girl in her arms and gone out as soon as her brother-in-law came home from the synagogue talking about the new prophet and his particular power. Now she sat on the stone step in front of the door and waited.

A strange entourage of maimed and miserable beings gathered around her, broken and poor people with their crutches and neglected wounds. The crowd increased with relatives and the curious. The small alleyway was full of people. As it grew darker, it also grew quieter. Those who only came to watch went home. Those who really needed help waited patiently. Some lay on cushions in the street; others sat by the wall. A crutch fell and made a clamor outside. An old man hummed his psalms, and a couple strong men spoke calmly to the lunatic they held between them.

It was almost dark. Above the flat roofs, palm trees imprinted their silhouettes against the sky. A single little lamp flickered within a small opening in the wall. A donkey bellowed in the distance, and a child cried somewhere within the crowd. Then everything was completely quiet. Someone removed the brace behind the thick wooden door to Simon's house, the woman with the child moved aside, and door opened to throw a flood of light out onto the crowd outside. It shined upon the dark faces and the white eyes as everyone gazed in the same direction.

He stood there, in the midst of the light. Someone carried a lamp and there was a whole entourage of young men surrounding him. He stepped out with them and began to walk around. He spoke with some. He passed by others. He was strict with some, some he comforted. He did everything with the same authority. He talked much of faith. He helped some; he said, "Your faith has made you well." He seemed to be able to see straight through people. He often spoke of their sins. He told some that their sins were forgiven, and others he told they would not be forgiven if they did not reconcile with their enemies. When he came to a dirty and broken wretch, it seemed as if he only saw him. One could believe that he had come out this evening for his sake alone. But he was the same way with everyone he spoke to.

Sometimes it was completely quiet in the alley, almost as if everyone held their breath. Every neck stretched, and everyone waited to see what would happen. At other times there was crowding and shouting, cheers and dancing upon the cobblestones when someone hurried home to tell the story. Even from far down the alley by the docks, one could hear how they praised God and how they trilled, shrilled, and cheered like a man does at a wedding. Sometimes the wild cry of a possessed person pierced the night. It was as if someone guarded themselves with insane anxiety. Then the Master's voice was always heard, stronger and more commanding than normal. It was like a strong hand that grabbed the piercing cry in the midst of the darkness and humbled it.

*

It was late into the night when the last psalm of praise was sung and Simon could stretch out on the floor. He blew out the lamp and lay listening to the breathing of the others who had made beds for themselves on the few bed pads or slept in their coats on the floor. He was having a hard time sleeping. Their world had changed since morning. This was the first Sabbath since he had become a disciple. He had continually felt the presence of the incredible event that would happen ever since he laid the net aside on the beach. The kingdom of heaven was near. John had said this too. But down there by the Jordan, there they all waited. There they all repented in preparation, but they did not have that which they talked about. Today, he had thought about what the power of the kingdom of God meant. It had begun in the synagogue. It was as if the radiance of God himself had descended upon the Master's words and filled them with a reflection of the glory enthroned upon the cherubim. And it had been exactly the same that evening. Here was something that really had not ever been before. The people would say, "We have never seen such a thing before."

But what now was this? Was it a precursor to that which would come? How would it be when the Lord's judgment came and God seized power? First and foremost, the people thought that the Romans would then be chased out of the country. The heathens would receive sevenfold for their arrogance and oppression. The fallen house of David would be restored in all its glory. The temple would be purified and the Messiah would reign in the land, and the grapes would be as big as waterskins and the kernels of wheat like apples. But the most important and primary thing was this: the Messiah would ascend to the throne of his father, David, and break asunder the Roman yoke.

But not a trace of this was seen. The powers that were now stirring did not seem to direct themselves against the Romans in any way. Jesus never spoke about them. He spoke about the kingdom, but he did not say what would happen to the Roman power. It was strange.

Already with the Baptist, Simon had received a lot to think about when it came to this kingdom. John preached that it would come. This was why so many young folk came to him from Galilee. Many of them had kept swords hidden in their homes since the day Judas of Gamala was defeated. But John didn't talk about swords. He talked about the ax the judge had set to the root of the tree. And he spoke about it in such a way that one felt as if he himself were the tree that was to be felled when the judge laid the edge of the ax to the bark and swung the first blow. John gave no order to brandish one's sword and wait for the signal. He told them to confess their sins and then wait for the one who was to come. And the one to come would judge. He would baptize with the Spirit and fire. But how would it go? Was this now the judgment? No—perhaps there would be judgment, but not in this manner.

Simon did not understand this. He put it away for the future. He was a disciple. He did not need to know everything but to listen, learn, and see . . . fortunately.

*

When the first roosters began to crow and there were still a couple hours remaining before dawn, the vegetable vender behind the synagogue lit his lamp and went out. He wanted to send a few baskets of onions with a camel driver who would leave for Bethsaida just before daybreak, and he had not done anything about the matter when the Sabbath had ended. So now he got up while the whole city was sleeping and went up on the roof to get some onions laid out up there to dry.

To his amazement, he discovered that he was not the only one up. Down in the street, he heard footsteps—not the sleepy shuffling of the fishmongers, who were normally on their way to Chorazin at this hour, and neither the soft solid steps of some woman with a burden on her head. It was the rushed and determined manner of a young man walking. He looked down over the wall at the edge of the roof and saw a white shape hurry by and disappear on the street that went out to the country. Yet for a long time afterward, he could hear the short small cracks of sandals against cobblestone. It was apparent that the man over there had left the road and took the steps up the mountain, whatever his business there might be.

Just two hours later, the vegetable vendor was given reward for his vigilance when Simon and his brother Andrew came and asked if anyone had seen Jesus of Nazareth. They weren't the only ones inquiring around the houses. The whole city stirred about. It was already crowded in front of Simon's house at daybreak, and it was alleged that people were still coming from Genesaret with their sick. But no one knew where the Master was. It was a proud moment for the vegetable vendor when he could put his thumbs in his belt and talk about onions, camel drivers, and his strange sightings.

Simon had been ashamed to be awoken by his mother-in-law, who told him the Master's bed was empty. It had been even more shameful to meet all the people in the street looking for Jesus without being able to give them an answer. Now he had finally gotten this lead and was on his way up the mountain. Andrew followed on his heels, as did all the other onlookers.

The mountains went almost straight into the lake at Capernaum, and along the whole shore, they lifted the land in massive slopes. The path that wound its way among the black rocks almost disappeared in the dense greenery. The huge buttercups looked like drops of red blood, and the umbels floated like foam at his elbows as Simon broke through the green luxuriance. He was red and sweaty but he did not give up. Only when he had climbed for a half an hour and reached the cusp of the first ascent did he straighten himself out and look around.

At his feet, he had the city, the harbor, the boats, and all the steep slopes with their thousands upon thousands of flowers. The ground in front of him was just as studded with the glory of spring. It rose up against the big mountains in the distance. His eyes searched the landscape. There was boulder after boulder underneath the spring greenery. Only goats, sheep, and their watchers lived there. But there wasn't even a shepherd to be seen on the hillside, since the side of every road down by the beach provided enough grazing. Up here, there was only greenery, the fragrance of flowers, the humming of bees, and then a big gray, black-winged raptor hovering high overhead.

While he stood looking around, he saw someone stand up next to a stone slab just a little farther up. Simon immediately saw who it was and made his way through the flowers. He breathed heavily as he came up and, while still a long way off, yelled out, "Master, everyone is asking for you. There are just as many as yesterday. Everyone is looking for you."

There was the twinge of a little smile that showed in the Master's tranquility when he answered, "No, Simon. Today we will go to other districts, to the villages over there."

He lifted his arms and pointed along the sea, where the small villages lay like gray flecks amidst the green fields.

"I have a message for them. I have been sent for their sake."

The others came along. They asked him to accompany them down again. But he shook his head and repeated what he had said. The gospel of the kingdom of God should be proclaimed to others also. This was his task.

Simon was quiet. It made him sorry for the people down there. It was a shame not to return with the Master and not see him continue the triumph of yesterday. But he was quiet. He had slept. The Master had spoken with God up here. And perhaps God had spoken with him?

So he wiped the sweat drops from his forehead, bowed to the others, and made himself ready to follow.

The Kingdom of Heaven Is Near

It was like a dream.

Simon rested on the oars and mustered the people on the shore. The gathering reminded him of those that gathered around John at the Jordan, but those were nothing compared to the masses that thronged here. Every inch of the steep shoreline was full of people. They sat on all the stone blocks. They had climbed out onto the rocks in the lake. They stood barefoot in the water, and they sat in row after row on the slopes until the last of them disappeared behind the steep bank. The crowd was so huge that the Master had to go out in a boat. And now he sat there speaking to them from the thwart in the aft.

A light breeze blew in from the lake, and Peter took the oars to prevent the boat from being driven inland. It was already evening, the banks on the shore were shaded, and the heat was no longer suffocating.

The Master spoke. The wind caught his strong voice and carried it high up on the hills. One could see them listening up there. As always, he spoke about the kingdom. The more Simon listened, the better he understood that there was nothing in all the Master said that did not deal with the kingdom. He blessed those who would receive the kingdom. It was the poor and the oppressed, those who hungered for righteousness that they didn't have, those who were small and humble at heart, those who forgave and wanted to be forgiven, those who suffered injustice without revenge, those who felt their sins and did not cheat them away when God came to rebuke them. To his own amazement, Simon had begun to believe that the Master really meant that the kingdom was precisely for these poor and small people that the Pharisees never acknowledged, all these who worked and slaved, who acknowledged that God's commandments were right, but who knew that they were not such as the law demanded. The Pharisees were inexorable on that point. They always said that the sort of people who did not know the law were damned. And it was not easy for a poor wretch to know all the statutes of the elders, and still less easy was it to keep them. The Master was also strict on the law. Not a jot shall be lost, but all would be fulfilled. He even said that righteousness that did not surpass that of the scribes was not good enough for the kingdom of God. He could lay out the law so that one wondered if he was any better than the worst publican. But it was different than with the scribes. One never stayed with them when they were at their strictest. One only became indignant when they said that it was breaking the Sabbath to draw a line in the sand with his sandal because it was a manner of plowing or when they admonished people to sew up all the loose cords on their Sabbath clothes because one carried a burden if one carried a loose cord on him. But when the Master was strict, one didn't contradict anything. When he said that it was adultery to look with lust on one's neighbor's wife, then men were ashamed of themselves.

Though the Master could cut like a razor straight into a person's most hidden sins in such a manner that there wasn't a single living person that could consider himself righteous, he was incredibly merciful at the same time. There was a predominance of great joy in everything he said. There was power and glory and beauty, something particularly great and overwhelming that blotted out sins and invited wretches and bunglers to come and be guests at the table with Abraham, Isaac, and Jacob. This was what the people felt when they came. Simon could see them up there on the shore: all these poor, quiet, timid and sinewy men with tanned skin and cracked nails and worn-out peasant wives with dirt on their clothes, carrying small children in their skinny arms.

Did they understand this? Sometimes they carried themselves in an infuriating manner. Like just now with that leper! He had rushed forward without bothering to warn anyone that he was unclean. He had cast himself down upon his knees and stretched his hands out to the Master. They were white with sores and sluffing skin, and the Master had mercy on him and made him clean. But then he had been told, strictly and earnestly, that he should not say a word to anyone but go directly to Jerusalem and sacrifice in the temple as the law demanded. It was as if the Master had wanted to get him away from Galilee as soon as possible so he thought to send the man to the temple which he loved. But instead of obeying, the leper ran around to all the villages and showed himself. He meant well, but for the Master it meant that there wasn't a town he could even show himself in. Rather, he had to go up into the hills and farther and farther away from the people. But they even came for him there. Rumors flew like swallows, and they came immediately, all the people in the villages and strangers who came from the farthest reaches of the land, from Hebron and Jerusalem, from the Decapolis and from cities by the sea.

It was like a dream.

All power and authority seemed to lie in the Master's hands. Nothing was impossible for him. The lame threw off their crutches and walked away. The blind could see. Evil spirits departed, and the craziest lunatics regained their wits and became calm.

When there were so many people by the lake that they couldn't even find time to eat, they had gone over to the other side. It was in the night, and the Master had slept in the boat. Then the stormy winds came blowing from the mountain. The winds created one of those really dangerous storms that turned the lake into a boiling pot of froth and foam. Fear took hold of them when the boat began to fill, and they woke the Master. He rose and rebuked the storm like a man rebukes a howling dog, and instantly it was completely quiet and calm. He asked them why they didn't have faith, why were they so afraid. They bailed out the boat and rowed farther, looking at each other in amazement. They all had the same question: Who is this?

And was this not the same question that must occupy everyone who heard the Master speak from the boat?

"You have heard it said of old. But I say to you . . . Not all who say to me, 'Lord, Lord,' will enter into heaven . . . Therefore everyone who hears these my words . . ."

Who was he who could say such things? He said it with an authority that was obvious. But who had such authority—but God alone? Who was this man?

He Blasphemes

They heard a loud crack and then another from the ceiling above them. The Master stopped talking, and they all looked up. Simon had noticed for a while that there were people on top of the house, but he thought it was someone that wanted to listen or watch through the hole in the roof. That was the reasonable assumption. The house was crammed with people. The garden outside was crowded too. It was no wonder that some of those who couldn't see or hear anything had found ladders and gone up on the roof.

But this was something different. The roof shook under the hard blows. Someone was working hard up there, ripping and tearing through the smooth wall plaster up there on the outside. Then they could hear rustling in the reeds between the rafters, and the next moment, the pick broke straight through the ceiling. A beam of bright sunlight broke through the darkness and played in the billowing clouds of limestone splinters and dust. Then the work was almost finished. All the reeds were ripped away from between the rafters. Debris poured down upon the floor, and a patch of sunlight fell upon all the rubble.

Simon brushed the dust from his face and squinted up at the light. What was this?

The next minute, the opening was filled with something that looked like a giant sack. It descended amidst a new landslide of mortar and twigs, slowly and carefully. A new flood of light followed.

Now Simon could see, and the situation became clear in a second. That which had been lowered was a common mattress. Straps had been tied to the corners, and a man was spread out over the cushions. He was immovable, with one hand folded on his chest in an unnatural position and with his legs strangely twisted together. The only signs of life within him were huge searching eyes. Up above, there were four other men, who looked down through the opening, all with the same anxious eagerness.

The mattress had reached the ground. The quadriplegic painfully turned his head. One could see how the muscles strained within his skinny neck. Simon looked at the Master, who had stayed where he was in the midst of the confusion. Now he rose from the rug and went over to the crippled man. He looked at him in the usual way, inquiringly, confidently, and encouragingly. Then he said, "Take heart, my son. Your sins are forgiven."

Simon had expected something different. Was *that* what the crippled man wanted? Perhaps, yet . . . in any case, it was what he needed most. Simon had known that since he was at the Jordan.

The lame man's eyes lit up with an anxious wondering. Jesus had turned from him. A few scribes sat just behind the Master on the carpet among the guests of honor. They had come from Magdala and Sepphoris to listen to the new teacher of the law. They hadn't said much today, but they listened very carefully. The Master turned to them while they were still completely unprepared and said, "Why do you think thus in your hearts?"

He looked at them as if he pondered their thoughts, and then he asked, "Which is easier to say to him: your sins are forgiven, or get up, take your bed, and go?"

There was a look of contempt in the eyes of the scribes, somewhat embarrassed and scornful at the same time. They were thinking that a false prophet can easily tell a lame man that his sins are forgiven. But to command him to walk? That he can't do.

Jesus looked at them for a moment. He was somewhat tentative. Then he raised his voice a little. It made a sound that for Simon always brought to mind the word of God's Spirit hovering over the great black waters.

"So that you may know that the Son of Man has authority on earth to forgive sins . . ." he said, turning directly to the lame man, who looked at him expectantly the whole time. Now Jesus lifted his hand and continued:

". . . So I say to you, rise up, take your bed, and go home."

Simon strained to see. The lame man brought his elbows back and straightened himself on the mattress before looking up at the Master, who nodded for him to continue. Then he sat up, bushed his arms to the floor and rose carefully:

He slowly straightened up, took a step, looked at the legs carrying him, and stammered:

"Blessed . . . blessed is he!"

"Blessed is the God of Israel!" The men up above answered. "And blessed is he who is sent."

The man bowed and scooped up his thin bed, took the ropes off of it, and headed for the door, half-faltering and half-dancing. Everyone made way and turned to him with wide-open eyes. There was a buzz out in the courtyard, and murmurs changed to cries of joy. Tongues also loosened within the house. One yelled, another screamed. They grabbed hold of each other's arms and said: "I have never seen anything like this!"

Simon looked at the scribes. They were reserved, perhaps a bit shamed. Maybe they also disapproved. Why had Jesus turned to them? What had they thought in their hearts? It could only have been that the Master didn't have any right to forgive sins.

Did he have it? Simon had never thought about the matter. They had wandered throughout the whole country, and the Master had proclaimed the great message that the kingdom of God was near. There had been power on the move that had never before been known. There was something that overshadowed those who were . . . Yes, what was it? Something that came from God. Something that was a piece of glory and power from above. Was it then so strange that also sins would be forgiven?

Simon looked at the scribes with wonderment. Did they really not understand anything?

Not the Righteous, but Sinners

The heavy pack fell to the ground with a thud when the camel driver finally loosened all the knots in the rope and balanced the burden over the edge of the large pack saddle. The camel that laid down by the roadside in the scorching sun seemed to squint at all the sweaty men with mocking contempt. The Syrian who owned the camel abused his help. He was livid about having to pack up all his bales yet another time today. He was positive that if he had given the publican twice as much as he rightfully should have, he would not have to untie a single knot. But this time, he had determined that he would come to Caesarea without paying a single drachma more than he had to. So he had to let all his wares spill out amidst the flies in front of every tollbooth.

Matthew sat in the shade under the arch and listened to the enraged parties. He was glad that he had come so far that he did not continue to argue with all the polished businessmen and fiery Galilean farmers. It was cool inside here, and he didn't have to do anything but take the money at the counter, take care of the correspondence, and keep track of the tariffs. It could be unpleasant enough. But he had become accustomed to all the unreasonableness.

Or had he? When the zealots called him traitor and promised to stick knives in him on a moonless night, it did nothing for him. They could yell if they wanted; it was still the Romans who had the power, and in the end, all would understand that it was the only sensible thing to do. But it stung his heart more when the rabbis passed by here on their trips and put their money on the counter with the extremities of their middle fingers for fear of touching him. It was just as bitter as when the Pharisees in the street would pull their coats about them and turn away as he passed.

Well, it had to be what it was. He had to live. Had he not become a publican, he would probably be starving along with the other day laborers who stood in the square waiting to find work. If God had given him a clear head and a brain for accounting, then the purpose was for him to use it. At least now he had a decent living. The Pharisees could say what they wanted. He didn't go to the synagogue. He knew that all this with the law and righteousness wasn't anything for him. He had his profession and work. That was enough. At times, he was taken by thoughts of uncertainty, whether it really was enough, but he pushed them away from him. Of course he had to make a living.

Matthew looked up and stared tentatively at the crowds out in the courtyard. The Syrian gesticulated with a shriek as he stood there between the camel burdens. One of the customs servants rooted through a sack. Some fishermen made their way, carrying a large basket between them. They came from the harbor and dropped off their catch. One of the merchants in the city came with his rickety carts laden with large wine jars. He limped through, though he came from Bethsaida on the other side of the border. The publicans just stepped to the side and nodded to him. They knew that they would have their share of the wine at Passover, and his wine was good.

When the rickety wine cart scrambled passed, there followed a cluster of farmers from outside the country. They spoke with lots of agitation and hardly noticed that they were at the customs station. One of them swore over and over again that it was true: He had stood up and left with his bed under his arm. One knows what he sees with his own eyes . . .

They were stopped by the soldier under the vault. No . . . they had nothing with them. What would they do in the city? Hear the Prophet, of course! See the new Elijah . . . Why else would they come?

They were allowed to pass, and Matthew watched them go thankfully. He had had enough of these sorts this last month. There was a jumble of rumors and endless talk, and Matthew didn't believe the half of it. They spoke of this Jesus as if he were a second Elijah. The Pharisees said one ought to wait and see. They probably didn't think he was scrupulous enough.

The Syrian began to finish up. His hired help came and enumerated a long list of dutiable goods. Now was time to keep one's head clear. Four and a half baths, five as—that made one denarius, six as, and two quadrans . . .

He paused in the middle of his train of thought and stared through the arch at the cluster of people in the courtyard. Between the camel burdens and the Syrian laborers came a crowd, first a half dozen men and then a whole swarm of men after them. Matthew fixed his stare on the first little group. There was no doubt . . . There were Simon and Andrew, and the sons of Zebadee . . . and Simon the Zealot, who had threatened him with the knife the day after the feast of Purim. Now they all passed with the Nazarene. There he was too. When Matthew first got the urge to see him, he didn't pass by this way any longer, so it was with great curious eyes that Matthew now looked over the tall figure. He went and spoke with the others, he pointed at all the unpacked treasures, and he greeted the farmhands though they were foreigners.

Then he came into the archway. Mathew had to hurry and start counting again. He did not want to show his curiosity, and he felt a bit unsure. This man spoke in the synagogues. He was a man who dealt with God. He was no one for Matthew.

Matthew sat looking down and tried in vain to add six and seventeen. His ears told him that the Master had stopped. He felt someone looking at him. He heard the steps come straight to his place at the counter. They were firm and resolute steps. Someone was coming who found what he sought. Matthew was completely still. He dared not look up. Under half-shut eyelids, he glimpsed the Master's figure; he stood right in front of him on the other side of the counter.

Now Matthew had to look up. The man of God had spoken only two words to him: "Follow me." These words were the most incredible words he could have said. They could have only one meaning, but that was precisely what Jesus could not have meant. Neither could he mean that a publican, a sinner, who sold himself to the Romans, who touched unclean things daily, who never went to synagogue, and who was the most impious in all of Capernaum—that he should come and follow him.

Follow me . . . Had one of the Pharisees said this, Matthew would have understood it better. He could hear how they would have laughed: short, cold, and threatening. It would have meant "Come along—God's people want to hold court and examine your soul. You should do evening prayer, or you shall be excluded from the synagogue."

But the Master had not taken this tone. Matthew dared to look up into his face. He could only read what the voice had already said. This prophet of God bade him to come along. Matthew would be his disciple. The Master had come here to find him. Had Matthew not asked for God? Then, in any case, God now asked about him through this man of God. And this must mean that God himself asked for him.

If it was so, then he would not hesitate. If God wanted to have something to do with him, then he would not think to say no. He had no idea what would become of all this. But he was not worried about the matter. He didn't need to know. He left that up to God. He pushed the accounting table and money away from him. Jesus had already turned to go just as matter-of-factly and as surely as he had come. And Matthew followed him, without hesitation and without looking back.

It was a great party in the publican's house. All the house could afford was brought forth, and those who could not find a place to lay down upon cushions around the table sat on the ground. The poor household goods were bought out into the courtyard, the Master had the place of honor, and the others flocked around him. Sticks with oil lamps stood in the midst of the circle and illuminated their faces. Again and again, Simon looked at the faces around the table. This was something so impossible, so lavish, so blissfully absurd that he could only think of the psalmists words: "When again the Lord establishes Israel, then it will be like a dream . . ."

Here, all these eyes hung on the Master's lips. They smiled and laughed; they listened and asked and listened again. Here were all the publicans from the tollhouse. Here, the old rascal from the inn at the harbor sat supporting his elbows on the Master's sofa. Here were both good-time girls from Magdala and all sorts of strange people from Bethsaida and Tiberius side by side with the honest fishermen and honorable peasants. Such as had not been seen in a synagogue for ten years mingled with men who had had their eyes opened at the Jordan. It was as if all the old was cancelled. All the toxic, sore, and dirty perversities sank into the past. Something new had come. God created and sent out his almighty word. The kingdom would be great and there would be peace without end. Here, the burden was lifted from the heavy-laden, and here, light shown upon those who sat in darkness.

Why?

The question kept coming back. Simon had not sorted it out. He knew that a new era stood before the door, but he did not know any more. And who was the Master?

There was someone who asked, "Rabbi, why do you not fast with your disciples? All the others fast, both John's disciples and the Pharisees."

The Master looked at the man who asked the question and looked around. He seemed to find the answer in their faces.

"Will the wedding guests fast when the bridegroom is with them?"

No, so it was so. Simon repeated the words to himself: "The wedding guests had the bridegroom among them." This is what was happening here. Abraham's God prepared a table for his children in the presence of their enemies. He let the cup of grace overflow and performed miracles and wonders. This was God's own exuberance, his spring of grace that flooded over all the banks and made the dry desert into a garden of delight. This was why sinners sat here and drank, and they who only had guilt went away rich. But the bridegroom—who was he?

There was someone who gently grabbed Simon by the arm. Simon turned and saw Philip standing behind the sofa where he had been laying at table. Philip bowed and whispered that he should come out for a minute.

Simon slid down from the couch and carefully stepped over all those sitting on the ground. The whole courtyard was full of people who came in through the gate from the street. Matthew had left it open on purpose. Tonight, everyone was welcome in his house.

Away from the gate stood a group of men who kept a little distance. It clicked for Simon when he saw their wide robes with corner tassels. They were the rabbis from the neighboring towns. They had been there when the lame man was healed. Their greeting was short and they talked with hushed voice. One could hear the resentment behind their question:

"Simon, son of Jonas, can you explain this for us: How can he eat with publicans and sinners?"

Simon didn't know what he should answer. To eat with a man was to be brothers with the man. Was then the Master a brother to the innkeeper and good-time girls?

It was the Master himself who answered. Simon didn't know that he had heard the question, and the scribes shrank back when he suddenly turned to them and said, "It is not the healthy who need a doctor but the sick. But now go and learn what these words mean: I desire mercy and not sacrifice. I have not come to call the righteous but sinners."

The scribes looked at each other. Then they went on their way without answering anything. Simon felt uneasy. Something had slithered into the garden that did not belong with the great joy. But then he turned to the tables and lamps and looked at all the faces from the harbor and neighboring villages. A few days ago, they would have been scornful or bored if someone spoke to them of God's law. Now they were open, inquisitive hungry beggars for the powerful word. Here was joy and light. Perhaps it was not found among men, but they saw it and it reflected in their faces.

Simon went back to his place. Not the healthy but the sick. Not the righteous but the sinners. Not sacrifice but mercy . . . This was really beyond all reason. But perhaps it had to be so when God's kingdom was near?

Greater than the Temple

"Are you the one who is to come?"

Simon turned John the Baptist's question over in his head. He mumbled the words to himself over and over again as he walked. It was somewhat a comfort for him that even the Baptist himself had asked this question. He too had been wrestling with the question, but he almost didn't dare admit to himself what it was that he was thinking about.

Everything had been simple down by the Jordan. There they lived in the shadow of the Almighty who would come. Everyone expected him. Everyone knew that he was near. When Andrew came running to him after his first encounter with the Master, he mentioned it as if it was the most natural thing in the world: "We have found the Messiah!" And afterward, they came to understand that the Baptist thought the same.

But then everything was so different from what they expected. What became of this baptism with the Spirit and fire? Where was the winnowing fork that would cleanse Israel of all the chaff? And who dared to say that Jesus was the Messiah anymore? Possessed people were the only ones, but the Master silenced them with an almost frightening power that stifled their scream and anguished confession. Jesus did not want to be called the Messiah. That was apparent.

Now, as he sat in his prison cell among the mountains of Moab, even the Baptist had begun to question it. He had sent two of his disciples. They had gone straight to the Master with their question. They were still dusty from the road, their faces still glistening from the burning sun: "Are you the one who is to come, or should we look for another?"

In that moment, Simon read the faces of the others and saw that they had the exact same question he had. They all looked to the Master with the same great expectation. But the Master did not answer the question directly. He asked them to see and hear for themselves, and then go back and tell John what they saw. It had all become so peculiarly matter of fact wherever the Master went: the blind saw, the lame leapt for joy, the deaf heard, and the poor had good news proclaimed to them.

They received no other answer. But perhaps it was answer enough to their question? Did not the Master mean that all this was evidence enough? Was it perhaps that he who had ears to hear and eyes to see must be able to sense what was happening here? "Blessed is he for whom I am not a stumbling block," the Master had said. Could he also be a stumbling block for some? Was he the rock where the stream of humanity was divided by an invisible hand, so that some were brought into the kingdom and others to judgment? And was this perhaps his intention—that this should be the case?

Simon stood on the hillside for a moment. The others were on the way down with the Master. They had just reached the edge of the little valley where the village lay with its synagogue. Simon turned to catch one last glimpse of the lake before he descended. It lay there like a bright eye between the mountains. The shorelines had turned white like an old man's hair these last few weeks. All the greenery on the slopes had been scorched. The mountainsides had the color of sun-bleached straw, and naked black boulders of basalt rose up from between the tufts of white grass. At this distance, the mountains reflected the summer's pale-rose color, and almost disappeared in the haze of the sun. The sun mercilessly burned everything from where it stood in the sky, and the heat in the valleys was heavy and brooding.

It was the Sabbath. They were on their way to the synagogue from their night camp up on the mountain. As usual, the people followed on their heels. Simon watched them hopping and sliding down the trail made from broken and dirty bits of limestone. The yellow grass clung to the folds of their robes, and their tunics were filled with thistle heads. Lean, sun-scorched and bareheaded, their naked legs torn by thorn bushes, starving and ignorant—yes, the Master was right: abused and abandoned, they were like sheep without a shepherd.

Once again, Simon started to descend. He stepped quickly with a long stride down the trail of scorching stone to catch up with the others. The small fields stretched out upon the seared slopes where the grain stood golden white between the fragments of stone. Yes, the fields were white for harvest. The Master had said that too. And it was precisely these poor and dirty wretches who he had meant. The harvest was huge. This is why they would ask the Lord of the harvest to send many workers to his fields. This is what Simon prayed for now, though he didn't really understand who would be sent and where they would go. In any case, he understood that it applied to this great gathering that the scribes condemned and to whom he himself had wrinkled his nose so many times.

"The poor have good news proclaimed to them." So strange that the Master mentioned that to John's envoy as the greatest and most powerful thing now happening. He counted it as something even greater than the deaf hearing or the lepers being cleansed. So this was the clearest evidence that . . . yes, that . . . at a minimum, the kingdom was near.

Simon passed by an old man with no coat or shoes snatching a couple ears of wheat and trying to chew the hard grain with his broken teeth. He wished him the Lord's peace and gave a friendly nod. The old man's face wrinkled when he smiled back, and the half-chewed kernels of wheat showed upon his dry tongue.

Was it wretches such as this who would inherit the kingdom? In any case, the Master invited them to him. Never did he speak anything but comfort to these toiling and heavy-laden people. They also noticed that the yoke of the Pharisees was heavy and hard, but the Master's was easy. The old man would not have dared to grab these ears otherwise. Of course, it was his right according to the Law of Moses. Every sojourner in Israel was to be able to eat from his neighbor's field as long as he did not come at the grain with his sickle. However, the scribes said that this was a manner of harvesting and therefore forbidden on the Sabbath.

Simon could sense that there would be conflict concerning this, and he had no more than come just inside the stone walls and fig trees on the fringe of the village before he realized his prescience. There was a whole crowd standing by one of the gates. He knew immediately what it was the scribes were talking about. One could sense a bitterness behind their hand gestures that they could barely hold back.

He heard one of them recite the Sabbath commandment as he drew near. All the others nodded and stared at the Master.

The Master recited the scriptures too.

"Have you not read what David did? When he and his companions were in distress and hungry, he entered God's house and ate the show bread, though neither he nor those who accompanied him were permitted to eat of that bread. And he also gave it to those who followed him."

"But that was David!" said the scribes.

Then the Master looked at them with a strange look. It was penetrating and sad. It was as if he wanted to say, "Yes, that was just David, do you understand nothing?" Then he said, "Have you not read in the law that the priests on the Sabbath broke the Sabbath in the temple and are still without guilt? But I say to you, there is something here that is greater than the temple."

Simon almost didn't dare breathe. Here again, he touched upon a staggering mystery. There was only one who was greater than the temple, and that was God himself.

The Pharisees went quiet. It was a sinister and spiteful silence. Then the Master turned to face the people and said, "The Sabbath was made for man, not man for the Sabbath. And the Son of Man is Lord even over the Sabbath."

That second, Simon was filled with a sharp, almost blinding clarity. He had been so blind! The Master called himself "the Son of Man" again. He had done this all the more often this last season. Everyone noticed that there was a particular note in the phrase, but for most, it only had its normal meaning: a child of man, a brother to all other poor wretches in this world. But this time it was crystal clear to Simon that the Master meant something completely different. There was also a different Son of Man, one spoken about somewhere in the prophets, one enthroned in the clouds of heaven, one who would hold court and rule over the people with an eternal power . . . It was him whom the Master meant. And he had spoken about himself . . .

They went to the synagogue. Simon saw and heard everything as if it had happened far, far away. There were completely different voices within him.

The Son of Man has power here on earth to forgive sins . . . Yes, so it must be. How had he not understood it! Who can forgive sins but God alone! The Pharisees were absolutely right about this. But Jesus forgave sins!

*

It was shady and cool in the synagogue. People continued to stream in, and everyone packed in so that there would be enough room. The scribes had taken their self-declared places of honor in seats before the place of the reader.

Simon stood and looked at them. Their faces were deliberately unfathomable. They looked straight ahead. They were in the synagogue, they knew what fit. Only when Jesus came in did they exchange a little surprised look. Then they looked purposefully to the side.

Simon understood. There was a man sitting there with a pair of large, expectant eyes of the type that were always seen along the way as the Master walked about. He kept his right hand tucked inside his robe, and from his habit of straightening his robe with his left hand, one understood that his right hand was not functional.

He was the one the scribes had glanced at when Jesus came in. Now they sat immovable and looking straight forward again. They too waited for something with sharp and watchful eyes.

This went on for a while. One could feel a wrestling of the will though nothing happened, but finally, the painful silence was broken. Jesus stepped forward in the midst of the scribes. But he didn't speak to them, he spoke to the man behind the column.

"Rise and come here."

The man rose rapidly and stood there with his eyes full of tension. Now the Master turned to the scribes.

"Tell me," he said, "which of these is it lawful for a man to do on the Sabbath: that which is good or that which is evil? May one save a man's life or may one destroy it?"

None of them moved.

"What do you yourselves do? If someone has a sheep that falls in a pit on the Sabbath, does he not take hold of it and lift it up? Is not a man worth more than a sheep?"

No one answered and no one moved. One could see that it tortured the scribes to be asked this in front of all the people. But they had apparently resolved to not let on about anything. They would not answer. They only wanted to know what he thought to do. They wanted to have something to accuse him with. They didn't even look at the man with the hand. What did he have to do with them?

Then the Master looked around. It was as if he wanted to see if there were any more hearts that were as hard as theirs. Then he looked at the scribes. At that moment, Simon had a feeling that they ought to have sunk through the floor. He couldn't understand how they endured. It was not the usual wrath and not the usual sadness in this gaze, but there was something reminiscent of God's own accusation over his unreasonable and obstinate people: "The ox knows its owner, and the donkey its Master's crib, but Israel does not know, my people do not understand."[1] Had it not been for their glaringly perverse hearts, he would have admired them for being able to sit there staring with such hard indifference.

The Master took his gaze from them and turned to the man who stood there waiting.

"Stretch out your hand," he said.

Slowly, the man pulled his hand out of his breast fold. Scrawny and twisted, it looked as if it belonged to a mummy. He looked at it tentatively, then he slowly moved his thumb next to his index finger. Then he rolled his fingers together and clenched them in order only to triumphantly stretch them out again. He lifted his arm. It was is if he held it up as proof for all the people.

Then the silence was broken by the scraping and chirping of the scribes' chairs as they impetuously shifted back. They had all risen, their robes rustled and their sandals slammed against the floor. They forced their way through the crowd and straight to the exit. Simon heard one of them say, "Is it right for such a person to live?"

Simon hardly dared to look at the Master. Was this what he meant when he spoke about killing someone on the Sabbath? He could usually see right through people. But was it really possible that Israel's teachers were in the company of those who had murdered the prophets?

---

[1] Isaiah 1:3 (ESV)

By the Finger of God

Now they have to see!

Peter was feeling a bit excited. There was murmuring and shouting, the same as at the beginning of a wedding procession. The day was beginning to cool off, and the mountains had regained their color. The last rays of sun shone upon the crowds. The courtyard was a swarm of colorful robes and dark faces glistening with sweat. The dumb man had just left on his way, shouting and half-singing in his delight. A whole swarm of men followed him. Those who remained spoke among each other in muted voices. Peter could only hear disconnected words. He had been startled a couple times. Hadn't he heard someone ask, "Is he not David's son?"

Peter made his way to the sycamores in the middle of the yard where the fine rabbis gathered in the shade. He wanted to see what they did for a few minutes. They had just come down from Jerusalem. Apparently, the scribes around the lake had called for them so that they could say their piece. Their greeting was a little reserved. A person could very well guess what stories they had heard from the Pharisees at Magdala. Now they would be able to see and judge for themselves. The Master had spoken as usual. He spoke with a powerful and clear voice concerning the narrow way into the kingdom, about loving their enemies and giving account for their words, about praying without ceasing and not gathering too many riches that moths eat and thieves steal.

And then someone came with this dumb man. The strangers had forced their way in so that they could see. And what they were able to see! Not only the power and authority in the Master's work, but also the goodness that healed. It could only be compared to a glance from the benevolent eye of God.

Peter was not the only one that had gone to the noble rabbis in order to hear what they said. They had stood around speaking softly to one another and with the scribes from the district. They twisted their beards. They glanced quickly over their shoulders. They whispered and nodded. None of it looked good.

Peter joined the crowd in front of them. A zealous woman shouted, "Say, will the Messiah do greater miracles when he comes?"

Someone hushed her. More of the others asked with low voices as if they were afraid of their own questions:

"Must one not be sent from God to speak as this man?"

"Has such a thing ever happened before?"

"What kind of powers are at work within him?"

The scribes turned to each other. They were able to silence the questions just as easily with their looks as they could with strict admonitions. Now they looked at the people with aloofness. Then an old man with a long white beard lifted his hand as a sign that he would like to speak. He waved his forefinger before their lips as a warning and then lifted it to his forelocks.

"Children," he said, "listen. Let yourselves not be deceived by a practitioner of the black arts." And then his voice sank:

"It is only with Beelzebub that he drives out the evil spirits . . ."

Peter felt the resentment rising up within him. He fought to keep it down. He knew that he should not get angry. It was not right. But this was still a foul ungratefulness for God's gifts, which . . .

"Fathers and brothers, will you come here? I have something to say to you . . ."

Everyone turned around. It was Jesus who had stepped out of the house and stood there in the sun, calling them with a voice that was open and full of confidence, like an outstretched hand, and yet so determined that it stopped any contradiction from the very beginning.

The scribes moved across the yard reluctantly. They looked at each other a little hesitantly. Could he have heard them?

They came in and he asked them to sit. He sat himself in the midst of them and began to speak in parables calmly and instructionally in his usual manner. The scribes looked at him inquiringly, prepared to test and weigh his words. But after all he said, their gaze sunk to the floor. Their heads bowed imperceptibly. They seemed to sink down between their shoulders.

Peter stood within the crowd at the door listening. The Master spoke about a kingdom that came into conflict with itself and destroyed itself so that brothers felled brothers by the sword and house fell upon house. And then he asked if they believed that Satan was at war with himself in this way. Did they believe that he devastated his own kingdom, that he hindered his own works? Did they believe that he drove out his own servant and let his prisoners go free?

Peter understood this. He could see everything in front of him: the wild gaze of their eyes, their limp and withered arms, their dumb lips that only grunted like animals. Yes, it was altogether Satan's kingdom. Had not God once created the heavens and the earth and all herb-bearing seed and man, who bore his own image, and made everything good and lovely? There was also an evil kingdom in the midst of all this, and to it belonged the usurer's crooked fingers, the curses of the camel driver and those that the drunken wine merchant let rain down upon his wife.

The Master continued:

"But if now it is with the finger of God that I drive out the evil spirits, so God's kingdom has come to you."

Peter wondered for a moment if he heard right. "So God's kingdom has come to you?" Had God's kingdom come?

The Master continued with another picture. He spoke of a strong man who sits on guard, armed to the teeth, with all his household goods around him. So long as he is there and watches over everything, his possessions are safe. But if someone even stronger comes and binds him and takes his weapons from him, then that person can also take his possessions from him.

Peter understood. Satan sat here armed to the teeth and watching over everything that he had gathered for himself. Therefore the people lay sick and tortured. This is why the curses, abuse, and bitterness continued. But now one came who was even stronger, and he threw the weapons out of Satan's hand. Yes, this was what was happening here around him. But then "God's kingdom has come to you." Did the Master mean that this was God's kingdom? No, the kingdom was something completely different. It would come with power and glory. It would give life to the dead and mean judgment over all evil. And still . . .

Peter thought about the mystery for a second. He looked at the Master. It was as if the kingdom was in him in some way, as if this power and this glory glittered around his word and streamed out from his hands.

The Master had begun to speak about something else. He spoke about forgiveness, about how all sins could be forgiven, even blasphemy, no matter how coarsely the man blasphemed. But there was a caveat. There was a sin that could never be forgiven, neither in this age nor the age to come.

No one in the room moved. There was something in the Master's words that gave them a particular weight, something that made a man feel that this was said at just this moment because there was someone in this room for whom life and death hung on these words. Everyone looked at the Master. Even the scribes had lifted their eyes again.

"He who blasphemes the Holy Spirit, he is never forgiven, but is guilty of an eternal sin."

Jesus looked at the scribes, and Peter understood that he spoke to them. Surely they noticed it themselves. There was a tension in the air, as if two eternal opposing dominions measured their powers against each other here under the low ceiling. Now this was life and death. They had just said that it was with Satan's help that he drove out the evil spirits. They had said that it was an evil and devilish spirit that worked within him. They had heard his gospel and seen his benevolent works today. They had been there when the stronger man came and bound the strong man who kept men in slavery. But when God's Spirit set Satan to flight and came so near to them that they ought to have felt how he slapped them on the cheek, then they said that it was Beelzebub!

Now they had received the last warning: If they hardened themselves against all that they had seen here, then there was nothing left that God could squander on their evil hearts. Here was he who was greater than David, greater than Moses, and greater than the temple. Here God had seen to his people in a manner as never before. He who did not want to see now and did not understand must be lost.

Were the scribes also lost? The leaders of his own people? The most pious in Israel? The old, strict, most-serious defenders of godliness? No one looked better than them. God had offered them the fullness of grace. He had offered them the cup of heavenly joy, and they spit in it and said that it came from Beelzebub. No wonder the Master asked them to be careful of the sin that could never be forgiven.

Had they understood?

It hardly looked like it. When they said farewell, they were certainly quiet and of few words. It seemed as if at least a couple of them had found something to think about. But when they came out into the yard, the oldest among them shook his long locks and shrugged his shoulders. Then he took the younger men with him like a partridge ushering her chicks to safety. Peter thought that a cleft had opened up here that would never in all eternity be bridged. If they had really and irreversibly said no to God's last invitation, then they would also be irreversibly engulfed by the other kingdom. Then there must also be strife with them in life and death.

Peter did not fear the strife. He had seen who was strongest among them.

Only Believe

The first ray of light lit upon the housetops and reflected back into the alleyways from the lake as Jairus made his way down to the harbor. The night had been unbearably long. He had gone up to the roof four times to look at the stars, and long before daybreak, he had sent the hired hand down to the harbor to look among the boats and ask about among those who came in after fishing during night. Just as dawn broke, the hand came back, breathing heavily and saying that Simon's boat had turned straight for the harbor.

Jairus shivered from the night frost and excitement as he left the shade of the alley, half-running over to the sunlit quay. The boat had just docked when he caught a glimpse of the Master's figure standing there on the thwart and lifting his hands to deter the pushy people. There were a lot of people on the beach. They had come down to get the night's catch. Everyone jumped out of their boats and gathered around the Master. The clatter of crutches could be heard from the nearest alleys, and people sprang up out of nooks in the street. Jairus hurried. He understood that he was not the only one waiting, even if none of them could have waited as he did.

The crowd around Jesus had begun to move. The sea of people billowed to the side and separated. Jairus seized the opportunity and pushed his way in. When he caught a glimpse of the Master he threw himself on the ground and grabbed his coat begging and pleading for him to come. He didn't ask but behaved like a beggar before a prince. His child's life was at stake.

"She's dying," he said. "Come before she dies. Lay your hands on her."

Jesus stopped. He looked at Jairus with his searching gaze, Jairus met it with a mix of anxiety and boldness and then took an even firmer grip on his coat.

"Just lay your hands on her that she may live."

Then the Master nodded, and Jairus understood that it would happen. The Master's movement lifted him from the ground. He pushed through, clearing the way. He caught a glimpse of Peter and James beside him. They pushed their shoulders against the crowd, shouting for people to make way. Again, the mass billowed away from the Master. You could hear the steps and a wave of clattering feet and cloth sweeping over the pebbles on the beach as the crowd headed up to the city.

In the alleyway, the crowd became so dense that they had to push the crowd aside to make their way forward. Jairus suddenly felt that he didn't have the Master behind him anymore. He turned around to see that Jesus was standing still and searching the people around him.

"Who was it who touched me?" he asked.

Everyone shook their heads. His disciples stared at him with astonishment.

"But don't you see how many people are pushing and shoving. And still you ask who touched you . . ."

The Master didn't look at them. He searched the crowd.

"No," he said calmly. "There was someone here who touched me. I felt the power go out from me."

A small hand shot out from between John and Andrew, and a pale little woman pushed her face forward. As soon as she saw Jesus, she sank to the street.

"It was me," she said.

Jesus stretched out his hands and touched her bowed head. He lifted it up so that he saw her face. Then she began to speak, stuttering at first, and then more and more boldly. Her whole history of suffering passed by, all the doctors whom she sought, the helpless evil that only got worse, how she had waited at the door over there, her determination to brush his clothes at a minimum, and then her desperate attempt to stretch her trembling hand out far enough to touch the hem of his garment.

And now she was healthy. She looked up into his face, pale and happy. Jesus only laid his hands on her head and said:

"My daughter, your faith has saved you. Go in peace and be healed from your disease."

The crowd was almost still. It was only farther down by the beach where no one saw or heard anything that anyone pushed or made and noise.

Just then there was someone touching Jairus's arm, someone who quietly came out from the crowd behind him. He twitched and turned about to see his servant's sorrowful eyes, which he immediately cast downward. The servant swallowed and said, "It is useless for you to bother the Master. She is dead."

Jairus controlled himself. Everything around him sank. All his strength flooded away and left him with a great empty meaninglessness. But he held himself upright.

Then he heard the Master's clear and strong voice a way off.

"Fear not. Only believe."

In the midst of his emptiness, he saw his Master's eyes, comforting, encouraging, and commanding. He nodded to them. It was impossible and yet it was possible when this man said it.

They started again. As if in a dream, Jairus saw the black walls pass by, these walls of which he knew every slot and every projection. Today it seemed unreal, temporary and unneeded. The only thing that was firm and permanent was this ancient voice that came like a flood of power from another kingdom. Ever since the first time he heard it in his synagogue, he had thought that everything else was small. It was this voice that was now asking him to believe.

Just outside the house, the Master stopped to have the disciples block the alley. No one would go any farther except for the three to whom he motioned to follow him.

Then they entered the yard. Jairus was ready to scream. There were the mourners tearing their clothes, beating their breasts, and screaming with toothless mouths. The old flautist was already there blowing a piercing dirge on his pipe. This was the entire entourage of forced distress, the hired mourning for a huge funeral. They were crying for wine and salty olives. And his wife in their midst, lost and distraught, unable to comprehend that it was her daughter who would be laid upon the rough bier and buried in a pit before the sun went down.

Jairus took his wife in his arms. He had to support her to keep her from falling to the ground. But what would he say?

"Why do you cry?"

Again, it was the Master's voice. It swept through the whole yard with its power. The flute was silenced, and the mourners went quiet. They folded their hands to their breasts and stared at him in amazement.

"Whom do you mourn? The girl is not dead. She is sleeping."

Then laughter broke forth. The widow by the wall had started it. The old basket weaver followed her, and it spread through the whole flock of women sitting there like ruffled black birds. They, of course, knew that she was dead. They had tried everything that could be tried before someone was laid in the ground. They had already begun the great lamentation that befitted a house like this. They would keep it up all day, and they would receive their payment, for this was a great sorrow. They laughed, they slapped their meager knees, and they laughed again. It was all shrill and mocking.

Jairus froze. It was as if a cold wave of disbelief washed over him, something that would snuff out and extinguish the little flickering flame that still shined in the great darkness. He understood the burning wrath that the prophets could feel against their own people.

Again, it was the Master's voice that filled the yard. Now it was like a storm that sweeps away the waste and chaff from the threshing floor. He swept them out with a single short command and a roll of the head. The laugh died away, the giggles exchanged for startled horror. They fluttered like a flock of frightened jackdaws out on to the street. An almost eerie silence swept through the empty yard.

The Master went to the gate and asked them with a glance of the eyes to come along. He gently pushed the door open and bowed as he entered. Jairus was the first to follow after. He stood with baited breath two steps in from the threshold. The tears rose up within him when he saw the girl lying there on the strange bed, alone in the middle of the floor, pale and immoveable, without a water jar or cup of wine at her side. But he didn't cry. The power of the Master's word carried him through. In the midst of all this that fell and turned to dust, the Master's word reached out as something endurable and unshakable, and he clung to it.

The Master slowly approached the girl. He bowed over her and seemed to look into her little pale face. Then he took her hand and spoke slowly, as if he was talking to someone who was sleeping and whom he didn't want to startle.

"Little girl, wake up. Get up."

Jairus stood completely still. He saw the girl open her eyes. She looked at Jesus wide-eyed, then she seemed to recognize him, and she smiled and sat up. He took her by the hand and lifted her up so that she stood on her feet. She looked around with wonder, saw the unusual bed, and let her gaze search around the room. Then she came to them.

Only then could Jairus move from his place. But he couldn't say anything at the moment. He heard the Master command the disciples at the door that they shouldn't say anything when they went out. Then he felt someone touching his arms as they gripped the girl hard. It was the Master. Only now did he think to thank him. The Master interrupted his stammering.

"Give her something to eat," he said.

As they looked for some bread, stirred the coals, and grabbed a fish, the Master told them one more time, stricter than before, that they should not speak of this but keep it a secret.

Then he disappeared. Only after he left did Jairus come to think that he ought to have asked what he should say to the neighbors. And there was so much else he ought to have asked about . . .

Today This Word Is Fulfilled

James, son of Joseph, pushed the little wooden door to the side and looked up the street. This time, it was the potter's oldest boy. His gangly stride did not fit with the steps in the stone pavement, which were calculated for donkeys. He wobbled his way up, with two steps on every other ledge and one on the next. He was the eighteenth of James's neighbors to have passed by in the last hour. And there was still another hour before the divine service would begin.

James would have liked to go there, that was the truth. But then he would have had to stay there. It was more than two hundred steps there, and an unnecessary walk would have cost him too many of the steps that he had the right to make on a Sabbath. Sometimes he envied the frivolous Galileans, who didn't question how many Sabbath trips they made between the houses when something special happened. But he had always said that it was better to be too strict than too lax when it came to the Law of the Lord. Today he had to show that he was no less careful, even though it cost him a real personal victory. He also stayed home now to wait for his brother Judas because they had agreed to go to the synagogue together.

He hadn't had a moment's peace since the rumors had come to the city yesterday. They reached him sometime before sundown, but it wasn't possible to go to Cana to have them confirmed. It could just as well be that they were false.

If they were true, then his brother would have had to come to the city yesterday evening, or he would have come today, in the morning. It would be a serious thing if he came walking today, on the Sabbath. It gave all the frivolous and dissatisfied people in the country ammunition against the righteous. But it was obvious that

Jesus did much more. The scribes sometimes came passing by and would often talk about it. James always had his house open to them. He loved all who loved the Law of the Lord.

They hadn't stopped speaking about his brother ever since the previous spring. James had defended him and said that he had never been a bad person. He had been an obedient son and had always gone to the synagogue of his own free will. Perhaps he hadn't loved the law as much as James and Judas, but he was very knowledgeable in the scriptures and had great reverence for them. The old experienced Pharisees had agreed that he had probably not violated anything intentionally. But he was confused. They would not say that he was a deceiver but that he was deceived. They were constantly coming up with new evidence of his confusion: He forgave sins. He made himself Lord of the Sabbath. He spoke against the tradition of the elders and denied the promises to Abraham.

So James spoke with Joseph and the other brothers, and they were of one mind that they had to get ahold of their brother so that nothing bad would happen to him. What they heard was being said in Jerusalem caused them to despair. He had successfully turned the entire Sanhedrin against him there. It was with even greater alarm that they heard that Herod had his eye directly upon him. It wasn't so remarkable, seeing as all the people down by the sea seemed to chase after him.

So they had resolved to seek him out. They had had a little trouble convincing his mother. She had been quite peculiarly closed off this last year. She went around quietly, and Judas suspected that she was also suffering. He knew what her firstborn meant to her, but no matter how hard he tried to fill that void, he had no success. It made him a little disappointed and perhaps even bitter. He thought he was at least as faithful a son as his older brother. And he could calmly say that he never caused her as much worry as she now bore for the sake of her firstborn.

So they had taken off on a sunny summer day. It was hard going up the plateau to Arbela, but when they turned to walk down to the lake, along the stony paths through the rugged valley, they almost languished. They rested their panting animals on the plain outside of Magdala and waited for the evening breeze, but when it finally came, its heat was as suffocating as air from a brick oven. Only when they neared Capernaum and the sun disappeared did a cool breeze blow off the mountains, allowing them to breathe again.

It was a strange entrance into Capernaum. They didn't need to ask directions. Before they opened their mouths, people pointed out the street and the house for them. There seemed to be only one thing anyone thought about here. In the street outside his door, there was a gathering of people, and they had to squeeze through the gate to get into the yard. It was quiet there inside. Everyone listened and tried to discern the voice of Jesus, which could be heard through the open door.

James instantly felt uncomfortable. A power emanated from the room in there. From inside, they all noticed the usual signposts on the street: the people in the gate who, in the midst of the crowds and heat, helped each other, and then the faces listening attentively outside the door. It was like the rings that form after a stone is thrown in the lake. In wave after wave, they came from one and the same place, and everyone carried the sensation of something powerful and captivating.

They remained standing outside. None of them dared propose that they should go in. Instead they sent a greeting and asked him to come out to them. But he didn't do it. He denied his family. He said that they who sat in there were his real relatives.

With this announcement, they took their leave. They felt shamefully excluded from all that filled this house and these people. James understood immediately that he was powerless here. These people believed in his brother. It was useless to try to convince them that this man was out of his mind. As long as they remained under this strange power, it was best to let them be.

So they had turned back. But he repented for having taken Mary with him. It would have been better if they had spared her that.

Steps were heard out in the street again. The people began to come in whole groups. It was apparent that there had been rumors in the city this morning, whoever the Sabbath breaker was that ran around telling everyone.

Finally there was a knock on the door. James opened it. It was Judas. He looked worried, half-afraid and half-annoyed. He came in and began to speak.

It was true that Jesus had come to the city yesterday evening. About an hour after the Sabbath started, he had come walking with many of his disciples. They had stayed in the shelter by the well, and a lot of people had gathered there. One expected that they would see some sign, and so many came with their sick, but Jesus was not able to heal them. Certainly, it was said that a dumb girl from Kislot received her speech back, but he had taken her aside so that no one saw when it happened, and one did not get much from the parents when they were leaving. In any case, it was certain that he would go to the synagogue today. The whole city was on its feet, and Judas had received not a few taunts on his way.

They had sneered at him and asked how it felt to be the brother of such a great prophet. One said that now he would finally be able to see if Jesus was as remarkable as he wanted to make himself out to be. Some only meant that it would be interesting to see him do some miracles, but most meant to laugh at the idea that it was God's elect envoy whom they saw bringing water to Mary and walking the pastures with the goats. It wasn't funny to be called Joseph's son today.

They went up the street briskly, without concerning themselves about the others looking at them. The others whispered behind their backs in the synagogue too, but here they were more protected. They were still respected Jews from David's stem, and James had stood up front countless times as the reader with the scrolls of the law between his hands.

It was Judas who first noticed that the others were no longer looking at them. There was something happening outside that had all their faces turned toward the door. For a moment, the whispers hushed, and then he stepped in with a whole flock of disciples in tow.

He greeted them just like old times. Yet he was not the same. James looked at him for a long time. It was hard to describe the difference. Long walks, poor night camps, irregular meal times, and the sharp sun on the mountains had done their part. But that wasn't everything. There was something new in his face, something that was both a great tension and a great peace, something very willful and expressive. Again, James felt uncertain and uneasy, just like that time in Capernaum.

After Jesus greeted all of them, he went to his usual place to the left, over by the pillars. A silence consisting somewhat of animosity but mixed with curiosity spread around him. Soon they were stirred up again by scuffling and trampling at the door. The shuffling steps and muffled giggles were those of two peasants bringing along the smith's widow as she limped between them. She was dragging one leg behind her that just didn't want to follow. They had taken her firmly under their arms, almost lifting her off the ground. The red-haired potter came in behind them with his lame daughter. He carried her on his back. Then it was the pale woman with anemia and perhaps a few more who weren't seen in the crowd.

The peasants dragged the widow forward and tugged the Master's elbow to get his attention. It seemed as if he remained in thought, as he looked away to the cabinets where the scrolls of the law were kept. He turned briskly and looked at the woman.

James was on edge as he watched the Master's face and movements attentively. He saw Jesus look over the old woman. His expression was opaque; it reflected both a great pity and something that looked like anger or uneasiness. Then he looked at the men, and his face became stern.

"But what do you want me to do?" he asked.

They grinned at him, half-confidentially and half-insistently.

"You shall heal her."

"You shall show what you can do."

Jesus shook his head so brusquely and dismissively that both men fell speechless.

"No," he said. "You I cannot help."

He pushed them to the side and took a step toward the potter. The potter held out his girl and curiously looked over her shoulder to see what Jesus would do. Jesus stooped down with open arms for the girl to come and stand before his knees. So she looked him in the face.

"Do you believe that I can do this?" he asked.

The potter didn't think about the question.

"It is that which you shall show," he said.

Jesus gave him a long contemplative look. Then he shook his head unremarkably and turned away. The potter got hot. He took a step after Jesus and grabbed him by the shoulders.

"But you helped all the others; surely you must help your fellow compatriot," he said.

Jesus looked at him again.

"If you believe, then it can happen . . . why don't you believe?"

He let his gaze meander about, looking at one after the other of them that stood there, tentatively. He seemed to be all the more amazed.

"But are there none of you who believe?" he asked.

Someone yelled, "Do a miracle; then we will believe!"

"You can't do it!" yelled another.

James saw how his brother seemed to grow where he stood. He met all the disbelieving gazes. Then he just said that it was an unbelieving generation that wanted a sign but that such a generation would never receive any other sign than that which the prophet Jonah gave to the Ninevites.

James understood what he meant. Jonah had preached repentance. He had not done any sign. Did his brother mean that he would give them a sermon of repentance without any sign for proof of his commission?

He whispered to the trustee to begin the worship service. It had already gotten bad enough.

During the song and the readings, the congregation settled down again. James was glad because he loved his synagogue, and it always tortured him when people talked during the exposition of scripture. He had never been able to understand the rabbis who stayed at home with their studies, saying that it was more valuable than going to the synagogue with the unlearned rabble.

Everything went calmly and according to procedure until the law was read and they came to the prophets. Jesus rose as a sign that he wanted to expound, and the trustee motioned for him to come forward. James saw him get the great scroll that contained the prophet Isaiah. Jesus put the prayer shawl over his head and lifted the book, rolled it open, and searched among the columns. Then he began to sing the holy words in the old tongue:

> The Spirit of the Lord God is upon me,
> because the Lord has anointed me
> to bring good news to the poor;
> he has sent me to bind up the brokenhearted,
> to proclaim liberty to the captives,

and the opening of the prison to those who are bound;
to proclaim the year of the Lord's favor[1]

Everyone was quiet while he sang. This was a dangerous text, a text about the Messiah, filled with all that which would come when God would send his anointed. When he rolled the book up and gave it to the synagogue's trustee and sat in the teacher's seat, no one dared to move. James himself held his breath in expectation.

Then his brother began to speak. He could not have started more boldly or more dangerously.

"Today the words of these scriptures are fulfilled before your ears."

From that moment on, the whole synagogue was captured by his voice. James could not help but wonder where he had learned to teach in such a particular and lively manner. Much of what he said was also right and true. When he spoke about a crushed heart and about the poor and oppressed that had nothing but God, and when he described how close heaven was to him who humbled himself and suffered for righteousness sake, James was with him completely. He spoke just as well and true about loving your neighbor as yourself. Again, James felt the highest demands of the law as he had them laid open to him by the greatest of Israel's teachers. But in the midst of all this, there was something frightful, something that caused James to feel the whole time as if he stood high up upon a pinnacle swaying to the beat of a battering ram. The whole time, he had the frightful feeling that Jesus meant that all this—grace, comfort, forgiveness, the kingdom—had come to them now. James wished that he was able to think differently. But once he got the fearful thought in his head, he thought that all his brother's words could be inferred to say that he meant God had now sent his Messiah into the world and that it was this Anointed One who offered the grace of God here in Nazareth's synagogue.

This blasphemous thought so plagued James that he could only pray to God that everything would end quickly and that the others would not recognize how blasphemous this speech actually was. He looked around nervously. Everyone's eyes were fixed on the speaker.

---

[1] Isaiah 61:1–2 (ESV)

Some were obviously gripped; others had grim wrinkles between their brows.

Then Jesus finished. Everyone moved. They whispered and talked. James heard someone violently say that he was just a normal man and that they had all seen how much there was to his miracles.

Jesus remained in the teacher's place. They noticed that he still wanted to say a few words before he went back down. He seemed to listen to the buzz and the whispers in the hall. Then he began to speak, and everyone went quiet again.

He knew very well, he said, that they now turned the proverb on him: "Physician, heal thyself." They demanded that he do miracles here like he had done in other cities. But now he turned another proverb on them: no prophet is accepted in his own city among his own relatives. If they did not want to believe the gospel, then neither should they expect any miracle. God was not indebted to anyone, and no one could demand anything of him.

He reminded them of how it was with Elijah and Elisha. There were many widows in Israel during the great famine, but Elijah was not sent to any of them but instead to a widow in the land of Sidon. And Elisha had many lepers around him. But none of them were made clean, only Namaan from Syria.

Now James felt as if the shaking wall had been destroyed under him. Jesus should not have said this. It was a presumption that everyone must have understood. He had just stood and compared himself with Israel's greatest prophets. He implied that this was a time of grace and visitation, now as in the time of Elijah. The people in Nazareth had reason to count both Elijah and Elisha as prophets from their own town. From the heights above their city, one could see Mount Carmel, where the fire had fallen over Elijah's water-drenched altar and where Baal's prophets were slain. At the other end of the plain lay Shunem, where Elisha had given life to the dead boy. The shadow of the great prophets still lay like a powerful protection over the cities on the Plain of Jezreel, and now Jesus stood here and said that he followed in the footsteps of the prophets, leaving his own and refusing them their obvious right—the right of the firstborn in this year of grace that he claimed had come.

James knew that it would go badly now. It was dangerous to tease the people here in Nazareth, and it was even more dangerous to make oneself a prophet among them. James didn't move from his spot. He looked straight ahead. He didn't want to hear or see anything. The stomping and shouting stormed behind him. This was blasphemy; this was making himself to be God. A blasphemer should be stoned; one such as this shouldn't live. They pushed forward and shuffled; they drove out the disciples. He himself was lost in the crowd.

Only when the whole shrieking swarm stormed out did James follow. He had never in his life been so helpless. He cursed the day his brother went to the Jordan. He reproached himself for not using violence to get his hands on him that time in Capernaum. He wondered how he could show his face to his mother ever again. And first and last, he wondered what would happen now. A blasphemer should be stoned. That was what was written. He would be thrown over the nearest edge, and then they would throw stone blocks on him. The whole excited crowd headed for the threshing floor. Apparently, they meant to put the threats into action at one of the slopes down on the plain. James increased the length of his stride. He had wanted to shout at them to calm themselves, to wait, to appeal to the Sanhedrin. But then he wondered if it was right of him to try to avert this. The whole time, he had the fearful feeling that Jesus wanted to be the Messiah. He would not truthfully testify in his favor at a trial. And was it right that he tried to save his own flesh and blood when it came to a matter of unrighteousness? Was this not to have partiality for someone?

They had gone down to the last house by the threshing floor. It was just as far as he could go without breaking the law. He stood. Never had it cost him so much to be a son of the law. But the commandment had been his joy in good times, so he would keep it in a day of distress.

The noise and shrieks dampened in the distance. His heart became evermore heavy within his breast. Was it already done?

He didn't know if minutes or hours had passed when he caught a glimpse of a few figures down on the path. He was just about to duck away so as not to encounter them when he saw that Judas was among them. The brothers approached each other. He had completely forgotten that he had gone too far. He yelled when he was still a long way off:

"He just went on his way! Straight through the midst of them!"

James didn't know if he dared to thank God. Judas came forward and spoke. They had gone a piece down the road. Jesus had gone along of his own free will. When they came to the place where the path went right over the mountain to Nain, Jesus turned aside. He had gone straight through the crowd. They had screamed that one should grab hold of him, but it was as if they shied away from him. He only looked at them and they turned aside and let him go. He looked back one last time, but they did not get any farewell. Then he continued over the mountain, calm and peaceful, as if he had been out wandering alone.

James still did not dare thank God. He was at the same time boundlessly relieved and infinitely tortured. Who could understand the ways of the Lord? He stared helplessly at Judas but didn't say anything. The thought couldn't be said out loud. The worst of it all was just this: there was a possibility that God could have intervened because he wanted to save his servant. James thought about the peculiar power that was in his brother's words. It had all been essentially edifying and clear. The only problem was that it sounded as if God's Messiah spoke. But if now . . . No, it was unfathomable. The thought could not be thought, and he had not thought it. Only one thing remained, a clear and wise truth that he dared reveal also to Judas: Jesus had certainly said a lot that was good and true, and one would do well to listen to him if it only wasn't for the unreasonable and disgusting fact that he wanted to be considered more than a normal man.

You Have Received for Nothing

The wind was cold and the lower houses of the village seemed to be pushing themselves flat against the mountain so as not to be blown away by the storm. The tops of the aspens bowed deeply and the heavy rain showers made the splotched golden slabs look like a leopard's hide. The villagers yelled and screamed.

Peter stood next to the last of the cairns for a moment to see if anyone followed him. Andrew was close behind him, but the others had stopped. Their invectives could be heard over the howling wind. A pair of rough figures came out of the alley to the left. One of them gave a threatening gesture with his cudgel and sent them packing.

Peter was quick to stoop down and remove his sandals. Then he lifted his foot and brushed his hand over the naked sole of his foot, where small stones, straw, and trail dust had all become stuck. As soon as he had put that foot back in its sandal he did the same thing with the other foot.

"The kingdom of God is near," he yelled to the men inside. "Sleep your sleep and continue in your sins. Now we shake the dust from our feet and go somewhere else. But this you may know: the kingdom of God is near!"

They fastened their sandals and went on their way. The men disappeared into the alley, and everything was quiet again. The only thing to be heard was the constant whine of the fall wind, and the screaming birds of prey fighting the squall.

Peter felt happy and free up here on the deserted ridge that lifted itself so high above all the surrounding land that Lebanon could be seen to the north under the gray rain clouds. They had reached the northern border of the land. They wouldn't go any farther because he had not sent them to the heathens. They did not know where they would sleep tonight. Not one of them had a knapsack with them, nor even a single copper coin in his belt or a crust of bread. They had nothing but the shirts on their backs and their open-toe sandals. This is how he had commanded them to go, and they had not lacked a thing on their way. On the contrary, they had never felt so rich. They had received for free, and they were sent out to share for free, lavishly and with full hands.

They should preach the gospel of the kingdom just as he himself had preached it. They would be his apostles and representatives with full authority to do what he himself had done. They would be persecuted because it was enough for the disciple if it went for him as it did for his Master. They would be as defenseless as sheep among wolves. But their word would be as powerful as his. Those who rejected it rejected him. Their greeting would be full of power, and the peace they offered men would rest upon them like a blessing or rebound off their thankless hearts and return upon the heads of those from whom it had gone out.

It all sounded so incredible. They would have laughed at it, had he not been the one that said it. But there were only two options when he spoke: to maintain that it was all unbelievable and deny him, or to believe him and try the incredible. Peter had felt as if he was being thrown from the tops of the cliffs overlooking the Ginosar Valley. But he dared to leap. He had parted ways with Andrew and went ahead without looking back. He had gone to village after village. He had stood by the wells in the squares like a herald crying out "The kingdom is near," and inviting everyone to forgive their enemies. He had laid hands upon the sick and anointed them with oil. Everywhere he went, his deeds and words were overshadowed by power and authority in the lordship of God that now stood at the door.

Now he knew more than he knew anything that the Son of Man had power: not only the power to forgive sins and heal the sick, nor mere authority over the Sabbath or to speak in God's stead, but he also had the power to send men in his name. He had the power to lay the very same authority of his word upon their tongues and reach the farthest extremities of the land through them. He had the power to work miracles through their hands.

So he did not fret concerning the fact that he did not know where he would spend the night or what he would eat for dinner. It all felt like freedom. It was a relief to have no knapsack with him. He attended his Master's business. More and more, he began to understand that he could no longer attend the business of anyone else.

Then Came a Convenient Day

He saw a dark-red shoe embroidered with gold, a green marble base and then a white mosaic floor with colorful garlands that seemed to sway in the wind. For the hundredth time, he let his gaze wander from the gold embroidery on his shoe to the petals on the floor, and then, slowly and carefully, it made its way across the floor until his eyes glimpsed a plain and worn sandal, a foot tanned and cured by the stone cairns of the desert, and then the broken seam of a faded coat.

Herod wouldn't let his gaze go any farther. He kept his head buried deep within his hands. He wouldn't look at this face. He liked to hear the voice, he was happy to catch a glimpse of the figure, but the face . . . it was just too much all at once. One had to control himself. And Herod had become incredibly weak.

The first time he called John the Baptist, he had meant to make short work of it. Of course, this was something completely unheard of. John had come out and began to reprimand him for his private life. Perhaps such a thing could be permitted for an Isaiah, and people could hear this taught in the synagogues if it amused them, but if they so much as presumed to try to do the same! The police had taken their opportunity when the Baptist was alone on the road with a few of his followers. They had thrown him in prison easily and without any trouble, and Herod kept him there a long time to soften him up. And then he sent for him to put him on trial and interrogate him.

He had expected it to be a simple thing. No evidence was needed. There could be only one punishment. At most, there might have to be a little regard for popular sentiment. But one could reasonably expect the guilty man to recant. When he no longer had any adoring entourage applauding his insults, then playing the prophet would not be so much fun. Then if he really was soft and remorseful, one might let grace pass for judgment.

It didn't go that way. The Baptist was not in any way remorseful. The strange thing was that even now, when he had everything to lose, he repeated all the accusations. It was even stranger that he did it without any bitterness. He was no agitator, not a royal reviler only wanting to throw dirt on the throne. It actually sounded as if he meant well, as if he said all this for Herod's sake.

Herod finally threw him in prison again. It did not do to let him say all this in the presence of his secretaries and guards. There had to be private hearings.

So it happened that he called him up time after time and let him stand here in front of the judgment seat. He had the entire court ushered out, and the guards had to stand outside the door. Then he allowed the Baptist to talk. It was then that Herod realized that this man's intent was pure and that he had no guile in his heart. It was a peculiar experience in this house where one flattered and lied, where intrigue and envy ruled and everyone attempted to lay traps for one another. In this perfumed environment where nothing was authentic or true, this had the aroma of a cool breeze off the desert mountains. Herod felt certain that this strange Baptist was the only one in the palace who told him the truth without circumlocution and who wished him well without expecting the payment of jangling denarii.

He listened to him often, so often that he began to call for him in secret. He had had a few cold conversations with Herodias for the Baptist's sake. She laid into him with her requests. She called him unmanly and indecisive. She asked him if he even loved her anymore. But he did not give in. The woman's wrath increased, and the Baptist would not budge an inch to satisfy Herodias.

Herod looked again at his golden-red shoe and then the Baptist's open sandals. Why were such men so calm and resolute? Why should they work with such conviction and be so happy? How could the Baptist be so much happier going down to prison in his worn coat than Herod was wandering around up here in his soft caressing linen tunic? He would have happily set the Baptist free if he only had a small spark of this man's powerful faith.

Today, the Baptist also spoke of the way of repentance for the forgiveness of sins. Herod listened carefully even if he pretended to yawn from time to time and played with the tassels on the seat cushion. As so often before, the Baptist spoke with the words of the prophets: "Behold, the Lord's arm is not so short that he cannot save, and his ears are not shut so that he cannot hear. No, it is your misdeeds that have separated you and your God from one another, and your sins hide his face from you so that he does not hear you. . . ."

The Baptist could skip the application today. Herod knew what would come now: God had created man and woman so a man should hold fast to his wife. He admonished men to be careful so that no one was unfaithful to the love of his youth. He told them that he hates divorce and that he is a witness between a man and his wife. He cannot suffer that one replaces the one that he should love and takes to himself one who had been given to another. "Would I be righteous," says the Lord, "if I kept stolen goods in the house of the mighty or let the dishonest employee take that which is not his with impunity?"

Now Herod lifted his head from his hands. This had gone on long enough. Was it not the Baptist who was the prisoner, and he himself the judge? Should he let the prisoner speak as if he sat here as the judge and held the inquisition?

"Silence," he said. "Don't forget to whom you are speaking, and do not take advantage of your lord's kindness."

The Baptist only answered with the word of the Prophet:

"Seek the Lord while he may be found. Call on him while he is near. Then he shall have mercy on you and forgive abundantly."

He was ushered out by the guards.

Herod remained a moment. Where should he go? He ought to have gone to his chamber of council to hear the palace counselors lying naked lies and explanations for the grand cost of the new building. That disgusted him. Should he go to his private chambers first? To hear Herodias's poisonous suggestions? He rose and shook uneasily in his coat. He had nowhere to go.

Perhaps still? There was still one who promised to forgive abundantly. But how would it then be with Herodias? No, that wouldn't do. In any case, not now. Perhaps he ought to clear this up . . . But there would be another opportunity.

*

Come time, come council . . .

Earlier in the evening, all worries were drowned in a stream of flattery and wine, the scent of flowers and tinsel, and the clink of heavy gold jewelry. Herod felt himself being carried away by an overwhelming wave of praise and tributes as he reclined on a swelling bed at the feast table and allowed his gaze to glide over the brilliant colors surrounding him. In the golden light of the oil lamps, all the men of birth and wealth in his land shone before him. Easterners met Westerners in uniforms of a Roman cut, chitons made from the finest of Greek fabrics and the heavy oriental splendor from Tyre and Damascus. Today, all the worries and friction of this scheming group were relaxed. Today, all the faces were turned to him. Everyone praised his wine and his building projects, his wisdom and his taste. The murmur, the adulation, the warmth, and the wine rose like a cresting wave around him, and he let himself be comfortably carried away by it.

Then the wave broke in a sparkling foam wreath of pearls. The rumbling faded and was followed by a great calm. Only the pearls continued to dance, wild and frisky, like white foam upon the enchantingly smooth white skin of her soft nubile body. All the dark eyes followed her with charmed amazement or half-drunk lust. Then she slipped away again, just as lithely as she came. The foam stain disappeared in the wine-colored sea, and again the waves heaved and washed their cheers and frothy acclaim to Herod. Drunk on wine and pride, he called the girl to him. He felt the promise gush from his lips, rich and lush in the manner of the orient and the girl slipped away again, soft and graceful, with a happy smile.

When she came back, the silence was deafening. Herod felt the tension like a light sprinkling of discomfort in his festal joy, and he looked at the girl questioningly.

She bowed gracefully before her noble stepfather and said the horrible words:

"I want you to give me the head of John the Baptist on a platter, immediately."

The whole wave of royal celebration, splendor, and generosity broke from under Herod. He looked down. His head was spinning. His ears throbbed with thunder as if the wave threw him against a craggy cliff. He was fighting for breath and space. He wanted to think. He wanted to be alone. He was screaming inside: "Not now, another time! I need time, I need counsel."

But there was no other time; no more time came. The decision that he wanted to push away had fallen in his hands, the hand of an unmerciful enemy that shoved him against the wall and gripped his throat so that cold sweat broke out on his forehead.

What should he do? Honor the girl's wishes? Let Herodias triumph in her devilish female scheme? Murder the Baptist? Silence the only voice that spoke truth in this house? Put an end to the only person who wished him well? Never!

But what would he do otherwise? Take back his promise? Hear the whispers and watch the heads leaning into each other in the hall? Know how they laughed in the bazaars: Herod has become pious, he is like wax in the Baptist's hands, now he is done with drinking wine and lying with Philip's wife . . .

And what would he say to Herodias?

He no longer had a choice. He had still had it yesterday. Yesterday, he still had his hand on the strange enticing word about going to he who forgave abundantly. Now it was gone. There was only one way to go.

He wiped the sweat from his brow and commanded hoarsely that the girl's will should be done.

Five Barley Loaves

The sail filled out in the wind one last time before it lagged and hung slack and dead. The water was completely calm and still.

Despondent, they took the sail in. For over an hour, they had tacked back and forth without getting nearer to the beach. The sun was already high in the sky and the shadows among the blue mountains had descended to the bottom of the valleys. Now they grabbed the oars.

Andrew tried to gaze at the beach on the other side. To the left was the hometown of his youth, Bethsaida. They had sailed by it at dawn. Farther away to the right was Hippos on its crag. There was a four-hour walk between them. There were only a few groups of houses along the beach. The cold, deserted mountains rose up behind them, broken only by the steep canyons that found their way down to the water. He looked at the green marshy meadows closest to the city with the tall aspens where he so often played as a boy. Farther east, the slopes swept up steeper and grew into powerful mountains whose greenery faded to blue against the horizon. There were no people up there—not a single house nor even a shepherd at this time of year. That he knew. It was there he promised to take them, so that they would be free to rest.

They very well needed it. They had come back with all sorts of stories from their travels. They had fulfilled their commissions to be his apostles, and they were obliged to give him account. Everyone gathered in Capernaum when he himself came again. But they had barely begun to lay the power and commission down at his feet and to give account, all of them eager to tell their story, when a crowd gathered out in the garden again. A whole day had passed without them even being able to eat. When they thought they had finally sent the last person away, a new person always came. Late at night, when they were finally alone, the Master said that they should go with him someplace deserted, where they could be alone and rest a little. And so they sailed away, before there was even a hint of day.

Andrew navigated for his friends. They had come so close to the beach that all the details were visible. A huge herd of water buffalo on the left had come down into the water, where they rolled around like huge gray-and-white monsters in the banks of clay. Well, the water buffalo would not disturb their solitude. More concerning were the people walking along the beach. Andrew could not remember ever seeing so many people here at one time. For certain, the Passover wasn't far off, and perhaps it could be people from the villages of Gaulanitis making the pilgrimage together to the feast. But what made him nervous was that some of them had stopped. Now one of them was pointing out into the water. It was suspicious.

While the boat was still several stadia out from the beach, Andrew understood the whole situation. Not a single one of them continued south. They all stood together in a group, and those who came from the north hurried up and joined them. More and more came along the path leading from Bethsaida. The younger among them were half-running.

Andrew felt as if he had failed again. He had bet his pride on carrying the Master to this one place. And then they had this unlucky wind. Naturally, someone had seen them when they headed out. In the dawn's light, they had been but a speck out in the lake, and then the wild hunt began again. The trail from Bethsaida only took a couple hours; and now they were also both discovered and intercepted.

He glanced toward the Master. The friends rowed with their backs to the land. They hadn't seen anything. But the Master?

He sat in the stern and looked at the beach. His face was turned upward a bit, and he seemed to sit and look straight up to heaven. He did this often, and the strange thing was that he never looked to be daydreaming. His face was just as lively, as if he spoke with a person. But what he was thinking wasn't easy to say.

Now Peter had caught sight of the people. He immediately sounded the alarm. Everyone quit rowing and turned around. They gesticulated as they spoke. Peter proposed that they should row farther south. As if that would have helped with a hundred eyes watching them from the shore.

The Master decided the matter with a wink. They would continue straightforward and beach.

Then they came up amidst a crowd of people all welcoming and asking questions. What should they say? They couldn't say where they were going! The disciples pointed them to the Master, but they wouldn't ask him. They only stepped aside reverently.

Then the Master began to go ashore. They walked quite a ways, until the lake lay before their feet and the land around them was robed with grass and wild flowers. It was a strange train that made its way through the sticky greenery. Andrew went and looked at them. It was apparent that they had hurried off in the morning. They were bareheaded, thinly dressed, and ill shod as they milled about. Many had taken the long walk barefoot under the sun. They looked even poorer and more ragged than usual. It seemed that not one of them had had time to grab a washed robe or coat that wasn't torn.

The Master had set himself upon a huge stone high up on the slope. He let the people come to him and showed them where they should sit down. He gave them plenty of time and let them rest in the sun. Then he began to speak while new people continued to come up from the lake, and the circle got bigger and bigger.

Andrew listened with careful attention. Ever since he himself had wandered about carrying the Master's full authority, he had begun to think over these things in a new way. For the most part, it was Peter who had carried the word to the villages. Although they had never been in disagreement as to what should be said, they often found themselves unable to answer when the Pharisees came with their difficult questions.

The Master always spoke about the kingdom. He spoke in parables that Andrew was now beginning to understand a bit better than before. That is how it was with the kingdom. It was a mystery. It wasn't just anyone who could grasp it. There were those who had hardened hearts and deaf ears. The more they heard, the deafer they became. The Master himself had said it: he spoke to them in parables so that they saw nothing, though they had eyes with which to see, and they neither heard nor understood anything, though they had ears with which to hear. To them, the gospel was judgment. It was just like the time Isaiah was sent to harden hearts and blind the people. The word of God's salvation destroyed them. Andrew had seen it himself: the more the Pharisees heard and saw, the more bitter they seemed to become, and finally, they said it was all the work of Satan.

The Master compared the kingdom to a treasure that a man finds when he digs in another's field. When he hears the spade scrape against the lid of the chest and perceives what it is, he becomes dizzy and wild with joy. Then he covers the earth again and carefully hides the treasure. He leaves possessed with just one thought: acquiring the treasure. So he sells his house and all that he has and goes and buys the field whatever the cost.

Andrew had to smile. He could picture one of these poor ragamuffins in front of him digging for a lousy penny out in the field under the merciless sun, and then he finds a fortune in the ground. It was just what one could expect of him: that he looks around and carefully replaces the dirt clods before he is overcome with joy in the evening. This was the Master's way of talking to people. They could feel themselves in it. And at the same time, one perceived that the picture was a picture of something else. The slave of mammon possessed by his lust for gold in the earth was a picture of a man who found the kingdom of heaven. He was possessed by it. He knew that it was worth more than everything. Whatever the cost, he had to have it.

Andrew understood all this well enough. But now they asked him, "Where is this kingdom?" He had said, "It comes." And this was true. He knew that. But at the same time it was something that he, after all, had found. He knew this also. Just as if he was a merchant who sought expensive pearls, like the one Andrew had seen as a boy in Bethsaida at the border station, where his greedy fingers dug through the leather purse of a traveling merchant and offered anything for a pearl that enchanted his expert eyes. This pearl, it was the kingdom of God. One would pay whatever the cost for it when he found it. But how had he found it? It had not just come. And yet it was found in some manner with the Master. Everything he touched, and everything he proclaimed was full of this mystery. Had he not said it himself? "Here is one greater than Solomon; here is one greater than Jonah."

The Master spoke for a long time. He paused only when people would bring a sick person to him, and that happened often enough. There was constant coming and going among the huge multitude.

Andrew looked at the sun anxiously. It had gone a long way down behind the mountains beyond the plain of Genesareth. There was not much time before evening set in.

He went over to his friend John and spoke with him. Together they turned to James. He was of one mind with them too. They rose to go explain it to the Master. Philip was already there speaking with him. Apparently he had had the same thought. The area was desolate. They needed to send the people away before it got dark so that they could go to the villages around and buy something to eat.

Sometimes, the Master could be quite incomprehensible. Now he told them that it would be better if they gave them something to eat here instead.

Andrew gathered that he was thinking of how tired and starving they must be. Particularly, the elderly looked as if they would not be able to cope very long into the evening. But this was still hardly an excuse for such an unreasonable suggestion. Philip spoke straight from their hearts when he said that if they had a fortune to buy bread with, then it would only be enough for everyone to have just a little bit. Jesus seemed to smile at him, but he didn't say anything. He just asked how much bread they had.

Andrew came to think of the boy he had seen earlier. He was an attentive supporter from Bethsaida, one who went around with his basket on his head and sold bread in the city. He had surmised that he could do good business today and followed the crowd along the path.

In less than a minute Andrew had gotten ahold of him and could say, "He has five loaves and two fish today." But he couldn't just let that be; he had to add, "But what is that for so many?"

The Master nodded.

"It is enough. Bring them to me."

At times, there was something about the Master's voice that made a person think of the Creator's power and bow to his will, something that swept all obstacles aside and caused everything to occur according to his will. He had climbed up on the stone, and his voice was heard all the way to the farthest crowds. He invited them all to sit down in the grass and divide themselves up to eat in circles. He sent the disciples out in all directions to sort out the huge mess of people. When Andrew came back with the boy, they had already run out into the crowd and Andrew could see how they parted everyone and put them together in smaller groups. It looked just like a bunch of densely growing boxes between the waterways in a garden.

The Master commanded everything with his look and his word. He had laid the bread and the fish upon the stone in front of him. Illuminated by the last of the evening sun, he was visible to everyone around him. He stood like the father of a house in the midst of the whole crowd and recited the table prayer with his face lifted toward the heavens and his hands held in blessing over the food before him. He praised God, Lord of the world, who with his miraculous powers brings forth bread from the ground and gives food at the right time to all whose eyes look to him. Then he blessed the bread, took it in his hands and broke it, calmly and gently, as if he held something holy. He extended it to the disciple who was closest and pointed with his hand to where he should go. With the same almost reverent solemnity he broke a new piece of bread and yet another and put them in Andrew's hands. As Andrew walked away with the bread of blessing in his hands, it became clearer than ever to him that this was God's gift that he was carrying. He thought about the black rocky earth where this barley flour had been created from out of the dust. He thought in particular about how it had grown out of the dead earth and would become one with living bodies of men, how it would enter them and nourish them and take the form of muscle and thinking ability, hand movements and talking lips. He thought about what the Master had said, about the heavenly Father letting his sun rise over both the evil and the good. So today this bread of blessing would feed both prostitutes and publicans. What he now carried in his hands was proof that the Master up there on the stone slab made them all his friends and guests at his table. It was as if he invited this whole broken and starved crowd to feast in his Father's kingdom.

Andrew passed the bread out and was surprised that it stretched so far. Then he turned back. The Master had more bread. It was so heavy as he laid it in his arms that it was work to carry it.

He didn't know how many times he went back and forth. He hurried as much as he could. He didn't need to ask if he was welcome. All the faces lit up for him. The sun went down and gave all their colors their fullest look. As custom demanded, they ate in silence, but a wave of joy washed over the entire endless mass of rags and poverty. This was a true wedding feast, and the wedding guests had the bridegroom in their midst.

Finally, the disciples themselves were able to eat. Only then did they begin to seriously wonder where their Master had gotten all this from. They looked at each other. They dared not ask. They were almost apprehensive as they took the bread. But it was completely common barley bread.

Then the Master asked them to gather up all that was left over. Nothing would perish of that which they ate today. For the gift came from God's hand.

And Jesus Took His Leave

The heat was unbearable. Philip wiped his face as if he wanted to remove a stinging mask that the heat of the sun pushed against his cheeks. He wasn't sweaty at all. Every drop of moisture that oozed from his head immediately evaporated and left nothing but a sticky, shiny film that tasted of salt when he touched it with the tip of his tongue. The air around him felt like a thick mass he had to push through, and the blazing sun beaming straight down upon them pressed heavily upon his crown.

They had rested under some terebinths in the field, but the withered leaves didn't offer any shade. The ground was a single cairn of black stone, and the wind blew tormenting heat from the lake. It was impossible to get any rest. So they decided to keep going.

The dried grass between the stones rustled sharply. The men before him stopped to give warning. They pointed at the back of some reptile that had disappeared into a crack in this parched ground. If it had been three months earlier, they would have attempted to kill it. Now they just gave it a tired look full of ill will and enmity.

They walked straight up the mountain, over the harvested fields where the scorched earth broke out into a network of cracks and seemed to be crying out for rain with its chapped lips. The wheat remained at the edges of the fields, half-grown, bleached white, and so dry it cracked. It had come up too early in the thin soil and had dried up. The stunted and empty ears rattled in the wind. They were white against the stone slabs that cropped up where the soil came to an end.

They reached a field where the weeds had gotten out of hand. The thistles grew as tall as men. The wheat had been choked out, and no one had seen it worthwhile to come at it with the scythe. It stood by itself, waiting to be burned off.

Philip looked to the side to see if he could get around it. But the Master didn't bother himself with the obstacles. He went straight through the interlaced thistles. Philip lifted his hands above his head so as not to get them all shred to pieces. He heard the shards from the stalks snap around him as they whirled from the splitting stems that scratched and stabbed. Then they were through. He plucked the burs from his coat and brushed away the chaff that the wind had strewn through his hair and down his neck.

The heat did not seem to fade as they steadily made their way up the mountain. It was as if there was a fan blowing from deep within Gehenna down there. Perhaps there was. Philip thought the lake was cursed this summer. The longer he walked with the Master, the more mysterious everything seemed. In the beginning, he knew what he should believe. When he first got to know the Master by the Jordan, it was completely clear to him that he had found the one that Moses and the prophets had written about. When all the impressive mighty works happened, it was like a thundering knock upon the gates of a new age. He and all the people knew that the promised one stood before the door. The one who didn't seem to understand this was the Master himself. He took his hand from them as soon as enthusiasm rose to the point where the masses were like the quivering metal in a crucible that could be poured into molds and shaped according to will. It was then that he threw water on their fire and left them without direction. The evening after the feast, there was a forest of outstretched arms growing out of the twilight in the wilderness. It was filled with cries of tribute. They wanted to force him to be their king. He simply withdrew from them. And when they still sought him, he spoke more strictly than ever before, even more strictly than he had to those in the synagogue of Capernaum.

Philip shook his head. He who they believed to be the king of Israel did not want to be Israel's king. Instead of using his power to grab hold of the opportunity that heaven had offered him, he went around preaching that one should repent.

That was needed just now. Philip was in complete agreement with him on that. But it wasn't wise of the Master to push people away from him. He could have managed much more if he had made himself their lord as they themselves wanted and then written his laws for them. Now he gave them free will instead: they could do his word, and they could also despise it. It seemed to be all the more obvious that most despised his words. The people were like these fields. The Master himself had said it. Some were like the seed in the thin soil, the first to shoot up in the spring, but now their empty ears blew in the wind. Then they had stood like rolling fields around the Master when the summer came full of enthusiasm. But now they had grown tired, and their enthusiasm had wilted away. Then there were the others who were like thistles. They had also had their time when it looked as if they would bear fruit. But now there were only weeds remaining, and to go in among them was to stand amidst nothing but resistance and sharp grudges.

They stopped yet again. The slope that rose to the north was flaming hot under the afternoon sun. The heat pulsated up from the dry ground, and there was not yet the least relief in the fiery air drafts. Before them lay endless ascents strewn with black stone. Behind them lay the regions around the lake. There lay Capernaum, half-hazy in the sun. The houses of Bethsaida looked like white flecks trembling in the hot air, and closest to them lay the huddled and lifeless black basalt of Chorazin.

Philip thought about what the Master had said about these cities. They had not repented. They had seen his miracles in their streets. Things had happened in their synagogues that would have persuaded Sodom itself to change course. But they had only hardened themselves. Therefore the sinners of Sodom would find it more tolerable on the Day of Judgment than the people down there by the lake.

Philip knew that they deserved it. He himself would have deserved such a punishment if he now threw away the word that the Master spoke. He knew that Peter spoke the complete truth when the crowds thinned and the Master suddenly asked them if they too wanted to leave. Peter had answered for all of them when he asked the counter question, "To whom shall we go? You have the words of eternal life." One could not reject these words without rejecting God himself. And the cities down there had rejected them. People still came together to see signs and wonders, or to escape some plague. But they did not forgive their enemies. They did not quit cursing their brothers. They took every last farthing from their interest rates and wrote certificates of divorce for their wives.

And yet they had still offered the Master a king's crown. Why had he pushed them away from him? He could have gotten them all on his side. Why had he not seized the opportunity? Just a few months ago, the slopes were red and blue with flowers and the cranes went north in glittering flocks. Anything was possible. Now the land was scorched, a red-hot desert of black stone, of snakes and thistles, where the quivering heat seemed to rise up out of Gehenna.

Philip didn't understand a thing. The Master, the future, the meaning with all this was a mystery to him. But even as an unsolved mystery, the Master had power over him. So he wiped his hand across his burnt face once more and continued up the slope.

Bread to the Dogs

"Lord, Son of David!"

The woman's shrill voice cut through the still of the night and echoed from the other side of the valley. The day had cooled off, the sea glittered endlessly off to the west, and the sun fell on its steep path into its reflection on the surface of the sea. The last rays of light danced playfully on the tops of the mountains so that the snow on the heights of Mount Hermon behind them radiated with red. A slight breeze rustled the leaves, and in the depths under their feet, the frothy green river sang its song.

"Son of David, have mercy on me!"

Peter was sore. Now they had been discovered. They had come to relax in this lovely land where mature fruit hung alongside all the paths and where the green booths provided cool relief outside of every house wall. The Master had shut himself in over there on the hillside in the little white house between the walnut trees. No one knew why he was there. Only now, in the cool of the evening, had he left and gone up the valley.

"Lord, Son of David, have mercy upon my daughter!"

Peter looked at the Master as he continued to follow the narrow path. Naturally, he had heard it. The woman yelled so that the echo rolled between the hills. She had called him the Son of David. Would he let her do that? At home in Galilee, he silenced anyone who dared hint that he was the Messiah.

"Son of David, hear me! My daughter is sick! She is lying at home plagued by many evil spirits."

The Master continued along the narrow path. The woman, who went a little higher up upon the hillside, had come closer. She begged for him to come and make her daughter well. If this had been after nightfall, her voice would have woken every soul in the villages between the mountains.

Peter could not stand it. She would gather together as many people as were in the region. He saw that the others thought the very same thing. They went up to the Master and asked him to send her away. They could not let her follow on their heels and scream as she did. Would it not be best to do what she asked?

The Master shook his head.

"I am not sent to any but to the lost sheep of the house of Israel."

Peter had known this. He had seen it in all his Master's wanderings. He himself had received the command not to go either to the Samaritans or the heathens. So it must be. First Israel would turn back to its God, and then the light would go through Israel for all the gentiles. It was said by all the prophets, and yet . . .

Did the woman understand what they were speaking about? She had come down to them, and there she fell to her knees and took hold of the folds in his robe. She was definitely a heathen. She had heard about the Messiah because, up here, there were many people who went back and forth over the mountains between Tyre and Galilee. People had even come down to the lake shores from here when the Master began to preach.

Now the Master looked at the woman and shook his head.

"No," he said. "The children must first be satisfied. One does not take bread from them and throw it to the dogs."

Peter was astonished. Those were hard words. Certainly, it was true that every Jew called the heathens dogs. One should not throw holy things to the dogs, the Master had said. And all the lasciviousness and cruelty that they openly committed in their temples and amphitheaters showed quite well that they were not worthy to be named together with God's people. But still, to tell her that straight to her face—that was pretty harsh.

The woman looked at the Master with great sadness. She didn't look angry. She bowed her head conformingly.

"Yes, Lord" was all she said. Then she looked straight up at him again. "But the dogs eat the crumbs that fall from their master's table."

Then Jesus looked upon her as if he had rejoiced over her unexpected answer.

"O woman, your faith is great," he said, and then he added that for the sake of these words, she could go home in peace. It would happen for her according to her faith.

The woman kissed the hem of his robe and ran on her way. The Master resumed his hike, alone and quiet. Peter looked after the woman for a minute as she hurried along as fast and light-footed as a girl. There was no hesitancy with her. She had received his word, and it was enough for her.

"O woman, your faith is great." So this was a great faith. Nothing could be more humble than the woman who knelt there at the Master's feet and bowed her head to his judgment as she begged for a leftover crumb. Peter had heard the Master praise a person who had great faith before. It had been the centurion who sought help for his servant. He too had been a heathen. He too had stood there, poor and without claim. He did not even consider himself worthy enough for the Master to go under his roof. But he also had been as solid as a rock in his conviction that the powerful little words from the Master's lips were enough.

Was this the great faith? Peter thought about the poor and oppressed, the hungry and thirsty who the Master praised as blessed because the kingdom was theirs. He thought about the ragged and starving, the old and despised who gathered around Jesus. Did they too have great faith? Was this what the Master expected to find on earth—the great hunger that did not let itself be satisfied by anything other than the word that forgave and healed in God's own name?

Perhaps it wasn't so strange that he had found so little faith in Israel. How rich were his compatriots when compared to this woman. They had the law and the promises; they were Abraham's children.

But this couldn't be something wrong on their part. Was it not God himself who chose them?

Suddenly, Peter came to think about what the Baptist had said. If they prided themselves on having Abraham as a father, then they should also bear such fruit as belonged to repentance.

Was this where the mystery received its resolution? Were Abraham's children called to be the first who would repent in the fullness of time, and then the promise would be honored? But if they didn't repent now? Think if the Messiah came and his people did not receive him.

"Lord, Son of David," the woman had said. The Master had not silenced her. When he saw her faith, he gave her the bread that was intended for the children—Abraham's children. Had not the Master done the same for the centurion? Would not many come from the distant lands of the heathens and be guests at the table in the heavenly kingdom together with Abraham while the kingdom's own children had to stand outside in the dark?

That it could possibly go this way was something Peter had never really considered before. Now he let his gaze thoughtfully sweep from the eastern horizon, where Mount Hermon blocked the view of Damascus and all the lands east. Now he looked off to the west, where the sun sank in the endless sea and where two small ships were heading for Ephesus, Corinth, and Rome.

The Thoughts of God and the Thoughts of Man

Will the Son of Man find any faith on earth when he comes?

Peter thought about the Master's words all morning. A person had a lot of time to ponder while he walked, and it was possible that the Master had taken them here simply to give them time to do that. He was very quiet. He often prayed alone. Now he was alone in the lead again.

In the villages around here, there were only strangers. Straight ahead on the hills were the temples of Caesarea Philippi at foot of the great mountains. They were consecrated to strange gods. Their gables bore the images of the half-animalistic Pan, and no Jew was happy to set foot in that city because it was overshadowed by the Greek deities of lust.

Yet here the plains just outside the city were like the garden of paradise. The streams welled forth—not like the springs of Galilee, with a soft rippling between the stones, but like rushing rivers from the bowels of the earth. They filled the entire vicinity with the lovely sound of coursing water. Here the aspen forests were thick with tall white trunks. The wind sang in the glittering crowns, and the flecks of sunlight danced upon the rippling water. It was like an Eden for those who came from the scorched slopes of Galilee.

But shall the Son of Man find faith when he comes? The question returned.

A man should pray unceasingly. Day and night, one should cry. God would vindicate his chosen people. The Master had said it again, and they knew that he himself spoke with God both day and night. Peter believed he knew the cares that he spoke about. The Son of Man had not found faith on earth. There was a leaven of the people who poisoned and destroyed everything. He had warned them of it, and they had begun to understand what he meant. There was the leaven of the Pharisees. This was the art of making oneself unrepentant by being of such surpassing righteousness—the trick of tithing a tenth of one's mint, cumin, and dill to avoid giving your heart as a sacrifice. The Master had exposed them; they forgot both charity and mercy, and replaced them with their own statutes. They said that they had the key of knowledge, and could unlock the gates of heaven. But it was precisely this that they had lost. Those who had let the leaven infect their hearts would never rejoice in the jubilant message. To hear this ring of joy, one had to be poor. But they were rich, very rich, and satisfied.

Then there was the leaven of the Sadducees fermenting in the people. This was the art of making oneself unrepentant by being sufficiently pious. Everything was to be in moderation. There was moderation with Moses and the service of the temple. Life in this world was lived without any disturbance or reckoning. And the high priest himself spoke this way, so it was no wonder that the people followed. He who tasted this leaven never repented again.

And then there were the Herodians! They too, the Master said, had their leaven. They had taught themselves the art of saying no to God's kingdom for the sheer purpose of good order and peace in the land. They had set their hopes on the house of the king, to be given magisterial posts, on the right to own land and collect wealth. When a person offered them the kingdom of God, they never had time. First they would go away to check on their fields. Or they would have to consider if it was lawful, proper, and profitable for good order. And when the foremost of the land acted this way, it was no wonder that the people followed suit. So the Son of Man found no faith on earth. There were so few around him. And it seemed as if he no longer expected that there would be any more. Was he done with this unrepentant generation?

Still, the Master led them quietly. They didn't speak amongst themselves. If they spoke, it was mostly about inconsequential things. They looked at a waterwheel or watched a heron fishing. The day was filled with the dense, even heat of late summer, broken up by the shade on the banks of the cool rivers. It was almost like spring. The swirling black smoke of a burning field of thistles was the only thing that indicated the end of summer.

When Peter saw the billowing smoke and the two men who stuck their burning brands into the dry weeds, he thought about what the Master had once said about the word he had sown. It too could be choked out by the thorns. Did he already know then that it would go as it was now going? Was it so with the words from the lips of God—that most of them would be wasted? Was it foreseen that the Son of Man would not find any faith when he came to earth?

But why, then, did he come? The Pharisees had just now requested a sign once again. And again, he answered that they would not receive one. They would receive the same sign as the Ninevites and nothing else. The sign the Ninevites received was the powerful preaching of Jonah. In the same manner, the Son of Man would be a sign for this generation. They had heard his sermon. But they did not believe in the sign.

Peter knew all too well that they had said Jesus was a false prophet whose time was growing short. The Anointed who came in the name of God would gather God's people around him. He would stand like a banner on Mount Zion, and all the dispersed tribes of Israel would gather around him from the ends of the earth. But now they dispersed instead. They had wanted to make him king, but he had refused. So they turned away from him. If he did not want to be king, then he would also be without people.

This was a mystery for Peter too. When the Messiah came, he must gather his people around him. The government would rest on his shoulders. He would establish his kingdom with truth and righteousness.

He had pondered over this a lot. He had thought about what the prophet had said, that only a little remnant of Israel would be saved, a holy shoot from the decapitated and mutilated stump of Jesse. Was it not written that the people would remain blinded and hardened until only a tenth remained, and then a tenth of that would also languish? Was this what was happening now?

He looked again at the Master, who led them quietly and alone. He saw the blue robe that was bleached by the sun and the worn head scarf fringed on the edges. The Master had never before been so alone, and never had it been so hard to understand his mystery. Everything a man put his faith in before was being undone. Jesus had not held court as the Baptist had said. He had not established the kingdom of David as the people had wanted. He had proclaimed the good news, but the people disdained it.

But then, of all the squandered seed, there would be a little share that fell in good earth. And it would bear fruit. God would vindicate his chosen. The kingdom of heaven itself was a leaven that could do miracles.

It was not easy to believe it. Peter cast a timid glance at the others. They wandered along the river without a care in the world. They looked for fish among the stones. Either they didn't understand much or the mystery had become so great that they pushed it away.

This was truly an unsolvable mystery. The Messiah was the king of the age. He was the one around whom everything revolved in the history of the people. The living God himself would prepare his way. He himself would be present. He himself would gather his chosen people. The living God's work was full of glory and the power of victory. Was it not unreasonable and blasphemous to believe that the poor tracks of worn sandals, which were seen here in the road dust, would be the beginning of this work?

And yet there was something else. There was this that meant more than all reason, and you could never get away from it: The kingdom of heaven is like a mustard seed. It is least of all seeds . . . Fear not, little flock, for it pleases the Father to give you the kingdom. Blessed are you who are poor, for the kingdom of heaven belongs to you. And blessed is he for whom I am not a stumbling block.

It was unbelievable, but it was true. He could not be, and it was then so. This was impossible to believe, and yet Peter believed it.

Did he believe? Or would the Son of Man not find faith when he came to earth?

*

Jesus stood on the parapet. He leaned forward and looked down into the streaming water. Suddenly looking up when they were only a few paces away, he straightened himself out and said:

"Well . . . who do people say that I am?"

They stopped and looked at each other for a moment. Of course, they knew how much this matter was spoken about in every house by the lake, from the sukkahs in the vineyards to the palace of the prince. But they had never dared speak to him about such things.

"They say that you are John the Baptist who has risen."

"Or Elijah"

"Or Jeremiah, or one of the prophets."

Peter looked at the Master. What did he say to all this?

The Master did not seem to be surprised, hardly even interested. He nodded almost imperceptibly, as if he let the whole matter rest. But then he looked at them again, and now his gaze was searching and impossible to escape.

"Well . . . who do you say that I am?"

They were quiet. Peter had a feeling that none of them dared to look at one another. This was the first time the Master had asked them about their faith. They had gone with him, and he had instructed them, but he had never asked them about their faith. Peter understood that he now stood at a crossroads where he had to make a decision that would shape the rest of his life. He could still go. A man could follow a Master for a few months or even years and then say thanks and go. But there was a line when all freedom, all choice, and all the rights of an individual came to an end . . .

He took half a step forward. He knew that this step carried him over the line. He stepped into a realm where he would no longer prevail over himself. He heard his own voice clearly and openly say the unprecedented:

"You are the Messiah, the Son of the living God."

Jesus's eyes smiled at him. The whole of his face lit up with joy reminiscent of the times when he thanked his Father or laid hands upon the sick. He said something solemn:

"Blessed are you, Simon, son of Jonas, for flesh and blood have not revealed this to you, but my Father, who is in heaven."

Peter breathed deeply. So it was not in vain that he struggled in his solitude. He had struggled with the living God, and his eyes had been opened so that he had seen his work, even where it was hidden from all reason.

The smile of victory came back to the Master's face.

"I can also tell you who you are, Peter. You are the rock, and on this rock I shall build my church, and the gates of hell shall not prevail against her. I shall give you the keys to the kingdom. What you bind on earth shall be bound in heaven, and what you loose on earth, that shall be loosed in heaven."

Then he turned and went ahead of them, alone and thoughtful as before. They looked at each other in amazement and a little hesitantly. Then they followed him.

Peter also went by himself and thought. Here he had received the answer: The Master was the Messiah. He was the king above all kings, and he would also gather all his people. He had expected a word that the scriptures used for God's elect congregation. He was the king of Israel too. He came to gather the remnants who would turn to God. He would lay the foundation for the congregation that would be God's people for all eternity. He would build them up like a temple, holy to the Lord. And he would build this temple on the rock, Peter.

Once again, Peter felt completely overwhelmed by all this. It laid upon him like a burden that no man could carry. Who was he that he should carry God's new temple?

It was unreasonable and yet inescapable. It wasn't he who had chosen this. He had once thought that he had chosen to follow the Master whatever it meant. Now he saw that he was only a piece of clay in the Master's hand. Here, the living God operated through the Messiah. Here, he had no action nor right to choose. He had been chosen. He was called to be a fisher of men. He proceeded to a future that he did not control and did not understand. Still, he went because God's Messiah led the way.

The Master stopped and called them to him. There was something he wanted to tell them. They were not to reveal this to anyone for any reason. Again, he emphasized that no one should know that he was the Messiah.

Again, he went forward and again they followed him. Only now did Peter dare look at the others. He was almost afraid to do it before. Must they not look at him with wondering eyes and think ill that he would be the rock? He had been their friend and equal in everything. Why, then, would he have the power to loose and bind?

The others were very serious and very quiet. They had stopped looking at the birds and the water. They walked by groves of newly broken pomegranates, where the golden fruit shown in the opened casing, but no one touched them. It was as if they looked at something great that had come closer from an unknown distance. But Peter noticed no envy. If everything was to be kept secret, then it was all the same. They had to believe the promise despite what they saw and against the protest of reason. The only thing that separated him from the others was this: he had received a great promise that was even harder to believe.

"I shall give you the keys to the kingdom." Another time—they would have to wait. At another time, sinners would be called to repentance and given to be children of the kingdom. And Peter would even be the apostle who spoke with the full authority of his Lord. He who believed this word would be loosed; he who rejected it would be bound. And the keys would be held in his weak human hands. It was unreasonable—and still possible. He had already shown that when he went out in his Lord's stead and proclaimed the message in his name. He was sent by God's Messiah so that the message did not come from flesh and blood but from God's own lips.

"And the gates of hell would not prevail against her." No, it must be so. This was just as unreasonable and just as necessary as all the rest. The gates of hell shut themselves unmercifully upon every man. No one could hinder them from shutting again, and no one could break them open. But here, in the Messiah's congregation, among the Holy People of God, they would be impervious to this power. He did not understand how, but he thought that it must mean that no one would be able to kill the Master and stone his chosen. He remembered how the Master cheated death in Nazareth. He thought about everything that he had heard of Herod's evil plans. No, they would not be able to lay God's Messiah low. Would God not vindicate his chosen when he cried to him?

The Master stopped once again. He sat on a fallen trunk and motioned for them to take a seat. Then he began to instruct them again, as calmly and as matter-of-factly as ever. He spoke about God's Messiah, and they listened attentively.

It was a strange talk. They understood everything and yet nothing. There was a contradiction right at the beginning. The Son of Man would suffer much. And the rest was even more peculiar: The

Son of Man would be rejected by the elders and the chief priests and the scribes. They would kill him . . .

Kill God's Messiah? But who could kill God's Messiah? Kill Jesus? But who, then, would carry out his work and build his new temple? Peter defended himself with all his might against the idea. Then everything would be destroyed altogether. Had he found God's Messiah today, only to hear that he went to die?

When they went on, Peter dared to catch up with the Master. As soon as they were out of earshot from the others, he began to speak as seriously and thoroughly as he could. This would not happen. God was very gracious to his Messiah. He should not think in this way.

The Master had stopped. He looked at Peter. The others had gathered around and listened. When Jesus saw them, he said very firmly, very slowly, and very seriously, "Get away from me, Satan. You are a stumbling block in my way, for yours are not the thoughts of God, but of men."

And he turned again and left, and Peter remained standing. Finally, in a quiet group, they followed.

Blessed and Satan, it was too much on the same day. He had been called blessed for that which God revealed, but then because of that which God had not revealed, that which came from his own human heart, he was called Satan—the tempter—called a stumbling stone, and compared to a rock set in the Master's path to trip him. Was he so powerless? Did he stand in the way of God when he did his best? Did he stand in the way of the goal for God's Messiah, the goal God had set for him?

God's Messiah, and then rejected and killed—this was too much. It could not be accommodated in the same destiny and the same human being. Either one or the other, but not both. And yet the Master had said so . . .

He had received his answer, and yet everything was a new mystery. He knew who the Master was. He knew the secret of his being. God had opened his eyes so that he saw that the carpenter and prophet was God's Son. He who did not reign with the sword but only with his word, he who would not crush his enemies but save them, he who did not want to have tribute and praise but only asked for the fruit of repentance was God's Anointed, he who had been hidden from the ages, the one generations sought and prophets and kings longed to see.

This mystery was solved. But behind them was an even greater and darker mystery before which all reason was powerless. He who was the rock under the Messiah's temple had been a Satan when for the first time he let his groping thoughts seek a solution to them.

Peter lifted his bowed head and looked ahead. The others had caught up to the Master, and he had turned to speak with them. Peter went forth and followed with quiet embarrassment behind the pack. He heard the Master say that if anyone wanted to follow him, he must deny himself and take up his cross. He who tried to save his life would lose it. But he who lost it for his sake—he would find it.

"The gates of hell will not prevail against her." There it was; Peter heard it again. Unreasonable but inescapable. But perhaps he believed it precisely because it was beyond all reason. His own human thoughts had backfired. Now it remained to see what lay in the thoughts of God.

Whiter than Snow

They were up by the last trees. John had taken notice of how the forest had become sparse, and the shrubs grew together. They seemed to crouch and creep along the ground and cling to the stones.

Then there weren't any more trees. John looked around amazed. He had never thought that the mountain could be so high that the forest could no longer grow there. Otherwise, this ought to have been a glorious forest. They walked over a tight carpet of tasseled grass and creeping willow. They continually encountered rivulets of cold water that noiselessly seeped over the rocks and wet gravel.

After just a few hours they had lost sight of the valleys around Caesarea Philippi. The entire city crept down and hid behind the foothills of the mountain. In return, new and unbelievable vistas opened themselves over their own lake, stepping forth from behind the heights, getting bigger and clearer the higher they climbed. They stopped again and again to look at the cities. There was Tiberias and there Magdala, they caught a glimpse of Capernaum, and Bethsaida peeking from behind the ridge. And at the same time, the lake came out of its hiding place among the mountains and met the horizon in the south. On the other side of the plain, Mount Carmel, Mount Ebal, and Mount Gerizim rose up among the hills of Samaria, and there behind them one could glimpse the ridges of Judah and even the surrounding area of Jerusalem. And still they climbed.

John looked at his brother with a wide happy smile. This was a journey that suited them. It was said that no one climbed up here of their own accord. Everyone saw this mysterious mountain, but no one climbed it. It was for just this reason they were happy when the Master asked them to come along. They felt as if it was a reward, just like the name that he had given them. It was somewhat in jest that he called them the Sons of Thunder. If they made noise and upset the peace in small things, they were also the first on the spot when there was a demand for courage or something demanding vigor.

So John was enchanted by the idea of ascending to these mountain meadows where no one had set foot before. In the west, the sea opened up its infinite expanse beyond the mountains of Phoenicia. In the east, there lay an endless desert. Before him was the mountain. Again and again, he turned to look behind him. Up there, on that crown, they must surely reach the top. But new crowns kept appearing on the cold heights. The climbing was less steep, but the mountain rose before them endlessly.

It was the first time James had climbed up to the snow. It was in a deep crevice between the cliffs. They sunk their hands in it and pressed it against their cheeks. Never before had they held living snow. They had seen it once before carried down to Bethsaida, packed hard in stretched leather wineskins, but that snow was dark and dripping wet. This was white and grainy, clearer than salt and so cold that their hands ached when they dug into it.

The sun kept going down. It was pleasantly cool and strangely easy to breathe. The blue shadows moved softly over their homeland down below; some singular clouds floated like white patches of wool over the surface of the lake. The whole deep valley between the mountains of Galilee was already enveloped by the twilight. Certainly, they had arrived now?

They never reached the top. They came so far that the mountain fell steeply to the east. Their eyes were full of amazement when they saw a city down there that had to be Damascus. It looked like a white jewel in a setting of green in the midst of the red desert. The forest of this great mountain fell like a giant across the plain and sped faster and faster toward the horizon. Then the blue twilight spread out over the land. Dust clouds across the desert were momentarily painted a reddish purple, and the small clouds over Lake Tiberius climbed like cut roses. Then it was all extinguished. The sun disappeared into the sea, and the intimidating darkness of night swept over the roadless expanse of the desert.

They prepared camp for themselves with sod in a deep ravine and ate their bread and figs. When the stars began to shine above them, the Master asked them to remain there while he went away to pray. Still, when it was completely dark, they could make him out against the horizon above camp. They heard him speak with his Father, but they could not make out the words.

John sat at watch for a long time. His brother slept between tussocks, and even Peter laid down. He listened. He would have liked to know what the Master said when he spoke to his Father . . . Again, he shrank before the great mystery that did not find resolution. He knew this and he believed it fully and firmly. And still he did not know what it meant or what it would come to mean. Here they had God's Messiah among them. The bridegroom at the heavenly feast of joy had come down to earth. They were also invited to the wedding. He had called them and appointed them to be his groomsmen, and he clothed them with authority like no other. They were the beginning of his people and heirs to his glorious kingdom. Yet nonetheless, they wandered about homeless and made their camp on the ground. It was the Master himself who said that foxes have holes, but the Son of Man has no place to lay his head.

He had dozed off for a minute, and the stars had journeyed a long way through the heavens. It was infinitely calm about them. There wasn't even a faded echo from the world of men below.

Then they heard the Master's voice again. He spoke softly to someone who was right next to him and yet infinitely far away. John listened for a long time. Did the Master never get tired? How could he speak with his heavenly Father for so long? It was a conversation he heard. The Master spoke and listened. He was quiet and then spoke again. It was off in the distance, but even when John fell asleep, he could hear the peculiar sound of boundless reverence in his voice. It addressed something of which he was a part and worshiped, him of whose being he himself was an echo.

When John woke again, it was at first with the sensation of the sun shining in his face. Drowsily, he opened his eyes and saw the deep-blue sky above him, as deep a blue as is only possible in the earliest hours of the morning when the stars first go out. Yet the sun shone around him. He pulled himself up, still heavy with sleep, and saw the Master standing before him.

Was it the Master? His face was changed, his clothes shone like light reflecting off a field of snow. His whole figure was made of light, interwoven and filled by light, a strange enchanting light that caressed the eye and blinded it. It filled one's heart with both joy and dread. Two figures stood next to the Master, they were perforated by the same light. The second John saw them, he knew they were Moses and Elijah. They had come down here to talk with the Son of Man. The foremost among those who had gone before the Messiah were standing here speaking about the work that they had begun and he would now fulfill.

At first, John wondered if he was dreaming. He looked around him. Yes, this was certainly a dream. He was floating in the clouds. The whole mountain floated in the clouds. They spread themselves out like soft waves of woolly foam. Yet they were still filled with the blue of dark night that had yet to feel the first red splash of the morning's blood. The soft sea floated about their feet and carried them. They were alone under the sky.

John took a drowsy step forward. His foot thumped hard on the gravel. His clothes were wet with dew, and his hands felt frozen. This was no dream. James and Peter stood there. They were just as drowsy and perplexed as John. Like children awakened too early, they drew closer to the Master.

In that moment, both figures bowed their farewell and prepared to go. Peter took a couple stumbling steps, and John heard his sleepy voice say something confused about it being good that they were here. Could they do them the service of building three booths, one for each of them? His incoherent words were drowned by a white clarity, a glittering cloud that was something other than a light. It was a glory and a power, something sweet and terrifying. John threw himself down on his knees and bowed his head to the ground. While he lay there with his head pressed against the willows, he heard the light fill with a voice that was not a voice, but a living word that filled him and permeated him like the light itself. And the word that came out of the clearness and filled his breast and head told him, "This is my beloved Son. Listen to him."

Still stunned by bliss and horror, he felt the Master's hand on his shoulder. He heard his voice say, "Rise, and have no fear."

He looked up. Jesus stood there alone. Nothing was visible behind him but the desolate mountain vastness and then the endless sea of clouds turning red with the first light of dawn.

John rose, unable to say a thing. Unconsciously, he took the bread that Jesus offered him. He followed him just as passively when he began to climb down to the shoreline created by the sea of clouds.

Timid and tentative, he exchanged a few words with the others. Had they heard the voice? Yes. Had they seen them? Yes. Was it Moses? Yes. And Elijah? Again, they nodded. What did they talk about? About that which would happen now in Jerusalem.

Then the Master turned to them as if he understood what they were speaking about. For the first time he mentioned the vision they saw. He forbade them to speak about it to anyone before the Son of Man had risen from the dead.

They nodded and continued down the steep trail in silence. Now the sea of clouds before them radiated with sunlight. There were tears in the shroud through which one could see blue ridges. When they came closer, it dissolved into glittering light and fell about them like a veil of white mist enveloping them in a sun-saturated haze. Then the air became clear again, and white fuzzy clouds floated above their heads. Below them lay the whole Galilean mountain range over the backs of which the blue shadows of the clouds meandered.

Once again, John slowly began to speak with the others about what the Master had said: that he was the Son of Man, who would judge the world. He was the only Son of the living God, who, though misunderstood, made his way to his glory. This they understood. He would go to Jerusalem and he would establish his power there. There, the mystery that was only known to the chosen would be revealed to everyone.

But this was a word that they did not understand. He said that the Son of Man would rise again. They knew that the dead would be resurrected. There would come a time when they would be esteemed worthy to be children of the new age and receive the same glory that they had seen a reflection of this morning. But the Son of Man? Would he rise again? God would wake the dead from their humiliation. But the Messiah was God's Son, partaker of his glory. And wouldn't Elijah come before the resurrection?

For the first time, they dared to test the great mystery with tough questions.

"How then could the scribes say that Elijah must come first?"

The Master's answer was clear and yet enigmatic. He said that Elijah must come first. This was right. He would establish everything again. But this was already done. He had come. But the men would not know him. They dealt with him according to their own evil desires. They would treat the Son of Man in the same way. Was it not written of him that he must suffer much and be despised?

The Master said as much, and they were afraid to ask anymore. They had received explanation about Elijah. They understood that he spoke of John the Baptist. But what did it mean about the Messiah suffering much and being despised? They had killed John. But the Messiah? God's own Son?

*

The air was heavy again, the sunshine was no longer playful and glittering. The heat was thick and muggy on the valley floor, and a breeze blew up from the village greeting them with the pungent smell of burning garbage. They were down among men again.

They could already hear excitable voices off in the distance. Huddles of people thronged about, quarreling. John could see Andrew and Thomas trying to defend themselves from the great flood of gestures and arguments with which the scribes showered them.

Just then, someone in the crowd caught sight of the Master. With wide-open eyes, he jerked his closest neighbor's arm and pointed. They both started running instantly. The crowd before them broke up and the square before them filled with approaching people.

John had never seen so many wide-open eyes at one time. They turned to the Master with a twinge of horrified awe. John had to look him in the face. Was there anything remaining of the shine from the mountain? In any case, he himself was still too blind to see it. He had looked into the sun, and his eyes were no longer able to see the weak reflection of splendor in a man's face.

It was the Master who broke the silence. He wanted to know what they were disputing.

A man bowed his earthen-brown neck respectfully and stretched his black furrowed hands open so that all the cracks on the inside could be seen. He began to explain the situation clumsily. He had one son, and he was a lunatic tormented by a dumb spirit that threw him to the ground so that he frothed at the mouth and gnashed with his teeth and became lifeless. So the father had taken him to the disciples and asked them to drive out the spirit. But they were unsuccessful.

John looked at the man's worried and disappointed face. He looked at his friends standing there, troubled and uncertain. He understood the man was speaking the truth. The ill-concealed look of triumph in the eyes of the scribes was proof enough. He gave the Master a quick glance.

Jesus lifted his face. It was as if his back straightened as he braced himself to take a heavy burden. He looked tired, plagued, and strong all at once.

"Oh, you faithless and perverse people," he said. "How long do I need to remain with you? How long shall I bear with you? Bring him to me!"

The father hurried up the village street. The whole crowd went silent. Never before had John heard the Master speak to his own people so sharply. Never had he sensed so clearly what a pain it could be for the Messiah of God to be amongst them. Usually, one had the impression of a great joy that flowed from an inexhaustible spring. But perhaps there was something behind this. John thought about what he had seen on the mountain. It was like catching a glimpse through the crack of a door to a banquet full of splendor never before seen on earth. He looked around the crowd that gathered about the Master: rough, dirty faces with low foreheads and stupidly staring eyes, torn clothing stiff with dried dung, a heavy odor of sweat and unwashed garments, and such a wind that struck up a dust devil of dirt and dried-out road apples. And then these disciples, powerless failures. The contrast was almost unbearable. He could not think the train of thought through. He could only sense that he touched upon a sacrifice and a self-impoverishment that went far beyond the limits of reason.

The man had come back with his boy, a pale, scrawny wretch, with jaundiced and dirty skin. He looked at the Master with huge and fearful eyes. His face began to twitch. He fell backward and rolled on the ground while foaming at the mouth. The men jostled and shouted. They sought in vain to hold him, but his thin boyish body flexed into an arc that no one could break.

"How long had he been like this?" the Master asked.

The man began to explain again: The spirit had had a hold of him since he was little. It often tried to throw him in the fire or in the water. This was how it wanted to destroy him.

Then the father looked at the Master appealingly.

"But if you are capable of doing something, have mercy on us and help us."

John saw how the sternness and tiredness disappeared from the Master's face. Again, he saw the spring of strength and joy wash over him.

"If I am able, you say? Everything is possible for those who believe."

Then the boy's father shouted with a shrill and helpless voice that seemed to cling fast to the Master's voice:

"I believe! Help my unbelief!"

The crowd had grown this whole time. The Master looked around for a moment. Then he quickly stooped down over the boy lying on the ground and spoke to him sternly. Everyone jostled and trampled. John barely made out the words: "I command you to come out of him . . ." Then they heard a wild shriek from the boy, who wallowed in the sand and then lay completely still.

The bystanders checked his arms and nodded to mean he was dead. But the Master knelt down, took his hand, and helped the boy to his feet. With the same authority, he broke up the crowds and sent the awkwardly stammering father home. Then he went straight to the house on the other side of the village where they would spend the night.

When they got inside, Andrew closed the door behind him and shut out the strangers that tried to follow. They stood there alone and gave the Master a timid glance. They hadn't yet said anything since they met. Now it came, troubled, hesitant, and almost accusing, though one didn't know who the accusation was directed against:

"Why couldn't we drive him out?"

"Because of your weak faith."

The answer came, curt and clear. They looked down. John saw that they were ashamed. He felt sorry for them. The Master continued to speak about faith. He was severe and short. If they had faith the size of a mustard seed, then they would be able to tell the mountains to get up and go, and they would obey them. Nothing would be impossible for them.

Now John looked at the ground too. He was certain that he would have fallen short if he had been there when the man came with his boy. But now he began to wonder if he himself had any faith at all. Tell this mountain to move? He would not dare do that.

Could the Master?

Yes, nothing was impossible for the Master, just as nothing was impossible for God. This he knew now. But why, then, did the Master not do it? Why did he not command the mountains out there to dance like children so that all his detractors would be dismayed and fall down and worship him? Why did he not think to use the power of his faith to gain respect among men?

"If you are the Son of God, then throw yourself down here." John was ashamed. He had just now had the same thought as Satan! He remembered what the Master had said about the time when he was in the desert and was tempted. That was precisely what the devil wanted: that he should show men his power in order to win their praise. But the Master had answered that one ought not put God to the test. Everything was possible when one believed, but faith only wanted that the Father's will be done.

John sat down in the circle with the others. The Master had begun to speak about what they would have needed today to have been successful: prayer and fasting. He spoke about prayer that knocks unceasingly at God's door because it knows there is help there and at that same time believes that it has already received what it asks for. He spoke about the fasting and denial that cuts out and drives away all that tempts a person to sin and refuses to look back like Lot's wife.

John thought about the call of distress from the father: "I believe! Help my unbelief!" This call of distress had been heard and has reached the mercy of God. It was a great comfort for him, when he tested his own faith. He believed, and yet did not believe. He did not believe like the Master. His faith was not all powerful. But he believed in the Master, and his whole heart was a cry for help against unbelief that was there.

He thought about all the helpless laying in the way of the Master, all those who stretched out their powerless hands to him, all who cried, "Lord, have mercy on us," and reached for the hem of his robe. It was sheer human weakness and human woe. But just there, in the midst of this distress, lived faith—a poor, woeful faith that screamed for help. And then when God's Messiah came, then there was strong faith that did miracles, healed and cured, a faith that forgave sins. Then this struggling, weak faith was filled with the riches of the heavenly kingdom.

While he sat there and listened, he was quietly thankful that he belonged to those who were able to see what all the prophets longed to behold. If he belonged to those who must pray for help with their unbelief, at least he knew to whom he had to go to.

Surely, he would never lose him? Surely, God's Messiah would never see death?

Now When the Time Came

"Whoever humbles himself to be like this child . . ."

The boy stood there, half-naked with dirty feet. His torn shirt barely reached his navel. His hair was matted, and he had a scabby rash on his arms. The Master had called him over and set him in their midst. Then he said they should all become such as him if they wanted to enter the kingdom of heaven!

They were fairly quiet when he asked them what they had been speaking about on the way. They had been trying to figure out which one of them was the greatest. This happened among the scribes and their disciples. It was a noble competition in Israel to see who was most pious, who could withstand the most deprivation and whose faith was strongest. Not until the Master looked at them and asked them what they were talking about did they suddenly have the feeling that they had half-intended to keep him out of the discussion. And then they were all silent. That was when he had called the laundress's dirty little boy and told them that they should be like him if they wanted to enter the kingdom of God.

They turned to the boy again.

Like this boy, a child was the humblest there was. Anyone could tell a child what to do. A child could be set to watch over cows amidst all the flies in a stone fold. A person told a child to operate the threshing sledge during the sweltering midday heat or to go out and pick up the fallen dates during a rainstorm when no one else would poke their nose outside. A child was everyone's servant. They had no rights, only duties.

The Master nodded as if to confirm their thoughts.

"If anyone of you wants to be first, he must be least of all and everyone's servant."

Peter wondered if the Master thought of him in particular. He had noticed that they had all prepared to leave Galilee in complete silence, and it looked as if the Master no longer thought of turning back. He thought about what it meant. Up there in Jerusalem the Master would get even with his enemies. Then something new would occur. It meant a new age and a new life even for he who would be the rock upon which the Son of Man would build his new church.

But—he was "everyone's servant." This was not what Peter had thought it would mean to stand as the foremost among the Son of Man's apostles. Had he again thought the thoughts of man and not thoughts of God?

*

"Because each person must be salted with fire . . ."

Peter was half horrified as he looked at the Master. Was it so serious? Every sacrifice was to be salted. Otherwise, it was not pleasing to God. Then it would be consumed by fire. Then it would be God's own. But what was this that would happen now? If every man was to be salted with fire, then it must mean that in order to be a sacrifice pleasing to God, every man would have to pass through fire, be sprinkled with fire, and be devoured by fire. His Messiah would baptize with fire. But was this not just for sinners? Did it not serve this generation well? Was it not to be worse for this generation than it was for Sodom on the day it was salted with fire from heaven?

The Master had said "every man." Peter began to feel an anxious curiosity about this journey. They stood with one foot on the route already. Every day, he expected the Master would give them the sign to depart. He knew that great things would happen and that the people would begin to move when it was known that they departed. He also noticed that the Master prepared them for something hard, something where you either stood or fell. One did not give his little finger to the enemy here. If one's own eye caused him to stumble, then it was necessary to tear it out and throw it away. For it was better to enter the kingdom with one eye than to keep both eyes and to stand outside.

It was either life or perdition, win everything or lose yourself. Outside the kingdom, there was only Gehenna. The kingdom was

God's; it was all power and glory there. Gehenna was the enemy's. There was nothing but darkness and horror, weeping and the gnashing of teeth in Gehenna. Its fire would never be extinguished.

But would every man be salted with fire?

> I was glad when they said to me:
> Let us go up to the house of the Lord
> Our feet have been standing within your gates Jerusalem,
> Jerusalem, the city built anew,
> Your houses are houses indeed,
> Wither the tribes go up
> The tribes of the Lord,
> According to the law of Israel
> To praise the Lord's name.

The old pilgrimage song again, with the same yet perpetually new joy, the perpetual new joy of pilgrimage, that belonged together with the new spring. The fields were red with poppies. The villages were circled by almond trees in bloom that looked like white clouds. The mud huts in the villages were covered in fallen apricot blossoms that reminded one of a dress fit for the daughter of an Eastern king.

They had crossed the great plain and journeyed up to the valley of En-gannim. Messengers went before them. They would announce his arrival in every city and every village. Everywhere they went, they met crowds greeting the first pilgrims. There was a sense of great things everywhere and an unsaid expectation that God's hour drew near.

They reached the village where they planned to stay the night. James saw the messengers returning through the fig trees that stretched their naked white branches against the blue evening sky. He was amazed to see that they did not leave their bags in the shelter. As they came closer, he could discern the reason on their red-hot faces: they had been dismissed.

James clenched his fists. These wretched Samaritans! Never even a drop of water, not even a morsel of bread, never an olive if one was on his way to Jerusalem! One ought to have been glad if he wasn't plundered and killed. And here, they now shut their doors in the face of God's Messiah! Now not even the Lord's anointed would be able to find a night's rest among them though he had always defended them and counted them as brothers.

He looked at his brother. Everything was possible for those who believed. Every man should be salted with fire . . . as always they had the same thought, and as always they were the first to act on their ideas. They turned to the Master who stood there speaking with the messengers.

"Lord, do you want us to call fire down from heaven and destroy them?"

Then the Master turned to them. It was rebuke they saw in his eyes.

"You know not the spirit of whom you are children. The Son of Man has not come to destroy souls but to save them."

They were quiet. The Master turned calmly and went back the same way he came. They followed him. They understood that he now went to Scythopolis and Jordan. He meant to go around Samaria.

Then they looked at one another. Yet again they had the same thought. If these people are spared by the Son of Man, who will be baptized by fire? If the Son of Man has come not to destroy but to save souls, what would he do in Jerusalem?

*

There were seventy messengers. The Master had sent a whole swarm of men before him. They went through the land two by two. In every city and village to which he came, they were there before him, proclaiming that the kingdom was near.

Peter felt his heart beat rapidly when the Master sent them out. He had come to understand that there were hidden meanings in all that the Master did. There was nothing provisional, and nothing was done at random.

He had chosen twelve disciples. It was a sign that he was the Messiah that was sent to the twelve tribes of Israel. That was the meaning of that great event. He would use them to establish his new church.

But this time he sent out seventy. The seventy represented the people outside of Israel. This time the message went to every town on his path, even where the Samaritans and heathens lived. It meant that God's Messiah had a message for every nation on earth and that his dominion would be to the ends of the world.

Was it possible?

In any case, not without a great miracle. Still, it seemed like arrogance and folly to believe that the Master who journeyed by foot, who was so powerless that a few rude Samaritans could deny him a night's lodging, should be the king of all the peoples on earth.

And yet, now it would happen. This was the great and final battle. Now everything that failed to measure up had to be destroyed. There was no one here who wasn't prepared to give his all. The Master dismissed anyone who showed even a sliver of cowardice or hesitation. Peter thought about the man who came and wanted to be with them, but asked first to go and take leave of his family. He was just told that no one was worthy of the kingdom of God if he looked back once he had set his hand to the plow. There was another who asked for just a day's respite. He only wanted to go and bury his father. He too was rejected. "Let the dead bury the dead," the Master had said. "But you go and proclaim the kingdom of God."

Let the dead bury the dead . . . outside the kingdom, everyone was dead. Where God's Messiah drew close, everything would live, even the dead. Here came the Incredible, who never damaged, who would fulfill all prophecy. Everything else had to take a back seat. To be there was to live; to stand outside was death.

Peter was there. He had taken his part. His nets hung on some wooden hooks in some dusty shed back home. Someone else used his boat to fish. He did not know if he would see his wife again. It was hard, and yet it was easy. Whatever happened now, it would happen only once in the history of the world. The big day was drawing near, the day the prophets longingly looked forward too.

Peter looked at the Master who went before him. A copper-brown neck, a faded robe with patches on the hem, a man of the people who walked with long resilient steps, accustomed to climbing over mountain ridges in the sun.

This was the king over the kingdom that was greater than the heavens and earth? Was this God's chosen and Holy One, who held the keys to the coming age in his hand? Truly, the thoughts of God were not the thoughts of man.

*

The terrible rumor reached them at the ford. The river was swollen
with the late rains, and the water flowed strong and cold over the
stone banks. It took time before the whole entourage could make it
across. Those who had already reached the other side rested in the
sunlight by oleander bushes as tall as they were and dried out their
clothes. It was there that both the brothers from Giscala came running down the riverbanks, warmed from the sun on the rocky paths
and hot with anger.

They had just heard it from a Jew of Gerasa coming from
Jerusalem. It had happened just three days ago when the first pilgrims came with their sacrifices. They were waiting for their turn
at the slaughter. They were poor people, and they didn't have many
sheep. Then suddenly a portion of the guard from Antonia formed
up and marched into the courtyard. It was almost empty at that
time, and no one realized what they were going to do. But then they
approached the Galileans. Then they split up, encircled the Galileans,
and slew them all so that they lay there among the sacrificed sheep.
No one knew why. Some said that all the men were zealots and that
Pilate suspected them for having instigated the terrorist murders
last fall. Others said that he only wanted to give all the Galileans a
warning, or one to whoever was coming to Jerusalem with a dagger
under their clothes. He was afraid of what might happen during the
Passover now.

Simon the Zealot was the first to wade back through the stream
to give the news to the Master. He didn't care that his clothes dragged
in the water. He was full of resentment. He feared that he had a couple
of old friends and perhaps even a relative among the dead. Certainly,
many of them were zealots, but he was sure that they hadn't gone to
the temple with any sedition in mind. And even if he had quit walking around with a dagger under his clothes and no longer wanted
to take part in an ambush, not even for Pilate himself, his heart was
still with them. At least they weren't lukewarm and indifferent. They
had some zeal for God in their souls. It was an honor to be known
as a supporter of the zealots when so many were lethargic and sold
both their freedom and faith for money. The only problem with the
zealots was that they didn't understand that all this they were waiting

for would come through God's messiah. They didn't understand that they only needed to bide their time for God's judgment and that the new kingdom that was already on its way.

He didn't find the Master. The entourage had split up. Some had remained and no one knew where the others were. The only thing to do was wait here at the ford, where all paths converged.

He told the news to whoever would listen while he waited. The resentment was incredible, the guesses crisscrossed each other, and then came the inevitable question a God-fearing Jew had to ask when considering such a fateful blow: What had they done to suffer so much? The two Pharisees from Pella who had been following them since yesterday were very certain in their judgment. Was it not written that he who sins shall die? If anyone becomes a ruffian, should he then live? No, he shall be punished with death; his blood shall be upon him. When the others mentioned that it was Pilate who was the ruffian, the scribes answered that it was true and that he was also guilty of misdeeds and would die. But these young men were deceived. They had taken the wrong path. Now they had taken the brunt of the guilt; they suffered in place of the guilty false shepherds who even now led Israel astray.

Simon knew the word was directed at the Master. It embittered him. These Pharisees would even blame Jesus for the unrest in the land and for the Romans who so unmercifully stifled any hint of rebellion with blood.

Then the Master came passing by. It vexed Simon to see the Pharisees take news from him and relay it to the Master. They gave it their own spin.

The Master looked around wide eyed, as if he wondered what men wanted him to say about this.

"You don't think," he asked, "that these Galileans were greater sinners than all other Galileans? No, I tell you: if you do not repent, you will all perish the same way. Or the eighteen who were killed when the tower of Siloam fell on them—do you believe that they were guiltier than all the other people in Jerusalem? No, I tell you: if you do not repent, you will all perish in the same manner."

No one said anything. Simon looked at the Pharisees. It seemed they had been given some bitter bread to chew. But he himself had been stung in the heart. He had not received a bit of relief for his resentment. It was as if the Master meant that Pilate's sins didn't concern them, and perhaps they didn't. If the people didn't repent now, everything was lost. There was a cutting accusation in the words against the Pharisees, for they had not repented at John the Baptist's preaching and even less for Jesus. But the people in Galilee had not done it either. And now came the great accounting when the plants the Father had not planted would be rooted up.

But to repent is to forgive your enemies their trespasses. The guilt of he who receives forgiveness but does not forgive others will remain. And if one was to forgive everyone, then even Pilate, with all his misdeeds, would be included in the forgiveness. It was so strange with this repentance. One had to start over again constantly.

The Master had begun to speak about repentance again. He used a parable about a barren fig tree that stood in a vineyard. For three years, it had not born any figs, so the owner gave word that it should be cut down and not remain there sucking up the earth. But the man who tended the vineyard pleaded for the barren tree. He asked to let it remain for one more year. He would dig around it, feed it, and see if it didn't finally bear fruit. But if it was not successful, the ax would find home in the tree.

The Master took off his coat and got ready to wade into the water. Simon asked to carry his clothes and followed him quietly. He thought that he had suddenly been able to look into the unfathomable depths of the Master's heart. He understood that the Master had thought about the Baptist again. The Baptist had said that the ax would be laid to the root of the tree and that every tree that did not bear good fruit should be hewn down and cast into the fire. Andrew and Philip and the others who had been at the Jordan had often spoken about this, and they wondered why the judgment tarried. It was now three years since John had preached the baptism of repentance. For three years, the fig tree stood barren as the Master had said. So the ax would swing. But there was one who loved the useless tree and pleaded for it, one who wanted to give it one last chance to bear fruit.

Was this why they went to Jerusalem? Was this why judgment tarried? Was this what the Master spoke to his Father about when he was alone all night on the mountain praying?

Simon looked at his Master. He walked with firm steps in the strong current and held the staff firm in his hand. Was that the hand that still held back wrath? Was that the hand that held back the ax of judgment from the old tree of Israel?

But if the fig tree did not bear fruit? If the last attempt was in vain? All would perish if they did not repent, he had said. He knew this, for it was the Son of Man who held judgment. It was the same Son of Man who now interceded for them all and who got them another year of suspended judgment . . .

*

It had been the first really hot day of spring. The wind came from the south, and the great desert blew its suffocating breath across the land. The sun shone dim through the haze, and the air was hot and sticky like the vapor from the body of an invisible giant. They sat to rest at the edge of a village, where the last rough stone walls joined with the garden walls. The arch of the gate gave them shade, but the desert's heavy breath could not be shut out.

When John came back with the other three who had fetched water, he ran into some women in the street asking for the prophet from Nazareth. He looked at them. They were common peasant women dressed in dirty blue clothes. They had jingling silver coins in a band on their foreheads, and children in their arms. Naturally, they were as curious as everyone else.

Rather sharply, he asked them what they wanted.

One of them held up a bundle of dirty swaddling clothes from which a little helpless infant head stuck out. She said they wanted the prophet to lay his hands on the children.

Were they sick? He asked a bit suspiciously. There were quite a few for that.

The women shook their heads. They wanted him to bless their children.

John became indignant. The Master had trouble enough with all who wanted to be healed or have him answer their questions. Now they should really leave him in peace. This was pure conceit. What would the children do here? Here was the great decision; here everyone that would not give their whole heart would be thinned out. Great, strong men would be great if they stood the test, and even they had to be humble before the wisdom of God that was spoken here. And now these foolish mothers came here with their children bundled in rags, and they wanted to share in it too!

John said no. The others obviously thought the same as him. They supported him strongly and made it clear to the women that they would not be able to see the prophet.

At the same time, they heard the Master's voice behind them. There was a moment when the Master's voice was like lightning and thunder at once. It cut through and struck with a force that made any protest impossible. He asked them to be quiet and let the children come. They should not hinder the children, for the kingdom belonged to such as these. He who would not receive God's kingdom like a child would never enter.

So he waved the women over to him and even went to meet them. He lifted the children out of their arms, laid hands upon them, and blessed them.

John looked on with very uneasy feelings. He understood that yet again he did not understand anything. The kingdom was the most holy and highest of all. It demanded all a man's heart. If one looked back when one put his hand to the plow, that man was not ready for it. And now there were these children who couldn't do anything, couldn't understand anything. The Master laid his hands upon them and gave them the kingdom. The kingdom was for such, he had said. And he who did not receive it like the little child under his hands would never enter. Who could understand this?

John shook his head and began to distribute the water.

*

There was something peculiar about this man. He was all hunched over when he came, as only those who are in real distress are. Peter thought that he would ask for his child or his father. But to his amazement, he heard that the man lying there in the gravel was plagued by something else completely.

"Good Master, what shall I do to inherit eternal life?"

There was the ring of scripture in his words. Certainly, he was one of those who held fast to the faith of the fathers. He was still young, and he was clothed like a man of noble birth. It was unusual to see a man of this sort kneel before the Master with a question.

Strangely enough, the Master answered him very curtly, almost reproachfully.

"Why do you call me good? No one is good but God alone!"

Peter looked at the Master. Was he not good? Was it not God's own divinity that dwelt in him? What was it, then, they had seen on the mountain? But then he understood: This was a mystery that no one knew and no one would know. To this man, the Master was only a master. There was a splash of flattery and human tribute in his words. It was this he was being rebuked for.

So he received his answer. Peter had guessed what it would be. He had God's own command and God's own law. He should keep them.

Then the man said, "Master, I have kept all this since my youth."

Peter noticed that he was not the only one who was shocked. Who was this who dared to say such a thing? Everyone looked at him tentatively, even the Master.

His face was open and sincere. It was obvious that he meant it seriously. He had kept all this, as far as he himself had understood it. He was a man with a clean conscience and clean hands.

But why, then, did he lay there on his knees? Was this not enough for him? Peter looked into his face again. No, this man had not been satisfied by all his piety. He was one who burned with a great hunger for righteousness.

Peter noticed that even the Master looked into this face with affection. Very quietly he said, "There is one thing you lack. Go and sell all that you have and give it to the poor—then you shall store up treasure in heaven. And then come and follow me."

A great thankful joy rose up within Peter. The man had stood the test before the Master's eyes. He had been considered worthy to take part, and he had been able to hear the word that had once put Peter and Andrew before the gates of heaven.

He was ready to go to the man to stretch out his hands. Then he saw that the man's face had gone dim. The excitement was gone; the shine in his eyes had vanished. Something unclear blurred his features, something that was at first alarmed and hesitated, which then turned into great sadness. He looked furtively at the Master and then cast his eyes down. His hands let go of the Master's cloak, and he rose heavily and doubtfully. Without lifting his gaze from the ground, he turned around and went away.

Peter stood and thought about how different human strides can be. He had moved with swagger and strength, with every step he swung forward. Now he was heavy. His feet were stuck to the ground. It seemed as if he were a speck of brown dust that had to work to keep himself upright, doomed to fall down and become dust again.

Even the Master watched him. He didn't look angry but rather sympathetic and contrite, as if he himself felt the man's burden.

"How hard it is for those who have money to enter in to the kingdom of heaven."

Yet again, the Master's gaze followed the man with the hanging head and the heavy shoulders. Then he met the astonished and staring eyes of the disciples. Then he said it again, very slowly and emphatically:

"Yes, my children, how hard it is to enter into the kingdom of God! It is easier for a camel to pass through the eye of a needle than for a rich man to enter into the kingdom of God."

Peter saw that the eyes of the others were still round. They had thought the same as him. He had left everything, it was true, but still . . . The boat at home was still his, the house as well. He was regarded as wealthy, the same as James and John. It was his own anxious question that came from the lips of the others.

"Then who can be saved?"

Jesus looked at them. It seemed almost as if he rejoiced over their questions and amazement. Did he want them to feel such trepidation before the presence of the kingdom of heaven? He only said, "For men, it is impossible, but not for God. For God, all things are possible."

For men, it is impossible. Peter dared not ask, but he was almost certain that the Master really meant this: to come into the kingdom of heaven was impossible for men. He had seen the demand become ever more strict and unreasonable and yet still completely clear. In God's reign, God's will should happen and God's name be honored by everyone and all. For this reason, a sinner must repent. For this reason, one should be the heavenly Father's child and forgive like him and love like him. One should leave all behind him. Nothing should mean anything to anyone but this: God and his reign. But it was just this that was so hard.

Or was it impossible for men? It felt as if it was so. Should it be possible despite everything after all? For God?

He thought about the children who the Master blessed. For such as them was the kingdom of God, he had said. But what had they done? Absolutely nothing! They did not even know what was happening to them.

For God, nothing is impossible . . . But was it only up to God?

He took courage and came forward with his question.

"Master?"

"Yes"

"See, we have given up everything and followed you."

The Master understood. He answered that no one who forsook anything, whatever it was, for him and for the sake of the gospel, would be without reward.

It was comforting to hear. And then there was something strange about this reward. It would be given within tribulation. So there would also be tribulations. This meant poverty, disgrace, and perhaps even torture. And the reward in the midst of this? Perhaps Peter still understood. When the rich man had just left for his earthly goods and his livestock pens, he felt that the rich man was poor and that he himself was rich—he who was able to continue to Jerusalem.

Perhaps it was best to quit looking for rewards according to the usual manner of men. In the kingdom, the first would be last. Was he himself first or last?

Once, he had asked if it was not enough that he forgave his brother seven times. "No," the Master had answered, "Not seven times, but seventy times seven." Then he had understood, and so he had stopped counting. Was it also so with the reward?

We Can

The merciless sun scorched the barren plains that lay exposed to its heat. An old dry bush stretched its scrubby branches out to offer them its round Sodom apples. James whacked them with his cane so that they cracked open, and the dry tinder inside flew out.

They had been quiet for a long time. It was heavy going today in the heat and clay dust. James paid little attention to the road he traveled upon. Again and again, his gaze searched the overwhelming heights before them where Jerusalem lay. They could see the ridge of Mount Olivet. Those with sharp eyes posited that they could see houses and olive trees up there. The Holy City was directly behind it on the other side. They would be there tomorrow or the day after.

Mount Olivet's ridge disappeared behind the horizon again, but the closer they came to the rock wall looming before them, the more precipitous and menacing it seemed. The matte brown bare rock resembled a predator's kill, and the prominent mountain giants gazed out over the plains like a pride of lions. The Galilean mountains were a lot rounder. They lifted themselves to the heavens, proud and dignified, sweeping themselves in a beautifully pleated coat of green. The Judean mountains were naked and rough. They seemed to have broken through the unfruitful ground with violence. They were stripped of everything that could have concealed their harsh nudity.

James had never liked these mountains in the Judean desert, but he had never thought they looked as menacing as they did today. The black hollows in the rock walls stared at him like sinister eyes, and shadows streaked down like bitter folds in the red stone visage.

This was the behemoth that bore Jerusalem on its back, the city that murdered prophets and stoned those who were sent to her.

The Master had said that about this city they were going to now. James sensed the seriousness in his word. Up there, the enemy sat in his stronghold. There, Pilate's soldiers occupied solid barracks. There, the Sanhedrin sat in the midst of the temple guard. There, the scribes and Pharisees bent the will of the people like soft wicker in their skilled hands.

James admitted to himself that he was carrying something within him that others called fear. He knew the others felt the same as him. They had already been tested by the hatred and recklessness of their opponents in Galilee. Yet there, the Pharisees didn't have any weapons other than sharp tongues. In Jerusalem, they had all the power that still remained in Judah, and it was said that they could also get the Romans to move if needed.

Yesterday, they encountered a centuria marching to the border. They were tanned and rough people, tall and well armed. They marched through the crowds of pilgrims in closed ranks. James thought they resembled a broad-horned buffalo calmly walking through a swarm of flies. Like a true Galilean, he straightened his neck and looked indifferently to the side. But he felt strangely oppressed. They were so few and so defenseless in their soft coats, all too easily put under by such a behemoth. And this was just one centuria . . . six centurias made a cohort, and it was said that there would be two cohorts in Jerusalem during the Passover.

James reproached himself for his feeble faith. Why was he concerning himself with centurias and cohorts? He followed the Messiah of God, who was on his way to the city of the great king, where God would make signs and do miracles.

He looked at the Master. He was on the road ahead of them, all alone. His eyes seemed fixed upon the mountain. He made firm steps that were a bit heavy and lingering, as a person would do when he was in deep thought. There he was, by himself on the vast plains, constantly advancing toward the menacing mountain wall. There was something eerie about his solitude. It was as if the slightness of his human stature was engulfed by the evil wilderness, and the unknown lying in wait behind the mountains on the horizon.

James looked at the others. They were quieter than normal. He looked on ahead and then finally took notice of all the small things on the side of the road.

The Master had stopped. He looked around and noticed how far behind they were. He waited for them at the side of the road. They thought he would continue as soon as they drew near, but he gathered them around him with the wave of his hand. Then he pointed at the mountain and told them they were going to Jerusalem now so that everything that was written of the Son of Man would be fulfilled.

James nodded. He understood. Up there, the scriptures would be fulfilled. They stood on the threshold of a new world order. God's Messiah would now stretch his scepter out over the world.

But then he didn't understand a thing. As the Master spoke, he dressed all his evil fears in words and aired all the thoughts and doubts that James himself would never allow to take shape. He said that the Son of Man would be handed over to the chief priests and the scribes. They would sentence him to death and betray him to the gentiles. They would mock him, spit on him, flog him, and kill him, but on the third day, he would rise again.

They could tell the Master wanted them to know what was hidden there behind the mountain and that they were the only ones who were to know it. He was quiet when strangers passed by. This knowledge was for them and only for them—those who had received full authority to be his apostles.

Yet none of them understood any of this! James went over to speak with his brother. They understood there would be a showdown up there. They understood he might be preparing them to give their lives. He had said that if anyone denied him before men, he in turn would deny him before God when he came in his glory. He had spoken of those that would be dragged before the Roman authorities and the judgment seats of the Jews. He had said that he did not come to bring peace but a sword and that they should not fear those who could kill the body.

So there would be a fight. They were Galileans. They didn't bother anyone about any fears they might have. They would die for him if they had to.

But then?

The Son of Man would come in his glory. There would also be victory. The enemy must take the short straw. They who denied the Son of God would see the truth of the song of praise; everyone who did not praise the Son would perish on his way.

But then?

*

Yes, because the Lord waits,
Until he can be gracious to you . . .

Salome lifted her eyes again. She looked up at the mountain and meditated upon the words of the prophet. Yes, the Lord waited. The time of humiliation lingered. The Chosen One was still misunderstood as he walked among men, and those who had seen his glory followed. But they were tired from the long journey and burdened by the mocking smiles of men. This was the time of expectation, the hours before the gates of the bridegroom's house would open. Yet the moment had not yet come when the Lord would be gracious to his people.

She set her tired feet as lightly as she could in the hot clay dust and hummed the words of the prophet:

Because he is enthroned on high,
Until he can be merciful to you.

Over there, the Lord was enthroned on high above the city of David. There he would have mercy upon his oppressed people and finally show his power and glory.

For the Lord is a God of Judgment
Blessed are those who wait for him.

And she, Salome, the wife of Sebedeus, waited for him. Ever since she was a girl, she had belonged to those in the land who waited. God's promise could not be an empty wind, and what he prepared for so many generations could not come to nothing in the end. The Messiah would come and fulfill everything that still remained mere omens, prophecies, and faded pictures. Some said that he would come from the heart of the sea. Others believed that he was in hiding in Rome, just as Moses had grown up among the oppressors in Egypt. He would step forth into power from insignificance. He would judge the world with righteousness. He would bring back the displaced, the world's empires would melt like wax before his face, and he would destroy sinners with the power of his words.

Salome felt both fear and jubilation in the assurance that all this would now be fulfilled. In a manner that the blind people could not conceive, the Messiah would step forward from his humility. What the prophet had spoken would be true: What they had never been told, they shall see, and what they had never heard, they shall perceive.

Up till now, he had grown like a sapling in dry ground, but now God himself would judge between him and his opponents. This is why he went up to Jerusalem now, unarmed and without an army. Was it not said of the Messiah that he would not put his trust in cavalry or bows, nor in gold and silver or war? That he would not build his hope for the day of battle on many people, but that the Lord himself would bring his cause to victory, and that with the power of his word, he alone would afflict the mighty?

With the power of his word . . . Salome could never cease to wonder at the blindness of these people who did not feel the power in this word. It was like a sword through the heart and a cool stream of balm for the soul. It was like a storm that swept away all ill-borne issues; it was a strong arm that lifted the sick from the ground. It was a high mountaintop in clear cool air that allowed the eye to see what it had never seen before. She could only imagine how it would be when this word went out in all its royal power, when it broke down walls and encircled the whole world, kneading it like a piece of soft clay in his almighty hand.

She drew close to the Master again, and saw that he had gathered the twelve around him. He lifted one hand to Jerusalem. She was filled with great expectation. She wanted to stand there and listen to what he said. But she had become accustomed to standing off to the side when he spoke to his twelve apostles. She was happy to have two sons there, but she thought they didn't always quite understand or appreciate the honor afforded them. She would have given anything to be privy to his secrets like they were. She thought that they took all these favors for granted. They ate and slept, took care of their sore feet, and gathered sticks for the fire almost as if it was just another Passover pilgrimage to Jerusalem.

Salome had noticed that the Master loved her sons. He loved them almost as much as he did Peter, in whom he had such great confidence. She wondered what it would mean when the kingdom came in all its glory. She had thought about this again during the journey. She herself was only able to be one of the others on the pilgrimage. She was happy to hear his voice from a distance and to catch a glimpse of his miracles. It could just as well be so in the kingdom too. She had never given thought to anything else and was completely satisfied with her lot. But with her sons, that was a different matter. They should sit in his presence. She once asked them what they thought about the matter. She received a half-reluctant answer. The Master had said that his twelve apostles would sit as judges over the twelve tribes of Israel. This must mean that they would be his chosen governors. Just as the Almighty had once raised judges from those who suffered as simple people and appointed them to guide in wisdom and righteousness, so also God's Messiah would lift her sons up out of their lowliness and make them righteous shepherds over his people when he established it anew.

The twelve had dispersed again. The Master went ahead of them, alone upon the great plain. Her sons walked together as they spoke.

She pushed her tired legs as hard as she could. Tough and persistent, she made up the distance between them and her. She didn't want to be noticed so she didn't run and neither did she yell. She was only a tad breathless when she reached them. They gave way to her where the path was most even.

She was careful not to ask anything. Instead she began to extoll her happiness because she would see the Passover that would be unlike any other since the Lord brought his people up out of the land of Egypt.

They gave her a puzzled look, and she asked them if they didn't think the fullness of time had come and that their servanthood under the Lord's enemies would now come to an end.

Yes, they believed this.

And did they not believe that lordship and glory must now come?

They nodded thoughtfully. Yes . . . they believed this.

She looked at them. Did they still doubt? She asked them flat out if they were no longer certain that the Lord's Day was near and that the Messiah would be victorious.

They were eager. That they knew.

She looked at them again, tentatively. It was as if they thought she didn't quite understand this properly. Finally, James said that there would be war first, hard fighting. It would not go as easily as some thought.

Salome noticed that something weighed on their hearts. In that moment, her sons' burden became her own. What were they fearful of?

They wanted to answer her, but her instinct told her that there was something ahead of them that wasn't quite clear to them, something that held them prisoner and occupied all their thoughts. They were like her brothers when they went out with Judas of Gamala. They had expected their baptism by fire on the Mount Gadara, the baptism of fire from which they never returned.

Her motherly heart was in stitches. What had the Master told them? That it was very well possible that the day of victory would remain far off? Would he not be revealed in his glory? Would they not be able to sit at his side on their own thrones?

Her maternal heart burned with this innermost secret, the question she entertained with delight. She had never spoken with anyone about it. She didn't want to say anything about it either. Instead, she asked about the matter directly:

"Will anyone die?"

They nodded so seriously and thoughtfully that she could no longer control herself. She asked them anxiously what would happen in regards to the dream that she had for them, the ones that occupied so much of her thought and which she was so certain would come true. Would they now be seated closest to him?

They could not answer. They both became very red underneath their sunburns.

"Has anyone said anything?" she asked.

They shook their heads.

Shouldn't they ask him?

All three looked at each other. Then they increased their pace.

*

They overtook him at the top of one of the plain's shallow indentations. He heard them coming and turned around. She fell straight to her knees and stretched her arms to him. He looked at her questioningly.

"What do you want?"

James looked the Master in the eye, bold but shy.

"Master we would like . . . that you let us have what we are going to ask of you now."

He looked at them even more questioningly.

"But then what is it that I should let you have?"

Now they dared to approach him with their question: Now, when he entered his glory, when the kingdom became his, could they both sit at his side, the one on the right and the other at his left?

"Say, Master . . . ?"

Salome looked up at his face with excited pleading. She seemed to read something there that resembled the smile a father has when he watches his boy try to push the boat out into the lake by himself. Yet at the same time that he smiled, there was an almost screaming seriousness in his voice.

"You know not what you ask," he said. "Can you drink the cup that I drink and endure the baptism that I endure?"

Salome heard them both answer at the same time with the same speed and confidence in their voices:

"We can."

Again, the Master's gaze smiled at them. The severity in his face was gone. He looked almost wistful.

Yes, he said, it was so: They would drink from his cup. They would endure his baptism. But the places of glory on his right and his left were not his to give. They would fall upon those for whom they were determined.

He nodded at them slowly and confirmatory and turned from them.

Salome remained laying there a moment in the trail dust, looking at him puzzled. What cup would he drink? What baptism would he endure? Why would he not give away the places of honor in his own kingdom?

When she first rose and beat the white limestone dust from her blue dress, she noticed that the others had gathered around them. She looked straight into their eyes and saw that they were upset. Philip said it straight out: They didn't think any of them needed to make themselves more important than any of the others. They all went with him. They would all take the same risks if it came to that, and they would all have the same right to the rewards.

This kindled a fire within Salome. Was it not right to want to be first when it came to enduring his baptism? They would be glad that someone went first on that day.

She never said this. The Master called to them. His sadness became severe again, but there, in the corner of his eye, there could still be found the puzzling glimpse of an almost ridiculing calmness.

He asked them if they did not know how it went among the princes of this age. Did they not establish themselves as lords and let the people feel their authority?

Salome watched them nod thoughtfully. Perhaps they thought about the legionnaires they encountered or of the aristocratic Roman whose black slaves pushed people out of the way when he came with his palanquin.

But it would not be so among them, the Master continued. The greatest shall be servant of others. And then he added, "Even the Son of Man has come not to be served but to serve and give his life as a ransom for many."

He turned and went on. None of them said a word. Salome was quiet and waited until they had all gone on ahead. Then she too continued on her way quietly, alone and thoughtfully.

Today Salvation Has Visited This House

When the great shadow of the mountain swept down over Jericho and the sun finished burning the flat roofs of the mud huts, a cool breeze stole in from the lake. Date palms rustled pleasantly, and the flowers lifted their drooping heads. They began to perfume the air again. Birds chirped and the donkeys brayed in competition with one another, hard hee-haws that sounded like the last strokes of a saw working through a tough bit of wood.

The street was already full of people when Zacchaeus made his way out. He looked farther down Jordan Street to find a place, but it was crowded everywhere. He tried to elbow his way in, but he was recognized, and the backs joined themselves tighter in front of him. He tried to stop a peasant with a camel and offered him a round coin to rent it for an hour, but the peasant showed the black tooth stumps of his smile and said straight to his face that he wouldn't let him defile his saddle for a whole sack full of the tax collector's ill-gotten gains.

It almost angered Zacchaeus, but there was something about this evening that made him restrain himself. He just turned around. He went a bit farther, stretched his short neck, and peeped between men, but every time, he found that, at his height, all he could do was catch a glimpse of the entourage about as wide as the palm of his hand as they passed by.

Then he decided to climb up the old sycamore at the cross roads. It had magnificent branches that stretched out over the street. He wasn't bothered by the wisecracks. When the cries and hustle began to be heard down the moorland road, they forgot all about him. He crept out as far as he could and leaned forward on a fork in the branch. It bounced a little but held him. With a strange feeling of hopeless longing, he watched the crowd roll down the street. There was an infectious joy in the air of this spring evening. At first, it was the usual festive mood that accompanied the week before Passover as the great crowds of pilgrims began to come from Galilee with their joyous laughter and songs around the campfires. But this year, there was something different. There was a great expectation, a mysterious joy that caused men to wink at one another and whisper as they held their breath in anticipation when someone came running with a new rumor. If one asked what it was, no one heard anything, and yet the great news could be read on everyone's face.

It was just this mysterious joy that was so bitter for Zacchaeus. He felt it so much and yet was shut out of it. He lived in the midst of it, and it was still his enemy. It was this that got him to climb up the tree like a little boy this evening, but it was also this that moved men to show him their backs so openly.

Who could understand it? Who could comprehend this talk about a great prophet and the whispers of a Messiah of God who would have such power over a heart that should have braced itself for the realities of this world so long ago?

He would have excused himself and not gone out this evening if it had not been for the rumor that the Baptist had risen up again. The Baptist had been strict, but he had also dealt with publicans as if they were people. It was said that this prophet did not shy away from eating with tax collectors and sinners either. The Pharisees called him a glutton and a drunkard, and yet he was still a man of God, powerful in word and deed. Zacchaeus had to see a man of God like that.

And there he came! The song crested down on the street—it was the pilgrim's song about the joy that would be like a dream when the Lord established Zion again. This song had a peculiar ring this evening. It was sung with an almost dangerous rapture that made Zacchaeus shiver with both joy and a bitter emptiness in his chest. He who had to be the prophet was walking in the midst of this singing throng. Zacchaeus looked to his left and his right. He greeted with a smile and then became serious again. His eyes searched the crowd unceasingly. Zacchaeus lay motionless against the fork in the branch. He saw the prophet come closer. He saw him look up. He caught the searching eyes for a moment. Suddenly, he was seized with fear. He wished he could make himself invisible behind the branches. He felt like a little boy caught with stolen apples. To his speechless despair, he thought he saw the prophet coming closer, approaching him directly.

The prophet stopped right under the tree. He looked Zacchaeus right in the eye, and then, as if it was that most normal thing in the world, he said, "Zacchaeus, hurry up and climb down. For I must stay with you today."

Zacchaeus felt the branch waver under him like the shaking of a storm. The whole crowd whirled around below him. But he could only see the eye of the prophet resting on him, wise and searching.

Within seconds, he was gliding down the tree. He didn't know how he reached the ground, but he knew that in that very same moment, he had entered into the joy of the people, into their great expectations, into the joy that is found only where God's promise finds fulfillment and then spreads to everything that a man can hope for or think about.

He bowed deeply and greeted the Master respectfully. He heard the prophet's voice. He noticed that Jesus walked up to his side. He felt like he was dreaming as they walked to his house. It was during the sweetest moment of the twilight, when the last bit of sunlight had gone out, yet the heavens were full of a golden glow that didn't burn. At that moment, there were no shadows. The land had lightened up and begun to blush like the face of a happy man.

They entered his house. He clapped his hands and called for his servants. He ran around. He gesticulated. He went out to the courtyard from the kitchen and ran up the stairs to the guest rooms on the roof. He ordered the front bed stands and cushions to be arranged. He sent for sweet milk and demanded that one should slaughter the fatted calf. He rushed down again and apologized to the prophet. The prophet smiled and asked about his wife and children. He called even the last among them and laid his hands upon them.

When Zacchaeus ran across the garden again, his wife came out to him. Had he heard what they said out in the city? No? Yes, one could guess that: the city was full of commotion because the prophet had come to them with his disciples. The pious people of the synagogue made sour faces and said that the prophet had gone to a sinner's house and that he should have gone with them instead!

Zacchaeus waved away her vexation with a great sweep of his hands and sent her to see that the food was ready. But when she was gone, he became motionless; for the first time he just stood there.

"Went with a sinner." He looked at his garden's fine stone slabs and the mosaic around the well. He looked at the magnificent mats that were rolled out and the embroidered cushions the servants had just brought for the couches around the dining table. He glanced over everything. He let his thoughts wander through the years. Again and again, they stopped at the tollhouse. It was a world of hateful voices and hard words. Finally, he remembered an evening three years ago that was strangely like this one. It was the evening his good friend and coworker came back from the Baptist. He was radiating with joy and tried to get him to understand that one thing was needful. Zacchaeus was afraid to ask his friend if he was done with collecting taxes, but he was not done. The Baptist had said that he should continue. He only needed not demand too much.

Zacchaeus didn't say much at that time. Afterward, he convinced himself that it was too unreasonable. Such conditions could not exist in this world of thieves and robbers. Then he buried the whole matter in silence and thought no more of it. Or rather, tried not to think about it.

Zacchaeus looked up to the mountains, where the stars were shining. He listened to the hustle and buzz in the joyous house, where he had the Lord's Anointed as his guest that evening. There had been a wall between Zacchaeus and the God of his fathers. God himself had broken this wall down today. Would he be so foolish as to build it up again?

He breathed deeply. Then quietly and solemnly, he went over to the soft carpets and entered the room where the prophet was sitting among all the people who had followed him in from the street. The prophet looked at him and offered him a place at his feet.

Zacchaeus stepped forward. Three steps in front of the prophet, in the midst of the circle of all these men from Galilee and from the streets of his own hometown, he bowed his head stuck out his hands and said:

"Lord, the half of my possessions I will now give to the poor. And it is so that if I have taken more than I should have from anyone, so I will repay four times again."

And the prophet nodded, but he did it so calmly and without surprise that Zacchaeus asked him to sit at the table. Then the prophet stretched out his hands again and offered Zacchaeus the seat at his right hand and said to the others, who looked on with amazement, "Today, salvation has visited this house, for he too is a son of Abraham. For the Son of Man has come to seek and save those who are lost."

Hosanna to the Son of David

It was good that they went out today.

The rabbi gave his two comrades a knowing look. Idle crowds were swarming on the village street in front of them and the road beyond the clustered houses. There was no doubt about who they were waiting for.

The three of them had just gone up over the back of the Mount of Olives to see the endless expanses open up to the east. The desert swept its white quilt up to the villages at their feet, and they could see men like small dark insects crawling out of the deep wrinkles far down at the bottom. They were getting ready for the final burning ascent to Jerusalem.

There was something scary about this desert, which almost came right up to the city's gates. There was no telling what would come from the great desert; it went on for days out there, to the horizon. Enemies could cross the Jordan at night, and by morning light, there could be marauding hordes in the cliffs down there, and then they would disappear again into the dried up labyrinth of stone, where they would be untraceable.

Yet threat and danger from the Eastern lands were not the only things to come from there. It was from the east that the prophet had seen the Lord's glory descend upon the temple. On the great day, he himself would set his feet on the Mount of Olives. The Messiah would come from there.

Strangely enough, this great hope that the Highly to Be Praised had given his people was a danger for the simple people today. In the Sanhedrin, it had been long known that it was whispered that the notorious prophet from Nazareth was God's Messiah. There was no proof of him having said it himself, but it was bad enough that the people believed it. It was doubly bad because it was said of a notorious Sabbath breaker, a weak character who did not keep clear boundaries where publicans and apostates were concerned. The masses had regained their fever when it was known that he was on his way to the festival at the head of all his followers. The Great Council anxiously checked the pulse of this unruly and fiery mob day after day. They knew all too well that the blood had become hotter than was healthy.

Now they had the confirmation of all their fears right before their eyes. So many people so far outside the city could not be explained by saying that everyone just wanted to welcome the train of pilgrims from Galilee. One might be able to say this to Pilate if he was suspicious, but the council members knew quite well that it was for the sake of the great prophet that these people had run off. With a sigh of worry, they had to add that the people should not have gone so far just to see a prophet. There was reason to fear they expected greater things than what some prophet could do, and they expected that it would happen now during this Passover.

The rabbis were standing there and talking about what all these people would hear at home when the first Galileans appeared on the village street. There was a pair of young men, straight and rough, like all Galileans. They looked around a bit and then went up to a donkey that was tied outside the gate of a garden. They began to untie it without asking permission. A couple of peasants standing there in the crowd asked them what they were doing. The rabbis heard them answer, "The Lord has need of it." The owner nodded, and the men went on their way.

There was something in the voice of these men that made the rabbis very uncomfortable. What kind of lord was this at whose beck and call one could untie a donkey and lead it away? If this was the prophet in question, he had an uncanny power over the sensibility of others.

It was him. There he came now, riding on the donkey! They had laid some coats on it, and it tripped up nicely with clipped ears and wide eyes, watching the spectacle that now wound up the village street.

The eyes of the council members were just as wide. There were some along the parade who had thrown off their coats and spread them before the prophet. Others had snatched twigs from the olive trees and waved them in the air. And at the same time, they began to sing. It was something taken from the conclusion of the Passover's great Hallel:

"Blessed is he who comes in the name of the Lord!"

In that moment, it was as if the floodgates broke loose. The people pressed and cried; the stream swept by and caught the council members up with them. The song grew into a noise where disjointed verses and freely contrived slogans of tribute met one another and flowed together as one great stormy wind of jubilation.

"Hosanna! Blessed is he who comes!"

Flowers and boughs rained upon the train, coats flickered when they were spread out and lifted again. The whole crown about the Mount of Olives was a swaying field of green branches. The gold limestone rock on the road was bestrewn with leaves and branches.

"Hosanna! Blessed is David's Son, he who comes in the name of the Lord!"

The council members pushed and scuffled with the crowds. They shook their fists and cried out for the people to be quiet. This was madness! It was playing with fire on a threshing floor.

"Hosanna in the highest! Blessed be the coming kingdom of our father, David!"

Now it had gone too far! This was almost a rebellion. This was to make the prophet out to be the Messiah. This was to proclaim him king in Jerusalem!

They shrieked and beat their way through raised hands and waving palm branches, and then they reached the little donkey. The rabbis seized the halter and cried out, "Master! Silence your disciples! Tell them to be quiet!"

They met the Master's eyes. They were calm and clear, remarkably cool for having received such a greeting as this. He shook his head and said, "No, if they were to be quiet, the stones themselves would cry out."

The rabbis let go of the halter angrily. The yelling escalated higher and bolder around him:

Blessed is the King
who comes in the name of the Lord

Peace be in heaven
and glory in the highest!

They had reached the crest and the whole breathtaking view of the Holy City rose up to meet them. The powerful temple walls towered up on the other side of the Kidron. The temple lay there like an entire city of pillared halls and marbled squares. Behind it spread a swarm of flat roofs and narrow alleys that climbed up toward the town's crown. Everything was firmly behind the city's defiant walls and angular towers. The hills around it were dotted with olive trees, vegetable gardens, and white suburban houses.

When the pilgrims reached this point, their jubilee swelled into an effervescent running, born by joy and longing. The rabbis were carried away against their will. They watched these poor Galileans who were able to see the temple—this miraculous work that the rabbis could ponder every day—only once a year. They had walked day after day, and today they had climbed hour after hour up through desert valleys. Now their elderly stood there, leaning on their staffs. Today they had thirsted and felt their legs waver under the relentless sun on the slopes. Tears now streamed from their eyes. They stretched out their arms as if they want to hug the city down there like a loving mother.

Again, the flow of people carried the rabbis to the prophet's side. They looked at him testily, with wonderment. He didn't take part in the jubilation. He sat completely still on the donkey. He cried. Tears washed down his cheeks. Were they tears of joy?

The Master looked out over the city, from the city of David to the pool of Bethesda in the north. Even he seemed to caress it with his eyes.

"If you had known, even you, what makes for peace! But you would not . . ."

Yet again his gaze swept over the hills and the walls, and then seemed to look far off into the distance.

"The time shall come upon you," he said, "when your enemies encompass you with siege engines and enclose you and penetrate you from all sides. And they come to beat you down to the ground, you and your children who live in you, and they will not leave one stone on top of the other because you did not take advantage of the time you were given."

The crowd started moving again. Two of his disciples led the donkey. He rode upon the coats strewing the ground as if in a triumph, between the hedges of cheering people and swaying green branches. The echo answered from the temple mount on the other side: "David's Son."

The rabbis found the other council members. They were all just as upset. While they regarded the bustling crowd below them on the slope, they anxiously spied the Antonia Fortress on the other side of the valley. They could see the legions' red helmet brushes showing over the battlements. But nothing happened. They thanked the Highly to Be Praised that it wasn't any worse than it was. No sword had been seen. No one had uttered a curse against the Romans, and that one sung psalms on the road to the festival, even Pilate had to understand that . . .

But what was this really?

The prophet had taken a donkey. David's Son ought to have come on a stallion if he wanted to come like a king. And then there was that strange prophecy in Zachariah about Zion's king, who came riding on a donkey, righteous and victorious, but poor.

Poor? A poor Messiah?

They shook their grizzled locks. He wanted to be the Messiah, and yet he came without weapons, in humility and poverty.

In any case, he had presented himself as a prophet. He had dared to speak unreasonable words against the temple. Did he not mean that his fate should depend on whether or not the people listened to him now?

They laughed as they walked down the slopes. The train had reached the valley floor and began to climb up the short slopes to the city gates. They themselves could still look out over the endless courtyards from which rose the shiny marble-pillared forest of the temple. Before this golden facade whirled the black smoke of the burnt offering.

They smiled again. The temple would not perish just because some self-proclaimed prophet from Galilee prophesied its destruction. And he who prophesied ill fortune ought to at least hold a firm hand over his own followers so that they did not draw misery over the temple and her people with this childish prank.

If they were quiet, the stones would cry out, he had said. Suddenly the rabbis were thoughtful. Had he meant that after Jerusalem had been destroyed, these stones would cry over these people if they had not cried hosanna to his glory? Again, the same blasphemous arrogance!

Did he really mean that the Lord's temple stands or falls for his own sake?

The rabbi shook his head in serious exasperation. Now he had an approximation of what he had to report to the Great Council. Perhaps this man was not a rebel. In any case, he was far worse: he was a blasphemer who claimed to be in God's stead and to speak in his name. Either way, he was a dangerous person. The Great Council would do its duty and see to it that the people were not harmed.

And Every Day He
Instructed in the Temple

The wall reached for the heavens where there were two magnificently sculpted doors that opened into a long underground street. Sloping steps rose up through the pleasantly cool darkness and into the blazing sunlight of the archway. It led them straight out into the court of the Gentiles . . .

Peter's eyes were blinded. He had to squint as he looked around, but the temple's glory overwhelmed him. This temple was not a house. It was a city so grand that Peter thought any city from his homeland could easily fit within its walls. Rows of new pillars rose up all over the place. Smooth yellowish stone shimmered in the sunlight, and the golden roofs on the pinnacles contrasted against the blue sky with their glittering tips. The temple stood over all this like a lion with his head held high looking down on all the people between his paws.

Peter couldn't think of when he had ever before seen so many different ethnicities at one time. Both the impure and heathen could intermingle here in the outermost courtyard. There were Greeks, Egyptians, and Ethiopians alongside Jews from every corner of the world. He heard a man from Italy speak broken Greek as he complained about the price of a lamb. A moneychanger tried to explain to an old man with red eyes from somewhere in the land of the Euphrates that he could not get more for his particular silver coin. There was a hustle and bustle along the southern edge of the basilica that was reminiscent of the bazaar in Tiberias. The hawkers of sacrificial animals shouted out their wares, and sheep bleated. Women bargained as they squeezed tethered pigeons, whose eyes were big and reproachful as they hung in great bunches lashed together at their feet.

The echoing bang of something falling on the stone pavement caused Peter to turn around. Another table fell at the same time, and he saw the Master pointing authoritatively toward the exit. The moneychangers stared at him with terror. They whisked their things together and half ran as they made their exit. If anyone tried to say something against it, he wasn't able to open his mouth before he was silenced by the authority in the Master's voice. Just as calmly as when he spoke in the synagogue, and with the same obvious authority, he turned to the people. As always, he cited scripture, and as always, he silenced the opposition. It was written that the Lord's house should be a house of prayer, and they had made it into a den of thieves, now as in the days of Jeremiah.

Peter straightened up and looked around happily. This was the kind of powerful action that the people understood and that the people longed for. Even one of the Pharisees clapped his hands. The Sadducees had vested interest in the marketplace. They just stood there perplexed, anxiously looking around. They saw what the people were thinking: a great prophet had come forth again. Had not Amos also stepped up with the same authority at the temple in Bethel, and had not Jeremiah prophesied against the unrepentant who believed themselves to be safer in the Lord's temple? There was faith enough remaining in Israel that one could still sense the spirit of the prophets.

But, one wondered, would they still shout their approval of the Master if they really understood what was happening? Had they not noticed his words: a house of prayer for all peoples? Was it not in the days of the Messiah that all the peoples would come and worship on the Lord's Holy Mountain? Was it not the Anointed who would come to his temple and purify it?

Who understood this? And if they understood this, would they then repent?

Again, the Pharisees began disputing with the Sadducees. They spoke earnestly, but in hushed voices so that the people would not hear them. And the people clung to the Master. It was mostly young men surrounding him, men with strong bronze arms and faces. One could see traces of a half-expressed expectation on their faces, a secret tension that seemed to ask for a sign so that the action could begin.

Peter was doubtful and placed himself in the crowd behind the Master. He was no longer as full of enchantment for victory. It was all well and good that they stood with the Master. But did they really understand this bit about repentance?

*

The twilight was already dark enough that embers of the burnt offering on the altar could be seen glowing like a campfire from across the Kidron Valley. The red billowing clouds of smoke in front of the temple square soared up over crest and swirled away like black clouds across the golden sky of evening.

On the other side of the Mount of Olives, it was already night. Only the white steps in the limestone rock could be seen, and the black crowns of the olive trees lifted themselves like sparse trail markers against the sky.

Suddenly, Peter stopped. Against the blue sky, he saw the silhouette of a strange ghostly tree whose naked branches seemed to be fully draped with sleeping bats. He ran a few steps closer, touched the dead black flags, and then shouted as if in anguish, "Master! Look!"

The others stopped with amazement on the road. He could hear how their lagging, tired steps on the stone pavers slowed up and grew quiet. He yelled again, "Look! The fig tree that you cursed is dead!"

He was sure it was this tree. It was one of the wild fig trees here on the slopes, and they had taken notice of it the morning when they went into the city because it was so quickly judged. The Master had gone there to see if there were any figs. It already had leaves, so it ought to have had some of the green austere fruits from last year's shoots. But the tree belonged to the rickety weed trees that were richly green but did not bear fruit. The Master had looked it over and then almost mourned when he said that no one else shall ever eat of it.

And now all the new leaves of spring that had made the bush look vibrant and green were hanging black and limp on the white branches. Peter was almost terrified to feel as close as he was to God's power within the darkness. This was something that was in line with

the severest actions of judgment found in the prophets. He remembered how Jeremiah had purchased a huge clay jar and took the
elders of the people with him down to the valley of Hinnom. There,
he broke the clay jar into a thousand pieces and prophesied that thus
would God beat asunder this stiff-necked people and send upon it
such a misfortune that it would reverberate in the ears of everyone.

Did not this blackened fig tree mean the same thing as the broken clay jar at the Potsherd Gate? Was it not there that the Master told
of a fig tree that had not borne fruit in three years and that had now
received its last period of grace? Had he thought about Jerusalem
in the morning when they stood around the tree that had so much
promise but nothing to give?

The company was silent on the road. A quiet fear had had fallen
upon them all. It was almost as if they cowered under the threat of
this infinite power that ruled over life and death, over grace and
judgment.

What the Master himself thought was not easy to say. He only
told them that they should believe in God. That they should be able to
tell this mountain to throw itself in the sea down there. That when they
stopped and prayed, they should believe that they had already received
what they prayed for. But they should also forgive everything that they
had against anyone . . .

So there we are again, Peter thought. Repent, for the kingdom
of heaven is near. It was always the narrow gate of repentance, always
the incredible power of the kingdom and opportunity.

But if the people don't repent now?

*

The white priestly figure walked ceremoniously up the high steps
to the altar. He lifted the bloody bull shank with outstretched arms
and threw it high up so that the white tendons glittered like silver
in the sun. It fell upon the glowing embers with a hissing thud. The
fat from the intestines was already melting away in rust-colored
rivers while the black clouds of smoke spread a pungent smell of
burning flesh.

They had stood on the people's ledge below the altar in order to
pray and came out on the half-round stair between the heavy copper
doors of the Nicanor Gate when they noticed a silent crowd waiting

for them. It was ordered like an envoy, with some of the oldest and most distinguished priests up front and a large entourage of rabbis and lords behind them.

The Master stood in the middle of the stairs and looked at them. Peter tugged on Andrew's coat and pulled him down to the stone pavement of the courtyard.

The priests greeted the Master ceremoniously. There was tension in the air, but they were not hasty. It wasn't simple enmity that lay in their questions.

They wanted to know with what authority he did this. Who was it that gave him the authority?

Peter understood that they were asking him about driving the crowds out. But perhaps it was also about how he cured the sick, instructed the people, and allowed the children to sing hosanna. He looked at the Master. It was a dangerous question. The Master could not deny the mystery. But what would happen if he confessed it?

The Master gazed over the whole crowd, as if testing their intentions and their hearts. Then he said, "I also have a question for you. If you answer me then I shall tell you with what authority I operate."

They were surprised. They stared at him with puzzlement. He continued:

"The baptism of John? Was it from heaven or from man? Can you tell me that?"

It went quiet, and then there was a gentle whispering within the distinguished throng. Peter smiled. He could see other people in the crowd smiling too. One did not need to see the scribes glancing at the crowds to know what they were thinking. All the people knew that the Baptist was a prophet. If now they said his baptism was his own creation, they would risk being stoned. However, if they said that it was from God, then they condemned their own unrepentance. It was just as strange as when the publicans, soldiers, and good-time girls had repented before John's preaching, but the Pharisees had refused to receive his preaching of repentance.

The elders turned around and spoke with the other councilors. And again, they stepped forward as the spokesmen.

"We cannot answer that," they said.

The Master nodded.

"Then neither will I tell you with what authority I do this."

He went down the steps and continued across the court to the Beautiful Gate. Peter could see the dark expression on the faces of the council members. They looked like servants who had received a scolding but remained defiant at heart. But here and there, he encountered approving glances. Once again, the Master had spoken as wisely as Solomon and with the authority of Elijah. But did they really understand? Of course, he had meant that he who had believed the Baptist could also understand he who came after him. But to understand all that would be to bow before the preaching of repentance the Master shared with the Baptist. If one repented as God demanded, then one could grasp the mystery of his Messiah. But if one did not want to repent, then it served nothing to try to explain that the Master had full authority. How would it help the conceited and smug Pharisees out there to know that the Master was the Messiah?

And what help would it be to the young men here who smiled and bowed and approved with clear eyes if they only wanted to have a Messiah who drove away Israel's oppressors but did not put their own misdeeds away?

*

A man planted a vineyard; he framed it with fences. He dug a winepress. He built a watch tower . . .

Peter shut his eyes and leaned against a pillar. He felt the presence of the crowd in the air's warm tremor, but he heard almost nothing. They were so quiet. Finally, far on the other side of the courtyard, there was a murmur, and bare feet scraped softly on the stone pavement.

Peter opened his eyes again and looked at the white cornice over Solomon's portico shining against the heavens. He imagined hearing the prophet Isaiah's voice echo through the halls. He understood that the Master intended to shape his words so that they would sound like the song in which the Prophet spoke about the Lord's beloved garden. That was the land of Judah, for which God did everything that could be done, but which bore wild grapes when he expected that it would bear real grapes.

He looked around. He read from the expectant, listening faces that he was not the only one who wondered what was coming.

The vineyard was rented to tenants, and the owner had left for a foreign land. When the time was right, he sent a servant to receive his share of the vineyard's fruit. But they took hold of him and abused him, and sent him back empty handed. Then he sent yet another one to them. They beat him over the head and treated him shamefully.

It is the prophets, Peter thought. As many as God has sent to this city, they have been beaten and abused.

But when the lord of the vineyard had sent all his servants and they had all been abused and murdered, then he had only one left whom he could send: his son, whom he loved. Finally, he sent him, for he thought, Surely they will honor my son.

Peter held his breath. Now it burned. They had to understand now. It was so unreasonable that a vineyard owner would send his son when the servants had been murdered. Naturally, he would send mercenaries upon them with swords and shackles. There was only one Lord who would send his son instead.

But the tenants did not honor his son. They conspired together and murdered him. They even dishonored his dead body by throwing it out of the vineyard.

Now, when the lord of the vineyard comes, what shall he then do with the tenants?

Peter barely dared to look around him. The Master talked firmly and quietly, as if he instructed them about any of the well-known old truths. A couple of old priests responded, mundanely and with condescension, as if the question had really been too simple for them.

"Because they had been so bad, he should be just as bad and destroy them. And he ought to rent the vineyard to other tenants who give him the yield when the time is right."

Peter stared at them. Their wrinkled faces were completely unmoved, but there was a little movement in the corner of their eyes. Perhaps that meant they did not want to let on that this parable had anything to do with them.

The Master nodded with confirmation as he usually did while he was instructing.

"Yes," he said. "So it is: He shall come and destroy them. And then he shall leave the vineyard to others."

"No! That is impossible!"

It was a pale man with black locks and huge burning eyes who had yelled. He stood, very upset, and appealed to the others with outstretched hands. A mumbling was heard. Apparently, they had understood.

Then the Master looked at them and asked if they had never read in the scriptures where it was written that the stone the builders rejected had become the cornerstone and that this had happened by the Lord's power.

Yes, this was written. In the conclusion of the great Hallel that they would sing anew when they ate the Paschal lamb, this was written. It was written alongside the word that they sang on the Mount of Olives, the word of the Blessed who comes in the name of the Lord.

But what did this mean? The very same cornerstone that they understandably cast aside, but which became the cornerstone by the power of the Lord—it must be God's Messiah. Would he then really be so rejected? Would it happen to him as it did to the son in the parable?

Now it was Peter who wanted to get up and shout, "Impossible, this shall never happen!" But he stayed quiet. When he saw the hate in the eyes of the scribes, he thought that they at least would not let anything go undone, so that really would happen . . .

*

Judas stopped and observed the people. He could never see the true measure of all those expectant faces. They were like noble horses harnessed to a four-horse chariot in the Hippodrome, nervously dancing in the stall and clattering their hooves, just waiting for the sweeping sound of the charioteer's whip to throw themselves into the race. He looked at all the smiles, full of the joyous victory that went through the crowd like a breeze over water when the Master stopped the mouths of his opposition. He noticed how the endless silence and the meaningful whispers pulsed like an upset breath through the crowd as soon as the Master gave the slightest indication that the great day was near. The vast temple engulfed this heated and impatient crowd with walls more solid than any castle and taxes greater than any king's. Where would the violence begin if not here?

Now the Pharisees came to the Master again. They had tried to convict him all day, but they had been thwarted. Perhaps they had

had enough. Now it was their followers who came with their questions. Judas watched with pride as they bowed deeply, though they were learned and wealthy. They stood off at a distance, respectfully, and they began to praise the Master for teaching the truth about God's way without beating around the bush and without partiality. Now they had an important issue to discuss. They and many others with them had wondered about this a lot, and now they would like to have the answer.

Judas looked at them where they stood, bowing reverently, hardly daring to lift their gaze to the Master as he stood like a ruler on the marble ledge before them. It was like a picture of the future, a first beginning to the restoration that had to come after all the years of humiliation. But what did they want to know?

They hastily looked up at the Master and asked, "Is it permissible to pay Caesar's tax? Should we pay the tax or not?"

Judas was as stiff with tension as the others. This question, asked here in the temple, in the midst of this feverish expectation, with thousands of witnesses and within view of the oppressor, was like rattling keys in the lock of the lion's cage. Anything could happen now. And now the Master would be pressured to answer, to give the answer that Judas himself had been impatiently waiting for for months.

The Master seemed to understand it. A wrinkle formed between his eyebrows, and he looked alert. The clarity of his voice was almost scary in the midst of endless silence.

"Why are you trying to trap me, you hypocrites? Bring me a coin for the tax, so I can see."

One of them fumbled through his purse and offered him a denarius. They all stared at the Master, who held it up for them and asked, "Well, whose picture is this now? And whose name is written here?"

"Caesar's," they answered.

"Well, then give to Caesar what belongs to Caesar. But give to God what belongs to God."

One could see that the men were crestfallen. Judas could begrudge them this because they hadn't come with the right intention. But he was bitterly disappointed himself. Once again, nothing had come of all the expectation. Once again, the Master had allowed the opportunity to fall on the ground. Once again, he had pushed aside the issues that burned in the hearts of the people, and instead he fell back on the old song and dance that one should give to God what belonged to him and be like a child to his heavenly Father.

Judas had a hard time holding back his bitterness. The Galileans were good people. Though he himself was a native of Judah and spoke his mother tongue purely and without accent, he held the Galileans dear for their burning faith in God's Messiah. But it was strange that this faith was losing tooth and nail among the apostles. Who wouldn't get a stale taste in their mouth from all this talk of being small and last, of being a servant? Who was it who had the power but was not happy to use it? Was not the victorious success of David proof of God's favor for him? Would then David's Son, the Beloved, be inferior?

Judas turned away unwillingly. He thought he could see on the faces around him that there were many who thought as he did.

*

The evening sacrifice was carried forward.

At the sound of the trumpet, they had thrown themselves down with their heads against the stone pavement for the last time. The priest at the top of the stairs lowered his hands of blessing, and the echo from the great choir of the Levites trembled like a frail tone within the halls.

Peter rose up, adjusted his coat, and looked at the altar one last time. In the vast entrance of the peoples just before the celebration, they had been able to stand among the worshiping crowds in the outer courts of the Israelites, but through the vast gates, he could see how all three sacrifices were brought forward, just as he had seen forgiveness touch him when the priest went into the temple to light the offering of incense. The temple house soared so high above all the surrounding courtyards that one always felt like he was standing before it, no matter where he found himself in this labyrinth of gates and stairs that held all the pillar-lined streets together with a multitude of small dark chambers and wide sunlit courts.

Even the Master looked to the temple's pardon. He still seemed to be praying, like so many of the other pilgrims. Then someone poked him in the side to get his attention. Peter saw an old priest tugging him by his coat and laying his hand on his arm with an expression as if he had waited long enough. He was not alone. Three or four others standing behind him all looked as if they belonged to the high priest's family. The linen of their clothes was almost as soft as a woman, and their beards glistened with oil.

It was obvious that they only waited for an occasion to ask their questions. The question concerned the resurrection.

Yes—did the Master believe there was a resurrection from the dead? And did he also believe in Moses? Good, then they would ask their question.

Peter read their faces: they rejoiced in this moment. Like all the Sadducees, they were men of the world, marked by education and an old fine culture. Their faces were controlled and measured. And yet there was something shrewd and derisive about them, as if they thought they had gotten something over on the Master.

They began to speak about a man who died childless. According to Levitical law, which they received from Moses, his younger brother should now marry his widow and give her a son who could carry on the dead man's name and lineage in Israel. But now the brother also died, and the woman became a widow again. Luckily, there were five more brothers in the family, and for the third time, the woman was married within the same circle of brothers. But misfortune continued to follow her. All seven brothers died, and all seven had been married to her by law. Finally, the woman also died.

They looked at the Master with an untold mocking respect and then asked the question: Which one of the seven would have her as his wife in the resurrection from the dead? All seven of them had been married to her . . .

One could see from their faces that they expected a long silence to be followed by the laughter of the people and the Master's embarrassment. But the Master's answer came instantly, crisply, and curtly.

"Does not your question show that you understand nothing of either the scriptures or God's power?"

The wrinkles of merriment quit playing upon the faces of the high priests. With an expression that was something between helplessness and vexation, they stared at the Master, who looked over their heads and spoke to the people about the resurrection of the dead: Then, there would be no wedding celebration, and there would not be any marriage like on earth. All such things belonged to the present world and would pass away with it. But they who entered the new age would be like the angels who were not born and did not die.

Peter nodded to himself. He received affirmation of something he thought he could understand. The resurrection was not as the Pharisees seemed to believe and as he had heard as a child. It would not only be the old life that came back with new power. There would not be fig trees, grapevines, wheat fields, and housewives and children in the new kingdom, just as now but only much better. It would be something completely different. The world would be born anew. A new age would come, and God would make all things new, just as he once created everything by his word.

But how? And when?

The Master continued to speak about the resurrection. Even Moses had said that the dead should rise. Scripture spoke of the burning bush where God called himself "the God of Abraham, Isaac, and Jacob." Did they believe that God was the God of those who no longer existed? No, for God was not the God of the dead, but only the living, and for him, all lived.

"You are wrong," he said and turned from them as if he meant that there was no purpose in bandying about words with them. They retreated without answering. Once again, their faces were important and aloof, but Peter thought that they boiled within. They could not help noticing that the people looked at them derisively. And that was probably the hardest thing for them to endure. They presided over money and education in the land. They had the best articles of clothing and the finest food at their feasts. They knew how to carry themselves among the Greeks and Romans too. They were never shamed, not even by their measured and tolerant faith. They had found themselves so wonderfully well and comfortable . . .

Peter looked at them almost compassionately. Was not that what the Master meant when he talked of owning the world and still losing everything?

*

Very openly and undisguised, he looked into the Master's face. He belonged to the scribes and was certainly a Pharisee. He had listened to the conversation and nodded in agreement when the Master stopped the mouths of the Sadducees. There was nothing ambiguous in his voice when he came with his question now:

"Master, which is the greatest of all commandments?"

Peter thought for a moment and noticed to his satisfaction that the Master answered just as if he anticipated it. He responded with the two commandments concerning loving God with all your heart, and loving your neighbor as yourself. He had also understood the matter rightly.

The scribe agreed. He spoke rightly, he said thoughtfully. To love God with all your strength and your neighbor as yourself, this was really greater than all burnt offerings and sacrifices.

Now it was the Master who looked at the scribe with a long appreciative glance.

"You are not far from the kingdom of God," he said. Then the crowds separated.

Peter would have loved to exchange a few words with the man. He was also close to the kingdom of God. He had understood those which were the greatest and foremost in the commandments. It was just this that the Master meant when he spoke about giving to God what belonged to God and letting the Lord of the vineyard receive the fruit of the vineyard. God was the creator and owner of everything. One was indebted to him for his life and strength, his soul and his body, his understanding and his heart. To give God what belonged to God was to give yourself and all that which one had called his own before. It was this that was the fruit of the vineyard. It was that which was called repentance. It was this that God expected when his kingdom came.

And yet this was not God's kingdom. It was only when the Master came that one could feel a bit of the kingdom's joy like a cool breeze. It was there and yet not there. It was like the morning sun that still lingers behind the desert's edge and yet fills the heavens with light. It was like the buds on a fig tree that are smaller than a fingertip and still fill the branches and leaves with sumptuous fruit. All this was in the Messiah.

And for this reason, the scribe was not far from God's kingdom. He had met the Messiah today and met him with love and reverence. He had opened his heart. He was willing to give God what belonged to God. But there was something lacking in him also.

Peter looked at the people who pressed in around the Master. That it should be so hard to be children of the kingdom! That they would have God's glory in their midst and stand at the gates of heaven but still be excluded if they did not bow their hearts in repentance.

He was gripped by a feeling of near hopelessness. Why should it be so hard? Was there really no other way?

The Kings of the Earth Rise Up

The forecourt around the altar was already entirely engulfed in shadow. The sun hid behind the temple so that it only illuminated the golden pinnacles high up on the wall. It strained the neck when a person bent backward to look up there. One could stack ten Galilean houses on top of each other and not reach the top of this monstrous building that was higher than any tower and yet broad and immense like a castle.

The two disciples moved slowly along the edge of the permissible range. One only set foot between the temple and the altar during the great procession at the Feast of Booths or when one came to the place of slaughter to offer a sacrifice. They watched the site with timid reverence. This was where they had murdered Zechariah, son of Berechiah, and left a pool of blood that cried to the heavens. But all this righteous blood would fall on their heads.

The cold wind blew over the mountains in the evening. They went into the shelter under the colonnade and pulled their coats tight around them. There was a desolate atmosphere about the great courtyards, where the people shivered as they went home as soon as the last ray of sun left the leeward side of the wall. Only a few Pharisees remained to pray at the altar. One could see how their hands shook in the cold and how their uplifted faces tightened under the pressure of their shivering bodies.

They exchanged a few short doubtful words. There was a nasty atmosphere in the city that they couldn't come to terms with. They had a feeling that the cold hostile wind was blowing in order to disperse the people from around the Master. They didn't need to ask where it came from. They constantly encountered this peculiarly hard piety that knew no compromise and yet was nothing more than one big compromise. It was just this that the Master reproached the customs of these pious people for: They gave a tenth of all sorts of culinary herbs even if it was just a matter a few small grains, but they couldn't be bothered with mercy and love. They laid heavy burdens on people. They wove together an entangling web of statutes that only they could steal their way through, and they closed heaven to those who would come there. They kept their self-made commandments of men. They cleaned up the appearance of their life to look like perfection, but they still had a heart that remained full of desire to be seated first at feasts, to earn money, to be greeted in the square, and to be noticed for their charity.

There was something frightening about these men. They were always to be found around the Master in the temple. They whispered and pointed. They slipped through the people, and they kept alert until the temple gates closed again. They were ready to travel over land and sea in order to make one proselyte, but when they won him over, they made him into a child of Gehenna, twice as bad as themselves. So the Master said.

Yet the most frightening thing was this: they were right. All that they said was what man should do. It was not with less righteousness that one entered the kingdom of heaven. When they demanded all for God, they only said the truth. The problem was only that they said and didn't do.

But who could be saved? Did not the Master himself lay a burden on man that no one could bear? Was not the kingdom of heaven shut to each and every one of them?

They had gone down the great semicircle of stairs and stood in the lower court where they would meet the Master. He sat on the stone bench across from the treasury and watched the people deposit their gifts in any of the thirteen trumpets that stood upright here; their open mouths seemed to cry for a handout. They clanged when the coins fell down, and it rang often with the rich and heavy sound of big coins.

The Master seemed to listen to the ring, as if he tested the gifts. He lingered there in the cold wind like he was expecting something. Not before one of the last in the court, a poor woman of the people, had dropped two small and thin copper coins did he get up.

He winked at them to come and said, "That poor widow gave more than all the others. They all gave from their abundance, but from her poverty she gave everything she had, all that was in her possession."

He threw his coat over his head and began to walk across the cold stone pavement. The disciples whispered to each other again. He had said it again: all that one had, and himself in the bargain, one should give to God. It was the law of the heavenly kingdom. He who tried to retain something for himself would find himself left outside. But there was something more in these words today. She gave of her poverty. He who was nothing and had nothing was always invited to be a guest in the kingdom of God.

Was there some similarity between this, to have nothing before God, and to give everything to God? Would God both have everything and give everything? Should one who gave everything to God also expect everything from him? Was this the only way: to be completely dependent on God? Was that the right way to live in God's kingdom?

They couldn't find anything more to ask. They dimly thought that this too was the secret of the Master's own poverty, of his entrance as the king who came to his people in humility and riding upon a donkey. But they put everything aside and continued walking in silence while everyone thought their own thoughts about things that lay closer to their hearts: of the glory that would be revealed, and the throne that he would ascend to in his Father's kingdom.

*

The winter cold crept along the thick stone walkways and filled the whole long courtroom. It penetrated everything so that the men edged higher up on the bench cushions along the wall. It was half dark in there. Some golden rays of sun peered in through the window latches. No one opened them up to let the warmth of the sun in. Everyone knew what it was worth to have a cool stone house when the month of Av came burning like a fire over the land.

Caiaphas rubbed his wrinkled old hands and ordered wine mixed with steaming hot water. Then he sent all the servants out and gave the door a tentative look to see that it shut firmly behind the curtain. Slowly and hushed, he began to speak again, with his eyes directed at the steaming beaker before him.

They were unanimous. Heaven had given them the responsibility for Israel's fate in this worrisome time, so they couldn't be idle. If it was a choice between one man's life and that of many, then it was better that one man died so that the people should live. Were they all agreed on this?

He looked up with a very quick and partial glance. Everyone sat still, looking straight ahead or nodding slowly.

So there was only one thing left for them to do: the heavy task to deal with. Were they all agreed on this too?

Now he looked up, challenging them with his inquiry. His old trained eyes caught all the nods, and if someone hesitated to give ascent to his feeling, he didn't release his eyes before the man woke up from his distraction, and nodded yes vigorously, half-appalled at his own negligence.

Caiaphas lowered his gaze again. There was timing to consider. It was important to act decisively and yet carefully. They all knew how these people were continually grumbling and obstinate toward them whom heaven had sent to be their shepherds. They all knew how awkward it was to stay on the path of peace during the festival, when there were so many confused or easily deceived in the city. So it was important to operate in such a way that those who would lead Israel astray would not have opportunity to start a riot or some bloodbath. So that which had to be done had to be done quickly and quietly, preferably at night, but, in any case, not during the celebration in front of the people. If one acted now, it meant that the judgment should fall the same night. Yes, of course, due process—one could hold an extraordinary session at sunrise in order to fulfill the letter of the law. But surely they all understood how important it was that the end was such that no thought could be given to unrest.

He looked around again. His father-in-law nodded his silvered head thoughtfully. His brother and brothers-in-law and cousins agreed. They apparently had the majority with them. But how was it with the laymen down by the door? Caiaphas almost regretted that he had made a gesture of reconciliation today, inviting these mocking Pharisees who always wanted to be more pious than the clergy. They always pretended to know more about the ways of God than the ordained sons of Aaron.

They looked straight ahead with inscrutable faces. They must know that everyone was looking at them, but they still didn't move.

Caiaphas stroked his beard and, with as much fatherly concern as he could muster, said that he hoped everyone here understood it was not for his own sake that he called them to this council. He had nothing to win here. It was simply what was best for the people.

An almost imperceptible shiver of cold mockery crossed over the faces of the Pharisees. They did not look at each other, and still, it was as if their eyes had met and a small mischievous smile curled upon their lips. Caiaphas blushed. Were they thinking of trading sacrificial victims?

Then the oldest of the Pharisees lifted his sharp dark eyes and looked at the high priest. This was very wisely spoken, he said. They were also agreed with this: that the judgment fell according to the law but as quickly as possible. And what the punishment would be . . . there was only one punishment for he who made himself equal with the Highly to Be Praised. Such judgment was not happily given to anyone, but was it not written, "Ye shall not respect persons in judgment. You shall not fear any man, for judgment belongs to God"? Everything depended on the evidence, so there was only one sentence to pass . . .

He looked searchingly at the high priest, who met his gaze steadily. Then Caiaphas nodded thoughtfully, and firmly. Yes, he had undertaken to ensure that there was clear evidence to be presented.

The Pharisees looked at each other. They were satisfied. They had received assurance that all righteousness would be fulfilled, and now they could give their assent with a clear conscience. They looked around and nodded their assent.

Were they mistaken? Or was there a special smile within the high priest's solemn visage when he saw how anxious his capable brothers among the Pharisees were for justice and righteousness?

A Preparation for My Burial

The oil lamps flickered whenever the door opened and the cold night wind swept in. The moon light fell in so clearly that it painted the rough stone floor a pale blue around the edge of the small flame's glow.

It was quiet around the table. The faces of the men lying about were visible in the candlelight as they silently tore the bread apart and formed it in their hands before dipping it in the dark bowls of course clay in front of them. It was apparent that they were tired and hungry. It was also apparent that behind the silence lay something that weighed heavy upon their hearts, something they wanted to talk about, but they were unable to find the words.

The door opened again. No one thought about it. Countrymen and strangers came and went. Pilgrims suffered a shortage of everything. They needed to borrow fire. They had broken a pot. They wanted to use the oven. Dark shadows perpetually stole out into the moonlight, and new ones came in their place.

It was only when someone approached the table that the two tired men looked up. The next minute, they heard the brittle crushing of something small and fine shattering, and then the ointment poured out upon the Master's hair. He wiped the shiny drops from his forehead and looked up. The aroma of expensive oil filled the room. It was strange how it even broke through the smell of smoke, hot food, and unrefined wool. It was a breath of royal grandeur in the midst of this bleak existence. The shattered flask would have fit at the head of a great man's tomb, but it made a strange impression here in this circle of sunburned men with their course hands soiled by food in earthenware dishes.

The lamplight illuminated the stunned faces. Their half open mouths shut again. Their dark eyes looked at each other, and their tired expressions were washed with renewed interest. It was too late now, but they still had to have their say. Why would all this be wasted? The flask was worth a great amount of money. A person could have sold it and given the money to the poor.

The Master looked up at the woman who had done it. Then he turned to the men and silenced them. Why should they harass her? What she did was beautiful. They would always have the poor among them. But they would not always have him. She had anointed him with this ointment in anticipation. She had prepared him for his funeral. It was a preparation he would otherwise have gone without.

It was even quieter around the table than before. Stunned and timid eyes met and then looked at the Master again. What was this? Was he anointed—for his burial? Was this healthy, strong body consecrated for death? But he was God's Messiah. He ought to have been anointed king. Was the Anointed christened for death instead?

They shook their heads mournfully, unable to understand. But the woman smiled almost imperceptibly in joy over the Master's words. She understood that this man, the guest here at this table, had more meaning than wisdom. She knew that she who held a shattered flask in her hand had found the pearl of great price for which one would give away everything else, give it with wanton joy, and be all the richer for the more one gave.

*

The oil lamps in the artfully forged candleholders swung in their chains and flickered when the curtain was pulled aside. The servant bowed deeply and nodded knowingly. Then he dared to speak clearly, bowed deeply again, and disappeared.

The buzz quieted in the hall. The flames glistened upon their long curly beards and the fine, soft skin above their bushy eyebrows. There was the slight smell of delicately perfumed oil, of old expensive wood, and of clothes that were stored in heavy boxes of aloe and cassia.

The heavy rings on the curtain rustled again, and the servant returned with the stranger. He looked around with great hesitance and shyness. Caiaphas urged him to come closer with the usual nod.

Hesitantly, he stepped forward as the servant silently disappeared. He slowly answered the high priest's questions. They could tell from his accent that he wasn't a Galilean, and they were reassured that he was a Judean. This strengthened their confidence. They spoke cordially to him, and soon his tongue loosened up. There was no doubt about the matter. He was willing to help them. He knew everything that he needed to know: the timing and all the secret hangouts. It could all happen as soon as this morning.

He gave them a quick glance from below so that they could see the whites of his eyes flash from his dark face.

"What will you give me?"

They looked at each other. Caiaphas winked at one of the young men who went away and rattled the lock on a box. Then he came with a little scale. The shekels rang as they dropped upon the scales.

"Thirty," Caiaphas said in a voice both hushed and harsh.

The man stroked them in his hand and let them disappear within his coat.

"As soon as possible then?"

Caiaphas nodded. This morning, if he was given occasion. At whatever time . . . It was all good.

They followed the stranger to the door with their fatherly looks of appreciation. Their faces changed into looks of quiet amazement when he disappeared. Then the young man picked up the scales and said with wonder, "He was satisfied with thirty . . ."

My Time Is Near

He felt the edge of the lamb's skull under the dark forelock when he laid his hand upon its head. Never before had he so fearfully experienced the seriousness of this holy deed. As he read the confession of sin, he prayed for all of his unrepentant people. He prayed for mercy upon the thoughtless masses floating about out there in the forecourts, pushing and quarreling in the alleys. He thought about his Galilean countrymen in Capernaum and Chorazin who were now getting rid of all the leaven in their houses as they prepared to celebrate the Passover, though they had pushed aside God's own Messiah. He thought that he was failing under the burden of the punishment that these pardoned and hardened people placed upon his head.

Then he turned the sheep's muzzle toward the temple. The aid flipped it over quickly, and with a tremor of anxious reverence, he sunk the sacrificial knife into its throat. The priest collected the blood in a bowl before carelessly sprinkling it on the altar and draining the rest of it in the channel at his feet. Apparently, it was nothing but a boring everyday task to him. For Peter, it was something that cut through bone and marrow. Here at the foot of the temple that reached for the heavens with the rolling veil right in front of him, here, only a few steps from the holy of holies, the unfathomable and unseen that was said to be filled with the glory of heaven from the face of the Blessed One, here he felt the full weight of his people's enormous guilt. By the power of his word, the Almighty had called forth his children from nothing and formed them from clay and made them almost divine beings. He had given them his law and shown them his ways. To break with

his will was to rise up against the Lord who held heaven and earth
in his hand; such a rebellion could only end in death. Whoever
broke with his Lord and Creator and trampled his divinity and
holiness underfoot deserved nothing but death.

This is what all these sacrifices had to say. Year after year, they
cried from the stone pavement, a perpetually renewed reminder of
Israel's bloody sins. Now as he laid his hand upon the sacrificial animal's head, he felt the meaning of it as never before: We have to die,
but we shall ransom our crumbling lives. Still we atone for our misdeeds with the blood of calves and lambs. Yet every new sacrifice
cries out that it was we who ought to die for our misdeeds.

The priest folded up the hide and took the shoulder that he
should have. The fat was carried away and thrown on the altar. It was
almost impossible to follow all that happened within the crowds and
masses. Now they stood there with the naked body of the animal on
a rod.

He winked at John, and they hefted the burden upon their
shoulders. He took the lead and steered their way through the Sheep
Gate right out into the sunshine on the forecourt. He saw drops of
blood on the stone and avoided stepping on them with his bare feet.
Peter and John turned aside. They stopped. They pushed their way
forward again, and made their way to the exit. The nauseating black
smoke from the altar of burnt offering hung thick about them the
whole time.

How long now?

Peter looked at the billowing mass of people. How long would
God keep covenant with them? Never had he felt so clearly as today
that this temple was only a preparation, a temporary order of things
created by the long suffering of God to last only until something better would come.

And now something better had come, that which was greater
than both the temple and the altar. All that the fathers waited for was
now among them. And no one saw it!

Peter and John found their sandals. They pushed through the
archway and once again heard invectives thrown at them. They didn't
bother going through the small stairway at the side that was built for
the pure, so that they would be able to keep their purity. They felt
that the Master would permit them to walk here in the midst of the

gate even at the risk of bumping into a woman giving birth or stepping on the spit a heathen left behind.

They slowly made their way, carrying their burden across the
high stone bridge that traversed the Tyropoeon Valley carrying them
into the Upper City. On the other side, they encountered camels and
shepherds. They gave way to a heavy palanquin carried by six blue-
clad black men. They stepped over baskets with beans and figs and
were cursed by the mongers.

Then how long?

The more they were called, the farther away they went, the
prophet said. Now God had called them through his own Messiah.
But who rose up to follow him? Did it not look as if they planned to
turn their backs on him? And then what would happen?

They had reached in between the houses in the narrow alley and
walked up the long sloping stair path between the high stone walls.
Children played around them. A water vendor held up his ladle, and
a boy sat milking a goat in the doorway.

His brother he cannot redeem, the psalm said. No one can give
God the ransom for him. The ransom for his soul is too expensive; it
cannot be paid for all eternity.

Peter felt he would pay whatever it cost to buy his brother's
freedom—all these children of Israel who murmured around him
here in the street. But he knew that he could not do it. God had
invited them all in his Messiah. Had they not rejected everything
when they rejected him?

*

The alleyway became ever emptier the farther they got from the
temple. They climbed higher and higher, but they felt as if they
were descending deeper and deeper into a tangle of narrow alleys
between the curving stone walls. No rays of sun reached the bottom of these paths. Arches spanned across the street and cold rose
up from the black cellar holes. The pale and timid faces of women
glimpsed out from bay windows. One could see through a half-
open door into a stone-paved courtyard with green bushes and a
water pond. Otherwise, the gates were closed, and he who banged
on the knockers could be sure that he were pounding in vain if he
was not recognized by the tentative eye that watched him through

the peephole. The Passover was a tumultuous time, and one had to be careful who one invited as a guest on this holy night if they did not want the festivities destroyed by the temple guard or Pilate's soldiers.

Peter didn't think about the walls that exhaled their cool breath upon him. The last few days, he had encountered so much hate and suspicion that he thought he would take a path where the threatening sloping walls almost joined themselves over his head. He constantly feared that something might fall on him at any moment. He carried a well-hidden anxiety in his heart ever since the Master spoke yesterday about the anointing he received in advance of his burial. Now he understood that it was deadly serious.

And now they would eat the Passover lamb. They would celebrate this joyous night when even the meanest in Israel lounged at the table and let themselves be served like a lord so that even he would know that he belonged to the people who were freed by God's own mighty hand. They would celebrate the Exodus and the night of liberation, and rejoice in the covenant God had instituted with his people.

Could he really rejoice over this covenant? Even if God's people betrayed it? Even if, for the last time, they pushed God's grace away and broke the covenant, hopelessly and forever.

Peter shivered. He was sweaty from the burden and froze in the cold alley. And like a cold chill, the question came over him: Was the covenant broken? Was grace finished for Israel? Was this the last time his people would find joy in the holy night of the Exodus?

*

A warm spot of sunlight fell upon the wall around the door. He felt the lovely warmth caress him when he knocked so that it rattled in the vault. He already felt so at home here, as if he had lived here for many years.

And was he in actual fact a stranger? Could they be strangers, they who were brought together by God's eternal determination? When in the morning they saw the man with the water jar come, the man they were told to watch for, had they known that he came walking down a path that was staked out by God's invisible trail markers? They had followed him. They had spoken with the owner of the house. They had found the room above his house with the three table couches. They had equipped it with the unleavened bread, the bitter herbs, and the red brick made of dates and figs. All had been staked out, all had been fulfilled, just as it had been told to them.

The gate opened and the lord of the house looked through the door opening. With few words, he showed them to the oven where they placed the rod carrying the animal's carcass and closed the door. During the waiting time, they sat by the path to the courtyard and warmed themselves in the sun.

A few swallows shot past like arrows in the clear sky. They were on their way north again, a long path that the All-Powerful had staked out for them. Then he also must have staked out the way of the people and the fate of men. In any case, Peter was confident that he now stood in the midst of a sacred event that awaited its fulfillment through the ages, and for millennia since, it had been signed in the counsel of God. The prophets who had seen into God's counsel had seen it and spoke about it. Only now would it step forth in deed to take form in events and life.

"My time is near," the Master said when greeting the man here in this house. And his time, this must be the time of the ages and the fulfilment of everything. So perhaps this holiday that he now prepped with bitter herbs and a redbrick of dates and figs and a roasted lamb would give the answer to the thousands of unanswered questions.

His time was near. The Son of Man would follow the path that God had staked out in his counsel. But what was that path?

On the Night When the
Lord Jesus Was Betrayed

The last bit of daylight faded over the city as they made their way up the stone steps. They watched from the roof as the gold luster on the walls transformed into a pale blue. It was as if the city had died, and its fever-stricken face turned white as it went cold and lifeless. The full moon that marked the Passover hung in the valley above the village of Siloam like a huge silver shield filling the evening with blue light as the last rays of sun were extinguished.

They heard a joyous hum from the neighboring houses where the people had already begun their meal, but it was quiet in the alley. A horn sounded off to the north, disrespectfully shredding the evening's peace. It was followed by the heavy rhythmical stomp of ironclad feet marching on stone pavement. The twelve looked at each other furtively as they tried to discern whether the sound was coming closer. The Master was the only one not bothered by it. He opened the door to the upper room and entered the hall.

It was dark in there. They lit lamps but exchanged few words as they reclined at the table. Their ears were still ringing from the trumpet blast. A sickening sense that something had to happen had hounded them all day long. It was the same oppressive feeling that one has when the air is full of a dark haze forming into thunderclouds.

The Master had taken the place of the house father. He lifted the cup of wine to begin the meal with blessing: the first of the Passover's four cups. But just when he lifted his hands for prayer, he looked at them and said, "I have long desired to eat this Paschal lamb with you before I suffer. For I say to you that I will eat it with you no more until it is fulfilled in the kingdom of God."

They stared at him as they laid there motionless. He took the cup of wine, blessed it, and praised God, who created the fruit of the vine. Then he offered it to them, saying they should share it among themselves; for now, he would no longer drink of that which came from the vine before he drank it on the day when all would be new in his Father's kingdom.

They looked at him over the brim of the cup with large, almost frightened eyes as they drank. Was his hour so close? Was this the last time they would recline at the table with him? Would they never walk through the countryside with him again? He had broken bread with them; he had given the blessing so many times. They had been sealed in their communion, the visual proof that they belonged to him and that the kingdom belonged to them. They had long ago noticed that he broke bread as a sign of annunciation, proclaiming the joyous feast of heaven was near. And yet, could his hour be so near?

The feast proceeded according to its solemn rhythm, just as they celebrated it year after year. They washed their hands. They picked up the bitter herbs, the unleavened bread, and the brick-red fig dough, the reminder of the bitter years of slavery in the Egyptian brick kilns. They read the sacred Paschal text and sang the hymn "When Israel Came out of Egypt." A breath of fresh air swept through the hall and filled it with the great joy of the miraculous night. The distant noise of hasty steps and murmuring crowds faded into the darkness. It was replaced by an echo from a thousand years of joy that followed the Lord's solemn vigil from generation to generation. On this night, Israel had become a nation and was ordained by God to be his servant. On this night, the Lord had sat in judgment over the gods of Egypt and struck the oppressors with a hard hand. But the blood was a sign of salvation on the doorposts of the faithful.

And now was the last time. The last time, really? Did they now stand at the threshold of the unspeakable that would make all things new? Would they drink the next cup of blessing and go to the table in the kingdom of God?

They ate the Passover lamb in silence. Their thoughts wandered, first to the menacing trumpet blast in Herod's fortress, then to the evil will they encountered in the eyes of the Pharisees, then to the word that the Master said about the hour that was now so close. Perhaps this was a true Passover, filled with the threat of Pharaoh and the hate of the oppressors and, even more, filled with hope in the Lord who would save his people with a strong hand from this extreme distress.

The Master had taken the unleavened bread prescribed at this time. He thanked God again and praised him for all his benevolent deeds. Then he broke the bread and shared it, saying that they should all take and eat of it.

They looked at him again, their eyes full of wonder. They looked at the tough unleavened bread that was ripped apart into small pieces between his hands. They saw him offer it. They heard him say that this was his body now given for their sake. They should do this in his memory.

His body. Given. For their sake. In memory . . .

Heavy and full of meaning, these words fell from his lips and sank down into their hearts. They were as clear as crystal and yet impossible to penetrate.

His body . . . So he gave himself. That which he gave here, it was his mystery, God's own glory that he bore within him.

Given . . . this was also something that belonged together with suffering and death. It meant sacrifice and self-giving. It was related to the words about his suffering that would begin now, and the burial to which he had already been christened.

For you . . . This word was a mystery. The kingdom was now given to them—this they understood. But if he should suffer, surely it wasn't for their sake? Was it not because of the high priests and the scribes that his trials should come? But they had believed, they had accepted him, they had faithfully kept to his side in all trials and tribulations.

In memory . . . Here their thoughts could no longer follow him. When would his memory be celebrated? Would they not be able to follow him and share in his glory now?

They took the bread from his hands. They ate. They were silent. They understood none of this. Yet they still knew that they were his, partakers of all the divinity that he carried with him, and coheirs of all that would now come to completion.

The meal came to its conclusion. The third Paschal cup was already filled. He took the cup with the red wine and thanked his father again. Then he blessed it. Now they all looked at him intently.

Yes, this too was something new. This cup was the New Testament in his blood that was shed for many for the forgiveness of sins. This too should be done in remembrance as often as they drank of this cup.

They drank. The cup went from one to the other, and at the same time his words brought to mind a stream of pictures. They were pictures of the Old Testament that had been instituted at the foot of Mount Sinai, when Moses held the book of the covenant in his hand and sprinkled the people with the blood of the sacrifice. There was the picture of the New Testament that God promised to institute in coming days. Was this the hour that now had come? Would this blessed night be again a night of salvation when God would let his greatest promise be fulfilled? Would this cup of blessing always be emptied in remembrance of something that was greater than the rescue from Egypt? Would God gather his people again, the people he had called for himself, and bring them into a new future of glory and joy?

They drank. From mouth to mouth, the cup passed with the red wine that was the New Testament in his blood.

His blood? Shed for many?

Again, they reached the limits of understanding. Finally, they saw only darkness and riddles before them. Should the Messiah shed his blood? For the people? For the great masses? For the forgiveness of sins?

The cup stood empty before him on the table. They dipped bread again and cleaned their plates. They had eaten the Passover lamb for the last time. And then the door opened to a new era. They were carried away by the powerful flood that God allowed to break forth from the wells of salvation. It had carried their fathers. It had carried them out of the house of slavery and given them drink in the desert. For more than a thousand years, it had filled this holy night with songs of praise and joy. It had carried them the whole time they journeyed with the Master. They had had the bridegroom among them. They had drunk from the cup of joy that belonged to the kingdom of God. Homeless and tired, burned by the sun and shivering in the rain, they always drank again their strength from this cup, which he allowed to overflow with the power of the kingdom of God. And now he had opened the door of the future, saying that this last Passover was the first. The end was the beginning, and that which no longer would happen would still happen continually anew and in a new form.

No one could dress it in words. There were visions and ideas. At the bottom lay the ineffable limits. It was he who spoke, he who offered, he who gave. They were silent and received it.

*

When Peter placed the cup back on the table, he saw that the Master still had something to say. He had been very serious all evening but also calm and firm, as if he had finally done what must inevitably be done. But a half-hidden joy had bled through the seriousness. It was something that was at one with the Paschal evening's victorious joy. But just now, he looked to be in pain. There was this hint of pain in the seriousness that Peter did not recognize.

The Master put his hand on the table and lifted it slightly. Then he let it fall heavily enough that they all looked up.

"Behold," he said. "He who betrays me, his hand is with me here at the table."

They looked at him in despair.

"Yes," he said. "It is so. One of you shall betray me. The Son of Man goes just as it has been determined for him, but woe to the man through whom he is betrayed."

They bent down. They looked at him furtively—and even more furtively at each other. Then one of them asked with a voice fearful of the answer, "Lord . . . is it I?"

The others looked up. It was the same question that burned in every one of them. It was inconceivable that someone would be able to betray him. And yet it was so because he had said it. It was an evil mystery, so scary in its unfathomableness that they all crouched so as to not be hit by the blow. Their voices were indignant and yet as helpless as a child's.

Peter nodded to he who was closest to the Master and asked him who it was. He whispered to the Master and received an answer that Peter could not comprehend. Then the Master took one of the last pieces of bread, formed it into a scoop, and dipped it in the fat. But he did not bring it to his own mouth. He offered it to someone else as a host would do for a guest he wanted to honor. Peter followed his hand in wonder. He wanted to see who the Master thought to distinguish with his gift.

It was Judas Iscariot. Peter felt a little disappointed when the Master offered his hand out to Judas and looked at him with a look filled with all his benevolence. Strangely enough, Judas seemed to hesitate. He did not look up. It was as if he did not want to receive the gift. So he lifted his eyes hastily, only looking at the Master once, with a glance of uncertainty. He took the bread, thanked him, and stuffed it in his mouth. Was he surprised at the honor? His face had been strangely tight. He tried too hard to be at ease. Did he not want to show the others how flattered he felt?

Then Peter understood. It was as if a dead man's hand had laid upon his neck and slapped his back. His loathing and horror could not have been worse. He turned to see Judas's petrified face, his jaws ground as if he was chewing grass, while a single little uneasy wink pulled the expressionless eyes together. Then he looked at the Master. His glance rested completely on Judas. The good, open, inviting expression was succeeded by a calm and firm authority that did not appeal but commanded.

"Do quickly what you do," he said.

Judas turned around but did not lift his eyes. He swallowed, sat up, put shoes on his feet, and went out the door with strange ungainly steps that seemed quiet but had an unnatural echo in the hall.

The door seemed to open itself. Outside, the night was deep. Without looking, Judas stepped out and was instantaneously engulfed by the darkness.

None of the others looked up. They were not bothered by what had happened. The Master had given his command so firmly and naturally that it seemed to concern a long agreed upon matter. He could have told him to buy what they needed for the festival or to give some gift to the poor.

One thing was clear: it was he who had told Judas to go. If Judas went out into the night on his own evil errand, then it was all part of the very same event that was now to be fulfilled.

Now the Powers of Darkness Prevail

The whitewashed roof looked like a field of snow in front of them as they stepped out. They could see the limestone walls around them in the moonlight. The mountains behind the city walls seemed to bathe in the bluish glow. But the alleys looked like black jagged cracks between the white roofs. To the north, the heavy towers of two fortresses rose up out of a maze of walls and battlements. They too looked white against the mountain and sky, but their openings looked like empty black eyeholes, suspiciously watching to see who moved about in the alleys of the town below.

Where was Judas?

Peter felt the anguish rise up and grab him by the throat. He suppressed it again. They were just ready to leave.

"Simon."

The Master went over by the edge of the wall and looked out over the city. A weak echo of joyous voices was heard off in the distance, and the tired steps of the changing of the guard could be heard from the path outside the wall. The Master spoke softly without removing his eyes from the temple and the Mount of Olives.

"Simon, Satan has asked to have you given into his power so that he can sift you like wheat. But I have prayed for you that your faith should not be for nothing."

The Master must have noticed his amazement and look of despair. He turned his head and nodded to confirm.

"And when you have repented, strengthen your brothers," he said.

Peter almost felt nauseous at how perfectly his comprehension failed him. That they were going to be tested greatly, he understood that. But the Master didn't count on him? Did he not trust in his faithfulness? Did he not even believe he had repented? Peter looked again at the heavy fortress towers that brooded over their closed world of barracks and prison cells.

"Lord," he said with haste, "I am prepared to both die and go to prison with you."

The Master looked at him again. Perhaps Peter had dared to read a hint of approval in his glance, but there was something else there. The Master contemplated something sad and distressing that seemed to have accounted for everything that Peter now promised him.

"Peter," he said, "I tell you that before the rooster crows, you will deny me three times."

Now Peter didn't know what he should say. This went against everything he found to be reasonable or fair. When the Master stepped before the stairs and the others followed him, he stood for a moment and tried to gather himself together. Had he aggrieved the Master? Had he been negligent in his service? Had he not proven himself without using words that were too grandiose?

The courtyard echoed with a rattle when the gate beam was removed. Deep in thought, he went down and followed the others. John looked at him questioningly in the gateway. Had he heard what the Master said?

Peter tried to think. What was it like to die? If he was whipped with rods first? What was it like to sit in prison? If one was chained to a stone wall in an ice-cold cellar?

No, even then, he would take himself on. He had decided once and for all. He had followed his Lord, gone where he was sent, heard his words long enough to have understood them. He had been faithful to him in all his trials. He would do that in the future too, whatever happened.

Silently, they walked through the blue shadows of the alley and down the endless steps in the street that headed off to the east. Finally, the Master spoke to them. He asked them what it had been like when he had sent them out with no money, no bag, and no shoes. Had they lacked anything? They all answered with a confident and grateful no. They had lived like birds under the heavens that fall. They possessed nothing, and they lacked nothing.

"But now," the Master said, "now he who has a purse must take it with him, and the same if he has a bag. And he who doesn't have a sword ought to sell his coat and buy one. For I say to you that now the word must be fulfilled in me, that he must be numbered among the evildoers. Yes, all that which is written of me, that will now be fulfilled."

They looked at each other, puzzled. Some of them fumbled with their coats and dug in their folds. Half-afraid to betray their secret, they said, "Lord, see here: we have two swords."

He did not look at them.

"It is enough," he said and walked on. Puzzled, they followed him. But Peter pressed on to catch up with the one who had shown his sword.

"Give it to me," he said.

The other had no difficulty in doing so. He didn't seem to know what he should use it for himself.

They reached the Water Gate and came out on the hillside of the Kidron Valley. The moon was shining again. It was tremendously clear. The whole valley looked like hammered silver. On the other side, the beautiful Silwan necropolis was carved into the rock, with blue shadows in its Greek moldings. All over the hill, common, simple gravestones lay bare and disorderly like scattered sheep that had fallen asleep randomly in the wilderness.

When they had gone a ways from the wall, the Master stopped and waited until they were all gathered on the hillside. Then he began to speak again about what was going to happen tonight. Once again, his words were clear and unambiguous and yet incomprehensible. On this night, they would all take offense at him and fall away because of him. It would happen as it was written: "I shall strike the shepherd, and the sheep shall scatter."

This time Peter did not allow himself to be dumbfounded by his thoughts. He had thought the matter through. He knew what he was saying when he looked the Master in the eye and swore that all others could fall away, but he would not. The others were eager and joined in. But he turned them away with the same dreadful words he had said before. It was only because he said them with no anger and without disregard—but with only a great, fateful, and heavy certainty in his voice—that they stood in such helpless bewilderment. They quietly followed him with sorrowful steps.

A tiny brook of dark water trickled between the stones at the bottom of the valley. They crossed the basin on the flat stones and followed the path north to the slopes on the other side. The immense temple walls were already in the shadows, but the farther they went, the more the walls seemed to climb up into the heavens and throw their crown against the pale stars. The moonlight mottled the ground with the shadows of olive trees growing alongside the road. The night was cold, and it seemed as if all of nature shivered in the darkness when the moon hid behind a cloud.

But where was Judas?

Peter kept a firm grip on the sword he was hiding under his coat. He didn't want it to shine in the moonlight and betray him. His thoughts worked the Master's words over laboriously. Who would strike the Lord? Who would scatter the sheep? Who would number him among the evildoers? How would Satan be able to sift them?

It was obvious that whatever happened here would put their faith to the extreme test. The evil powers prepared themselves well for the great onslaught against God's Messiah. But God could not hand over his Anointed. He must allow him victory. Otherwise, God would no longer be God. In some manner, God must sit in judgment over his enemies. But how would it then go for the unrepentant people?

Peter could not escape the thought of the sacrificial lamb that he slaughtered up there on the other side of the wall today. God's patience was still exacerbated. But if the men now took it so far as to lift their hands against God's own Son, then God must intervene and destroy their power. It was the Passover. It was the night when the Lord's punishing hand had afflicted the evil Egyptians. Did fortune now visit his adversaries in this rebellious house?

He tried to find comfort in the thought of victory. But it was an empty comfort. First and foremost, he mourned for his people, and then it was this nauseating mystery that the Master spoke about the whole time, saying that he would suffer and that they should fail. And it would all happen on this night . . .

Where was Judas?

*

The high garden walls followed the road as it meandered up the hill. Every crook and every stone slab was becoming familiar to them, they had come here so often. They understood where the Master was leading them. When they drew near the gate, Peter ran forward and pushed it open. The limestone entryway was white in the moonlight, but they stepped into the shadows of the olive trees. They shut the gate again, and the Master asked them to stay there while he went and prayed.

Peter was thrilled when he saw the Master wink at him. He gave the sign to James and John also. Then he led them deeper into the olive trees. They followed in silence. They thought about the time they went into Jairus's house together and of that day when they climbed the mountain. They understood that his hour was near. Now, they thought, he would reveal his glory.

The Master turned and stood there before them in the moonlight. They stopped, petrified. His face had changed. It was marked by an agony and grief, a torment beyond description. It forced him into an almost audible cry of anguish.

He looked up at them with his tormented eyes and said that his soul tasted extreme tribulation, even unto death. So they should stay here and keep vigil.

Then he left them and went a little farther away, about a stone's throw. There, he fell on the ground. It was as if he broke under the weight of an overpowering burden that cracked his back and pushed him to the floor.

They stared at him helplessly. No one dared to look at the other. Tight dense clouds had settled in front of the moon, and everything was swept in darkness. Peter heard the Master pray, and he himself lifted his hands in prayer. But he found no words. He didn't understand anything. What was this that wallowed over the Master? Was it fear? Inconceivable! The Master feared nothing. He remained completely calm among the furious men in Nazareth, when they could have cut him to pieces. It was inconceivable for him to be scared.

But what was this? It was like a dark power, an unreasonable, crushing burden of something evil that seemed to bury him under its dark mass. What was it?

He heard the Master praying again. It was always the same: "Abba, Father, if it is possible, then take this cup from me. Nevertheless, not my will, but your will."

Peter sat down. He was not able to pray. He was dead tired, weighed by his own inability and all the unsolvable riddles of this eerie night. He laid himself against the olive tree's gnarly trunk and pulled his coat about his cold body. He laid the sword next to him.

The Master prayed.

What was this cup he talked about? Was it not his right as the Messiah to empty the cup of salvation and let it overflow for others? What was it that his Father wanted him to do?

Peter was very tired. The clouds had thickened. It was almost dark around him. He looked at the silhouette of the city on the other side. There was the temple, and there were the fortress towers. The enemy was there . . . and he was very, very tired.

He woke from his slumber when the Master touched his shoulders. The night was deep around him. The Master's face was unnaturally pale, but his eyes were filled with the dark anguish.

"Simon, are you sleeping? Are you not able to stay awake a short while with me?"

Shame welled up within him. He had nothing to say. The others slept too. The Master only said that they should wake and pray to withstand the great test. The spirit was willing, but the flesh was weak.

Again, he left them to go to the same place and pray. Peter stretched his shivering and stiff body. Then he knelt between the stones to pray. He stammered awkwardly. Once again, he found that he had no words. He was only a tired and aching body, and a poor helpless mind that stood, still unable to comprehend what was happening.

Then he sat again. A glimpse of moonlight glided past. He saw the Master lift his face. Heavy drops of blood poured like sweat from his forehead. His eyes were full of torment beyond all comprehension. Again, Peter heard him pray, "If this cannot be taken from me . . . if I must drink it . . . your will be done."

Peter thought about the two times he had seen convicted criminals tormented to death. It had not been nearly as horrific as this. It had only affected the body. But there was something here that touched the Master's soul. It was as if he must receive something in his spirit that meant unfathomable pain for the whole of his being.

Peter felt a helplessness numb his entire body. He understood nothing. He could do nothing. His head was empty, and his eyelids were as heavy as lead. He laid his arms crosswise over his knees and leaned his aching forehead forward . . .

Again, he jostled himself awake and lifted his forehead from his arms. He could make out the Master in the darkness again, alone and with unfathomable abandonment in his eyes. Peter looked at him timidly, with a feeling of guilt. He didn't know what to say. He did not want to make excuses. He had nothing to suggest. His mind stood still, his strength was finished. He was just infinitely helpless and infinitely upset.

Once again, he heard the Master's voice over there. Again, the tiredness snuck up on him. Again and again, he lifted his head and tried to shake himself from this degrading sleep that crept up on him from behind, putting its heavy hand upon his back. And then he was asleep again . . .

When the Master stood there a third time, his face had changed. It was marked by a torment that permeated every fiber of his being, but it was the face of a king, filled by the confident authority of one who had the right to rule.

He watched them as they shamefully tumbled out of their sleep. There was no bitterness in his voice. It sounded like he thought everything was in order when he said, "Yes, you have slept and taken your rest. It is enough. The hour has come. Now the Son of Man shall be given over into the hands of sinners."

He looked through the trees as if he was expecting something.

"Let us go," he said. "See, here comes the one who betrays me."

*

The smoke billowed around red flares, lamps swung, and candlelight flickered on the walls as it played between the branches of the olive trees. A stream of dark figures flowed through the gate; quick steps spread to the left and the right. Then the other eight came running, all agitated and confused. Breathless, they stayed behind the Master, who calmly walked through the trees.

Someone pointed and screamed. A bent-over figure ran toward the Master, lifted his face to his, and kissed him hastily.

"Judas, do you betray the Son of Man with a kiss?"

The Master's voice caused Judas to bow again. He looked on anxiously. Those who had come with Judas had stopped as if they were forming up. The Master went to meet them. His voice sounded clear and authoritative again:

"Who do you seek?"

They answered, "Jesus of Nazareth." And he walked into their midst. His voice was so calm, it was almost scary.

"I am he."

They slipped, tumbled backward, and fell to the ground. He stood in the midst of the crowd and asked them again who they sought.

"I have told you that it is me. If it is me you seek, then let the others go."

Peter rushed forward. When he had seen them slip, as if swept away by an invisible hand, his first thought had been that the Master would walk right on through them as he had done in Nazareth. But the Master stood there, completely still. The others gathered themselves around him. More and more came in behind them. The dent of a helmet was seen here, there the stripe on a shield.

Now the eight came closer. Peter was still dazed and saw everything as if it was a dream. A tall man with a club in his hand shouted at the others to not be afraid. Then he drew closer, and as if on a leash, the others followed him with their heads bowed and their hands gripping sticks and swords firmly. He lifted his coarse fist to strike God's Messiah.

Peter waited a minute. Nothing happened. The Master stood there, tall and calm. Then he staggered. Dark hands fell upon his shoulders and grabbed hold of his clothes. They abused the Son of God.

Peter rushed forward. If no one was going to do anything, then he would have to intervene. Right has to remain right. He could not stand by as God's holiness was trampled underfoot. He swung his sword in a sweeping arch at the closest person there and felt it bite. Someone screamed wildly, and a dark river of blood streaked across his face shining pale in the moonlight. In the extreme confusion, the others turned around, throwing each other to the side. The Master stood there, free again. He lifted his hand with a short commanding gesture and asked Peter to put the sword away. Did he not understand that more than twelve legions of angels would come to help if only God's Messiah requested it? But then how would the scriptures be fulfilled? Would he not drink the cup that he had received from the Father?

Then the Master took a step forward, stretched out his hand to the one Peter had cut. The hand touched the dark streak and it went away.

Amazed and helpless, Peter saw the others regroup. He saw scribes and priests in the crowd, and there were Roman soldiers too, marching in step. The whole garden was full of trampling, cursing, and orders. Only the Master's voice sounded calm and penetrating:

"As if for a robber, you come with clubs and swords. And yet day after day, I sat among you in the temple, instructing, and you did not seize me. But this is your hour, and now the powers of darkness prevail."

Peter saw the soldiers move forward like a living wall, a dark wave of heavy armor that rattled as it swept over the ground and engulfed it. The next moment, he saw a quick shadow off to the side and behind him. He noticed that all the others had given him up. He let the sword fall to the ground and ran recklessly in the only direction that was still clear. He ducked under the branches. He swung down the terraces. He slipped down to the ground and got up again. Then he stood against the wall. He heaved himself up on it violently, swung himself over, and landed on the other side.

His heart was pounding as he listened. He didn't hear anyone coming for him. He saw no trace of the others. Off in the distance, he could hear orders being shouted, heavy steps scraping against the stone pavement. He could see billowing torch smoke rise up over the wall, colored by the firelight. They marched off.

When he came out on the road, he saw the light sway and swing on the other side of the valley. Like a slithering snake, it drew itself through the city gates. He followed cautiously after.

He would not think about what had happened. He still couldn't comprehend anything. He thought that it was the Master who went into the midst of the huge crowd at the very front. He had let himself be captured. Now the powers of darkness prevail, and he had let them prevail.

But Peter had to at least see where they took him. He did not want to fail, even if he had no idea what he should do. The torches illuminated the huge stone blocks in the wall, and the whole crowd was swallowed by the black gate. Peter increased his pace and successfully made it past the guards. He listened to the sound of marching. He half-ran in the darkness, he looked around the corners and bends in the alley and saw the lamp light flood over the stone pavement again. Then he slowed his pace and followed from a long distance.

The Master continued to the high priest's house. The soldiers separated themselves from the escort and marched farther up the street. They didn't have the Master with them. He had disappeared with the others through the wide black gate.

Peter drew closer. He tried to walk casually and carelessly, to look like someone out for a walk in the night. People came out into the alley. Lords of the council hurried into the high priest's house with long strides and wide coats sweeping over the pavement. Butlers came half-running up to the city with urgent bids. There was something unusual in the making, and there was something hostile in everything that happened in this house where the opposition gathered.

Peter observed the bare wall. It was built of smoothly carved stone block, the gate was flanked by pillars, and the lintel was richly sculptured. Otherwise, it was without windows or protrusion, dismissive and hostile. What hid itself behind there, Peter did not know. It was the enemy's headquarters, from which all his evil power proceeded. Once a man was consumed by the gate over there, he was helplessly within the enemy's power.

Peter caught a glimpse of someone at the gate, looking around. To his overabundant joy, Peter saw that it was one of the disciples, he who was at home here and also known to the high priest's home. He motioned to Peter to come in and then disappeared again in the darkness of the gate.

Peter hesitated a minute. The gate threatened but stood open and black before him. To go in there was to risk everything. It was like stepping down into a lion's den. But he remembered his vow of loyalty and took courage.

He tried to walk as firm and natural as possible as he entered the darkness. He thought he saw someone sitting by the wall, crouched over and looking at him suspiciously. He hurried through the gateway. Then a woman's voice called out after him:

"You . . . do you belong to his disciples also?"

He turned around as quick as lightening and answered, "No, I do not."

Then he removed himself to the courtyard. He found himself in the midst of a tangle of columns, stairs, and high walls with windows on many levels. So as not to look strange, he walked straight ahead, disappearing into the darkness under the colonnade, and then he came out into a grand courtyard. It was swarming with people. There were the high priest's servants, the judicial servants, and all the service people in this immense house. In the midst of the courtyard, there was a glowing fire where they sat and warmed themselves. Peter went in amongst them and tried to make himself as invisible as possible.

But where had they taken the Master?

He didn't dare ask. From the conversations of the others, he successfully gathered that there would be a trial already tonight. The lords of the council had just come together.

He stayed there a moment, and then he felt someone looking at him again. He looked up, alarmed to see the same set of sharp feminine eyes. Now she pointed at him and said, "He was also with them."

He defended himself as fast as he could:

"I know not what you mean. I do not know him."

The woman went away again. The others looked at him suspiciously. He pretended to look at something familiar off in the distance and pulled himself back into the darkness of the colonnade. From there, he came out into the outer courtyard. Now he saw that it was here that the grand staircase went up to the second floor. Armed soldiers from the temple guard stood there. Was the trial going on up there?

He had just begun to wonder if he should ask someone when he ran into someone. It was like being struck with a whip.

"But that man there belongs to them too!"

He turned around and saw a whole cluster standing there watching him. A woman gestured earnestly and squeezed her protesting fingertips together. The men came closer. Their voices were derisive:

"I saw you with them myself!"

"This man belongs to them!"

Peter felt the ground give way under his feet. Behind him were the stairs; before him, he saw the enemies circle close about him like a forceps. Now it was a matter of life or death. He lifted his hands to make an oath and kept swearing that he did not know the man.

Then a rooster crowed on the roof. It was the first crowing. Hoarse and piercing, it announced that sun and light followed this night too.

Peter was startled and turned around. Something compelled him to look up.

The Master stood there, tied from behind and between two guards. He turned around and looked at Peter. He gave a single long look, filled not with reproach, not with bitterness or harm, not with the triumph of I-told-you-so, but with ceaseless care and infinite mercy.

Peter threw his hands up in his face. He did not stand. He went straight out, and they let him go. No one seemed to think of grabbing him or stopping him.

When he got to the gate, he began to weep huge tears. He pushed on. He came out onto the street. He didn't know where to go. He sobbed the whole time with abandonment, helplessly, like a child.

Deserving Death

The high priest began to lose his patience.

From their place over by the door, the scribes could see how his round face reddened. His lips swelled ominously. There could be an outbreak at any time.

The clerk bit his stylus and looked at the others. They sat in the hall forming a wide half circle, shoulder to shoulder, quiet and upright. It was almost surreal in the lamplight. There were sleepy and bored faces with eyes half-shut and lower lips protruding sulkily. There were alert spying eyes that moved delicately and reflected every little shift in the hearing. The high priest himself was like a thundercloud. He had had uninterrupted failure with his witnesses even though he had interrogated them in advance and impressed upon them what was important to highlight. He had put the right words in their mouths. They had cheated all the way. They were coarse men, stablemen, and boozehounds that comprehended nothing. They all got mixed up on the decisive points. They betrayed an appalling ignorance of anything that had to do with the ways of God. The council could not convict anyone with such witnesses. They could only embarrass themselves.

It was strange that the prisoner was silent.

The scribes looked at him again where he stood in the midst of the half circle. He was bound tight with course rope. His arms were twisted together in the back, and the rope wrapped around his torso a couple times. One of the temple guards stood behind him holding the end of the rope. It was just as if he had been an animal tied up to be taken to the slaughter. But in the midst of this humiliation, he stood straight and looked calmly before him. He rested his gaze on the judges, though he lifted it a bit higher and seemed to gaze off into the distance. He looked like one who had suffered much, but he was not bitter. He looked at Caiaphas without hate and without fear. Had he not been bound, one would have wondered if he really was the one being accused.

The scribes began to have the nasty feeling that there was something superior about this prisoner. Why didn't he answer? It would be the easiest thing in the world to refute these poorly trumped-up charges. Did he think that he would never be condemned by such prattle? Then he did not know Caiaphas.

Two new witnesses stepped forward. At least they had heard what the prisoner said themselves. This Jesus had said that he would tear down the temple and build it up again in three days. But unfortunately, the testimony was not consistent, and it was not clear if he really said that he would lay hold of the temple. Still, it was the testimony with the most weight so far, and the Pharisees listened attentively. The clerk bit his stylus again. Now it was getting serious. Who could tear down the temple and build it anew but the Messiah?

The prisoner was quiet and looked at the high priest, who seemed to avoid his gaze. Instead, he looked around very authoritatively, and perhaps a little perplexed. If it was just the old sleepy Sadducees he had here, he might have dared to go up and ask if the testimonies had been enough. They would have just bowed and agreed. But with the Pharisees, it wasn't enough. They were clever men and implacable critics, and they would never have let him maintain authority after such a poor interrogation.

When Caiaphas noticed the uneasiness in the hall, he rose up, somber with resentment. He stretched his stocky frame and took a few impatient steps toward the prisoner. Then he looked up into his face, furrowed his eyebrows together, and asked with all his authority as high priest, "Do you answer nothing? What about what these men have said against you?"

But the prisoner was silent. He looked at Caiaphas with a look that was benevolent and yet frightening. When Caiaphas met it, he blinked a couple times, but he successfully endured it. His face was very hard, and his voice became sinister.

"By the living God, I command you to tell us if you are the Messiah, God's Son."

A quick breath went through the hall. The sleepy faces woke up; all eyes stared at the prisoner. The scribes would think, This is not lawful. No one can force a witness to testify against himself. Then the prisoner answered, "I am."

He looked at them all and added with an authority that seemed to spring up from bottomless depths, in eerie contrast to Caiaphas's rehearsed dignity.

"You will see the Son of Man sitting at the right hand of the Almighty and coming on the clouds of heaven."

There was a shiver of uncontrolled joy that washed over Caiaphas's face. Then he got a hold of himself, grabbed his coat collar, and ripped the soft fabric so that the sharp rustling tore through the silence.

With an easy tremor in his voice he said, "He has blasphemed . . . Do we need any more witnesses? You heard him blaspheme. What more do we need?"

The clerk worked desperately with the stylus in the wax to catch up. His whole body shook as he wrote down the tremendous words: ". . . sitting at the right hand of the Almighty and coming on the clouds of heaven." He knew how it would go. Had the Master just said that he was the Messiah, the matter would have been uncertain. But that he said that he was the judge of the whole world, the Lord who would come in the clouds—this was inexcusable. Provided it wasn't the truth!

A moment cut the terrible thought from him. He wrote and wrote, as fast as he could. He tried to record what was said, while new words flowed over him. He heard them spoken seriously, heatedly, questioningly, and maliciously, but all the same: "Deserving of death."

So fell the judgment. Unanimous.

He wrote it down. Then he exhaled and looked up. Everyone had risen; the whole hall was full of murmurs and shouts. They had gone over to the prisoner. Someone spit on him, and another grabbed his coat, threw it over his head, and then hit him hard on the ear and said, "Prophet, Messiah, who was it that hit you?"

They laughed loudly, and someone hit him with his fist in the face. The prisoner stood just as straight and just as quietly as during the whole trial.

The clerk turned away with disgust. Again, the dangerous thought crossed like a shiver through his body. What was it that happened here? Who was he? Who was it they treated like this? No, the thought was inconceivable. He pushed it away, gathered together the wax tablets, and left to correct his notes.

King of the Jews

Out on the street, there was a hot and sticky vapor that clung to them. The sun had just come up, but it had already burned through the heavy haze. An almost imperceptible breeze came in from the southeast; it was obvious that the day would be oppressively hot.

Despite the heavy air, they hurried up the ascent to the judgment hall. All had gone well up to now. They had held the council meeting as soon as it was day and finished it in less than half an hour. Thus there had been two trials and in the day. They could be pleased.

Now was the time to act, before the whole city got its legs. The high priest dried the pearls of sweat from his forehead and strove valiantly up the long ascent, gasping for air, while they went over the matter one more time. It was important that the procurator ratified the judgment. It would be best if one could shift the entire responsibility upon him. This meant framing the political side of the matter in language that Pilate understood. Above all, it had to be about the tax. If the Nazarene was the Messiah, it was obvious that this would threaten the Romans in their most sensitive point.

In short-breathed sentences, the scribes discussed the issue while they tried to keep up with the temple guard. Shouldn't one such as this be stoned by the whole congregation of Israel? Was it not written, "Take the blasphemer out before the camp . . ."?

Yes, but wasn't there something more important? Ought he not die on the cross? Was it not written, "One cursed by God is he who hung on the tree?" Ought not the people be able to see just this: that God had judged him and let him die the death of a cursed man?

They were stopped by the guard and had to wait. They looked around anxiously. Luckily, there was no crowd of people, and soon, the servants they had summoned would be there with them.

They had to wait again in the courtyard. The watch sat to the right under the archway, playing dice on the boards they carved into the stone pavement. A lone soldier went and swept the courtyard with a palm leaf. It was oppressively hot. The priest and his men stood there in the sun, and the hazy air felt like the touch of a feverish hand. They adjusted their coats and shook their sweaty clothes. It was insufferable standing here, but they still wouldn't go into the shade of the colonnade. That shade belonged to Pilate's home, and they would not desecrate themselves.

Pilate came out. The white toga with purple edges was elegantly draped over his shoulders. His movements were calculated and authoritative. He carried his strong chin high, and his eyes were set deep behind his eyebrows. But his complexion was sickly pale and a little too slack, and his bare arm was too fat to be manly. He gave them the sign to speak, and their earnest voices succeeded each other. In short and clear points, they were all thrown forward, until they laid before the procurator, a pile of accusations that seemed to tower above him: he was a rabble-rouser, a revolutionary leader, a self-made king, a tax protester, and an enemy of Caesar.

That was enough. Pilate made a decisive hand gesture that stopped their storm of words. He looked at the prisoner and asked, "Are you the king of the Jews?"

"Yes, I am," the prisoner answered.

Pilate's eyes widened. He gave the accused a long tentative look. The council members heckled with more accusations. If half of them were true, the man was dead. But the prisoner didn't answer anything.

Pilate asked, with wonder in his voice, "Well? You answer nothing? Do you not hear how much they have to testify against you?"

But the prisoner didn't answer a word. He only stood there and looked before him with an enigmatic face, the most secure and yet the most suffering human face that had ever sat before Pilate's judgment seat.

Pilate finally took his eyes off the prisoner. He looked absent and thoughtful. Then he turned around completely and went back into the palace without explanation.

*

"Bring the prisoner in!"

Pilate sank into his seat. It felt almost cold inside here when one came in from the glowing haze of sun outside. It was insufferable during these days when the desert wind came upon the land.

The door opened and the daylight fell in. The colors in the room livened up. The wall that appeared black was suddenly blood red. Small graceful cupids played with a border of yellow garlands, and the mosaic on the floor lit up in green and brown.

The door shut again, and the colors were extinguished. Pilate looked at the prisoner tentatively. He felt uneasy again. As deeply as he despised this people, he could not escape feeling something that resembled respect for this eerily imperturbable man who did not deny the accusations, did not defend himself, and yet appeared as if he were as high above these accusations they heaved upon him as the sky is above the earth. His face was neither hard nor blunt nor even defiant. Every muscle was characterized by an intense ability to be perceived strong and deep.

Pilate had felt sick about the matter from the very beginning. Certainly, insurgents were not normally brought before him. He would hunt them the best he could along all the winding valleys of this forsaken land. If this man had been driven up with the sun today, it was not because the matter was urgent for the emperor. Pilate knew all these foxes.

The prisoner met his testing look calmly. No, he didn't meet it—he answered it with something that was just as searching and trying, something that would have been intrusive and brazen if it was not so full of a natural dignity.

Pilate broke the silence and began the trial with the chief question. Was he king of the Jews?

Then something incredible happened that made Pilate grab hold of his chair. The prisoner answered with a counterquestion. This wretched Galilean—whose life hung upon a thin, thin thread—dared to interrogate he who sat here to judge him. The prisoner wanted to know if Pilate asked this because he himself wanted clarity or if he only asked because others had said so.

If the prisoner had not had this strange dignity in his own way, Pilate would have immediately had him carried out and made the process short. But because they were now alone, he could afford to continue the interrogation of this mysterious man, who seriously seemed to think that Pilate might personally be concerned with who he was. It was as if he stood here not to be condemned, but to teach Pilate something concerning the monstrous beliefs of the Jews.

"I am no Jew," he said irritably. "It is your countrymen who have given you over to me. What have you done?"

The prisoner was still looking at him searchingly.

"My kingdom is not of this world," he said.

Pilate stared at him. He spoke of his kingdom in the same matter-of-fact manner as Pilate spoke of his prefecture. He continued to speak about it: If his kingdom were like other kingdoms in this world, his servants would be fighting to the last so that he would not be given over to the Jews. But now his kingdom was not of this world.

"So, in any case, you are a king?" Pilate asked.

The prisoner again assented. He was a king, a king who came into this world to witness to the truth.

Pilate thought he suddenly saw the thing in crystal-clear light. The man was some sort of Jewish philosopher, one of those who thought the gods spoke to him. So he had come into conflict with the high priest and his party. And now they thought to use Pilate in order to have him eliminated!

The procurator felt a wave of delight swell within him. He had seen through them and asserted himself as judge. But in the next moment, he lost the secure feeling of superiority. The prisoner continued to speak with his strange authority. He said something to the effect that everyone who belonged to the truth and had a sense for the truth understood his witness and came to him.

Of course it was nonsense, yet it still cost Pilate a little effort to shake it off. There was something unsearchable and powerful in this man's being, something that demanded respect and that caused Pilate to dimly perceive the nearness of powers that he had always carefully avoided. Who had time to seek the truth!?

He shrugged his shoulders.

"Well . . . what is truth?"

He didn't expect an answer and neither did he receive one. He rang the silver bell with the dancing satyr, and the next minute, the henchman was there with the centurion behind him in the door.

"Carry the prisoner out," Pilate said.

*

The heavy copper doors squeaked on their hinges. The guard straightened up. The recorder and attendants jumped up from the marble bench, and the centurion let the watch march down to place themselves in a line before the stairs.

Pilate walked out with half-shut eyes and his strong chin lifted high so that the rolls of fat almost disappeared. He delivered the verdict. It read, "Not guilty."

The great silence that dominated the crowd was broken by a murmur of astonishment and resentment. Then the protests began. It was the cry of educated voices. Lawyers, speakers, and counselors were heard among the din and arguments. Pilate listened.

The cry grew in strength. It was incredible that a man such as this would be acquitted. He set the whole land on fire with his teaching. All people of Galilee had joined the movement and even here. For it was in Galilee that it had begun.

There was particular meaning with this talk of Galilee: that was the headquarters of the zealots and all disturbers of peace.

Pilate held out his plump white hand, and it was quiet.

"Is the man from Galilee?" he asked.

The answer came fiftyfold, bitterly and emphatically. Then Pilate squinted, and with the ceremonial voice of an official, with a triumphal undertone of mockery, he declared that the matter didn't fall under his jurisdiction. He would refer it to the proper authorities.

There was silence. Unsure and disappointed, they looked at each other. Pilate enjoyed a moment of triumph and drew back with dignity. The high priest counseled. There was nothing else to do but to send a deputation to Herod. But because the crowd of people was already great and there were constantly new people coming to demand a prisoner be set free for the Passover, the deputation would have to be small. It was best to stay here and see how the matter would develop.

*

Jesus . . .

Herod's eyes widened with joy and excitement when he heard the prisoner's name. The paths of fate could be strange. For more than a year, he had wished to see this notorious subject of his but never had occasion for it. And now here, in a strange house and foreign ground, he would see him—and sent by a Roman!

His eagerness to see Jesus was blended with a bit of fear. He felt a great relief when the prisoner was led in. The man, at least, was not the bitter type, like John, and there was also nothing of this prattle about the Baptist being raised again. But the more he observed the prisoner, the more his timidity returned. There was still a similarity. This prisoner even looked as if he was born to rule over his judges.

Herod began the hearing. He asked his usual questions. He had heard so much about this man and wanted to see him do one of his miracles. He had always wanted to see a miracle. He felt that if he could ever see a real remarkable miracle, one that could convince both him and the whole of his court, then perhaps he would take things seriously again, those things that had been so particularly important at the time when he had listened to the voice of the Baptist.

Herod didn't receive an answer to his first question. He asked again, but the prisoner was still silent. Herod felt insulted by his silence. It was as if he did not consider the king of his land worth an answer. There was no question whether or not Jesus heard and understood his questions. Neither was there any real doubt whether his silence was deliberate or unwavering. There was something prophetic and condemnatory in it, something that said, "Neither word nor deed will come to you from my God. You have already received your word, but you did not receive it."

Herod became ever hotter. He felt that he made a poor figure before the representatives of the great Jerusalem who stood there and accused the prisoner. Then he changed his tactic and began to mock Jesus and challenge his pride. But the prisoner's silence only became all the more penetrating.

It couldn't go on any longer like this. Herod nodded to one of his slaves and whispered something to him. Then he began to heckle Jesus, called him colleague and royal brother, and inquired about his treasury and his horsemen. The slaves brought in an old festive robe that had been modern a generation ago and laid it on the prisoner's shoulders to the jubilating chorus of the court. Herod asked him to wear it and behave royally, so as not to embarrass their high birth by walking around dressed like a carpenter.

The applause rattled. The court jesters joined in, and the poets cited the last comedy they had seen in Gadara. The little Greek from Antioch politely said that this was the best that life had to offer: to delight in the wit of educated people.

But the prisoner was silent.

*

They had done a good work.

During these hot midmorning hours, they had gone about in the crowd of people. They had spread out and regrouped. They had whispered and taken people confidentially under their arm. They had spoken flowingly and solemnly. They allowed men to gather in circles in order to reenter the masses and begin to whisper. They had asked the eager and young if it wasn't a wretched shame for all Jews that one of them would first speak as if one had power over heaven and earth and then give in without daring to lift a hand. No, it was different with Barabbas. He was a man who didn't just prattle about but could swing a sword. If someone deserved to be set free today, then it was Barabbas. Should they ask for Barabbas to be set free?

Yes, they should ask for Barabbas to be set free.

Then there was the rich fabric merchant from Alexandria, with the Greek cloths and the grand metropolitan, commercial smile. What about Jesus? Well, he should know that Jesus was a pious wind-bag of the type who prowled about all over the world, who spread their teachings instead of working and impressed simple people and most of all women so that they paid for him . . .

So the matter was explained in such a manner that he could understand. There was always something new to say and always some new viewpoint to share and spread about with whisperers in the waiting masses.

These lords were officers in the prince's court? Then they had of course heard of Jesus's shameful courting of the mob's favor. No? Yes, the poor should rule the earth, the quiet should be kings, all the poor people who died for nothing would be lifted upon purple couches. If one only kissed the saint's feet and anointed the great prophet's hair, then he would be in. Yes, neither was it a teaching for a man . . .

Yes, even the honorable goldsmiths were out in this terrible heat . . . yes, it was an old custom, and today it meant that Barabbas should be set free . . . Jesus? He was also a well-meaning man, unfortunately a victim of his own delusions of grandeur. And one could expect anything from his followers. They were blind in their admiration for him. It would be dangerous for them if he was set free again . . .

"For the sake of the poor? No, good people, do not believe that he takes up the cause of the poor. That is who he betrayed! Do any of you believe that anything can be made better for the poor because a man with a head full of muddled ideas runs around and says that you shall love your enemies and pray for Pilate and walk two miles with the centurion when he only forces you to walk for one? No, Barabbas had more guts. Don't you think we should ask for the release of Barabbas?"

Yes, they thought so.

Pilate looked out over the crowd that filled the immense courtyard. Carefully, he had called the priests and the scribes in order to keep them under his watch. He told them that Herod had also scrutinized the prisoner and sent him back. Neither had the tetrarch found any reason to take up the charges against him. Therefore, the most that could be considered was a disciplinary punishment. And then he would be set free.

Pilate raised his voice so that it would be heard in the farthest corners of the courtyard. He spoke ceremoniously, as if he led an assembly of the people.

"Is it your will that I shall set this man, who is called king of the Jews, free?"

A cry broke out from all corners at once.

"No! Not him! Release Barabbas! We want Barabbas!"

Pilate looked around, amazed. He had not expected such a united purpose in the crowd. The cry swept around him like a storm and caused him to feel uncertain.

"What then do you want me to do with the one who you call king?"

Again, the cry broke out against him, at first spattering from different corners of the courtyard and then in growing waves:

"Crucify him! To the cross with him!"

Pilate could not hide his amazement. His confusion was as obvious and it was just as dangerous as a breach in the city walls. The cry swept upward with double power at the exposure he showed with his astonishment. For the first time, his voice was uncertain:

"But what had he done that was so evil?"

"Evil?"

A weak echo answered: He has only done good. He has healed all and born all our distress as his own . . .

But the echo stopped within the hearts of those where it had awakened, and they were few. It was never explicitly said. It was drowned by a tidal wave of cries that threw its angry jetsam in Pilate's face.

"Away with him! Crucify him!"

Then Pilate gave in. He released Barabbas, the man who was thrown in prison for rioting and murder. But Jesus he delivered to be scourged.

*

The soldier cursed his misfortune. He always got the nasty orders when there was finally something real and fun happening in the barracks. He could hear the laughter of his comrades within the guard. They amused themselves with the king of the Jews. And here he would go alone to clean up after him.

Reluctantly, he picked the scourge up from the stone pavement, and threw it to the ground to shake off the blood and scraps of flesh. The broad leather belts slammed hard, and the pieces of lead that were tied into the straps rattled against the stone. He looked it over and found it acceptable. Then he put it back in its place under the stairs. He began to wash the pillars, where the prisoner had been bound, and finally he had the whole courtyard clear. He put the sponge on a cane and scrubbed again and again on the stone plates. It was remarkable how far it could splatter when someone cast the whip with the right rhythm.

Finally, he had mixed everything together and filled the bucket with a dirty slurry of gravel, water, blood, and scraps of skin. He poured it out into the gutter. Then he put the cleaning equipment back in the closet and wiped the sweat from his brow before hurrying over to the others in the guard.

There was an indescribable romp in there. They lay prostrate on the floor and haled the king of the Jews as they howled with laughter. They had draped him in an old officer's cloak, and had woven together a crown of thorny weeds. They put a reed in his hand as a scepter. He sat on the stone bench as if it were a throne, and this gave him a courtly image. Then they spat upon him and threw themselves at his feet and then spat on him again.

Oddly enough, he sat perfectly straight. The blood seeped through the coat on his shoulders and fell in heavy drops on the floor, but he had not lost consciousness. He had white patches of saliva and spit on his naked hands, on his forehead, and in his beard. His eyes were shut, his face was full of pain, but he still sat upright. He did not bow and did not turn away. If one had asked him to play king, he could not have done it better.

The laughter slowed down. The spectacular gibes began to be replaced with insults. There was something mocking about this Jewish king who remained so royal even under the crown of thorns. It was remarkable that they could not force this miserable worm to twist when one trampled upon him. They went up close and let the blows pummel his open face. They grabbed hold of staves and beat him again. They wanted to get him to at least swear or curse.

"Cease, soldiers."

It was the centurion. They jumped to attention from the benches and floor with a rattle and saluted. The cane fell to the floor. They stood around the Jewish king, who was still austere and upright.

"The prisoner is to go back to Pilate. Same guard as before. March . . ."

*

The heat was unbearable in the crowd. The sun had almost disappeared in the haze, but it did not mitigate the heat. It was as if all its heat melted into the heavy and sweltering air.

The little silversmith thought about going home. They had received their prisoner, and he could just as well hear about how it went for the Nazarene in the morning. That he was no messiah was obvious, because he had not been able to rise against the Romans.

He counted on his fingers. There had been not more than five days since the Nazarene had entered the city. The silversmith was almost ashamed. Even he had yelled hosanna when all the others did it. There was something exciting and full of expectation in the air that day. It had grabbed hold of both loiterers and noble people. But today, the same men stood here and yelled "crucify."

He had taken notice of them and wondered a little why they did it. He had a fourteen-year-old boy next to him, a half-grown scamp who had just received a fuzzy little shadow above his upper lip. What did he know about this Jesus? On the other side of him, he had a broad-cheeked and rough-armed woman down from Siloam, possibly a laundress or farmwoman. She stood and quarreled with a man who maintained that Jesus was a Pharisee, while the woman was sure that he was a disciple of John's.

Suddenly, there was silence. They stretched and peered up the stairs, where the doors opened again.

It was Pilate who came out. He walked quickly but stiffly, as if he was determined to show himself firm to the people. He stood, motioned with his hand and yelled, with a voice that was close to turning over, "Here, now, I am about to bring him out to you so that you can understand that I do not find him guilty."

The silversmith stood on his tiptoes and looked between two heads to glimpse first a soldier with black stubble and a contemptuously grim face, and then . . .

He stretched his ankles as far as they would go and held his breath. Feet shuffled around. People shoved, shuffled, and groaned in the heat while they strained to see. The scene was really something worthy of telling both his children and grandchildren.

They had whipped the Nazarene and dressed him like a king. They had crowned him with thorny branches, so that the blood ran down his forehead, and they had shrouded him in a purplish-red coat. He walked out slowly, with closed eyes. It seemed that every little movement caused him pain, because the heavy coat pressed against his back, which had been ripped open.

Now he stood there with his hands bound together, completely straight. He kept his eyes shut, and his head was bent back slightly. It was a tormented face—one of a man who had tasted everything awful and had been assailed with every affront and yet was still a living man who preserved all of his ability to feel, suffer, and love.

"Behold the man," Pilate said.

There followed a small moment of icy silence. It was as if the horror of the spectacle stopped every mouth. But then the Pharisees and scribes began to yell.

"Crucify him! Crucify him!"

Pilate swept his white hand out.

"You can do that yourself. I find no guilt within him."

Then the high priest screamed that he must die according to the law and custom because he had made himself to be the Son of God. Pilate seemed to crouch under their cry. He looked at the prisoner and then went into the palace. The Nazarene was led away again.

He was running away. Now the crowd raged and roared. They stomped and screamed, and the cries and wild threats fell upon the closed doors.

The minutes passed and the excitement rose. The silversmith looked at the boy next to him. His childlike head was full of wrinkles. His weak mouth was twisted, and the muscles of his throat made deep furrows in the soft skin. His eyes were wide with excitement. The laundress and the old man had joined their brown dirty hands and shook them in rage.

Now Pilate came out again. The yells slowed for a moment. He stopped at the door and pretended to be surprised that so many people remained.

Then the high priest's voice cut through the alarm full of threat:

"If you release him, you are no friend of Caesar!"

"He who makes himself a king, he has set himself up against Caesar!"

Pilate tossed his head. Then he turned around and spoke to the commander of the guard. Then he slowly went to the paved lot at Gabbatha. He sat in his judgment seat. He crossed his arms and looked disdainfully over the crowd. His face was that of a man of the world, but with half-shut eyes, one caught the glimpse of something helpless and uncertain.

The prisoner was brought out. Only then did the silversmith see that there was a great pool of blood in the place where he had just stood, and that his lingering steps left streaks of blood across the marble flooring.

Still, the man crowned with thorns stood there with his eyes shut and lifted his face. Again, it was as if an invisible hand laid itself upon the crying mouths and dampened the voices.

Then he opened his eyes for the first time. His gaze looked around, then swept over the crowd of people and met all the eyes that stared at him. When his eyes opened, his face regained life. It had rested in the agony. It had received its form from tortures and came to peace with its pain. Now everything broke forth again, all the atrocities livened up his face and presented it in all its vileness. And this was not the worst; the most incredible thing was that his gaze was not dark, not hateful, not sharpened by curses and revenge. In the midst of his unfathomable pain, he was good. He expressed compassion without limit for the people upon whom his gaze rested. It did not reflect hate, only mourning, a deep and pain-filled mourning that became a stinging rebuke, yet without accusation.

It was too much for the crowd. That this false prophet should now carry his head high—that he dared to stand here and play holy, to look reproachful, as if he considered himself too good to curse and revile, that he dared to pretend to be clean when he was punished—this was unbearable.

They screamed and railed. They swung their arms in the air. They stomped and jumped. Their cry was a rhythmic roaring that slammed itself against Pilate with the force of a battering ram.

"Crucify! Crucify! Crucify! Crucify!"

It was like a storm coming against the hated Roman. It was a sweeping wave that lifted everyone's fist in wild hand movements. It was an ecstasy that let the heart taste the gruesome sweetness far removed from the dull gray opportunities of everyday life.

Then Pilate gave in. Paler than anything, and with rings darker than usual under his eyes, he gave the order for the prisoner to be crucified. A wild cheer of jubilee followed him as he went back into the palace.

The crowd began to disperse. Only on the way home did the silversmith ask himself why he actually joined in with the screaming. And one of the scribes stroked his beard thoughtfully before gagging when he realized that he had also been among those who told Pilate that they did not want any lord but Caesar . . .

He Has Helped Others

He met them just outside the city gates. They filled the entire narrow street, so he pressed himself against the stone wall in order to let them pass. At first, it was a crowd of street kids, half-running as they whistled and looked over their shoulders. Then it was the adults, even rabbis and learned men. Then the soldiers came marching in lockstep.

It was only then that he saw the picket sign up front, written out in all the different alphabets of the world, and understood that someone was to be executed.

He licked his lips with a dry tongue. Simon of Cyrene was known for being a strong man, and in his African homeland, he had become accustomed to working even in the suffocating south wind. But today he had almost fainted in the field. His lips were numb and his tongue felt like a piece of wood in his mouth. His whole body was one burning desire for water.

The soldiers passed by, tanned with dry-patched coats and newly shined spears. Then there was a heavy thud as something hard broke and scraped against the stone. Some women screamed from a window, and the Roman officer issued commands in an unintelligible language. The soldiers stopped, the people pushed, and Simon forcefully elbowed his way forward to see.

It was the condemned man who had fallen prostrate. Up until now, he had been carrying the cross himself, and it was obvious that he lost consciousness and fell straight forward into the street. Or perhaps he was dead? One could see from the blood soaked clothes that they had scourged him hard. Many often died of this.

No, he lived . . . The officer allowed him to be picked up. He had bruised himself in the fall and bled from his chin and knees. There was already dry blood on his forehead from before. Simon looked at him with disgust but with a hint of commiseration too. The man did not look to have been a robber or of the rowdy sort.

Suddenly, Simon noticed that there was a Roman pointing at him. Then he had the two rough hands of a soldier upon his shoulders. They emphatically made it clear to him that he should pick up the cross and carry it. When he refused, they pushed him forward, laid the rough timber on his back, and prodded him in the side with the shaft of a spear to let him know he should move.

It burned him, but he knew refusal was futile. He saw one of the soldiers jostle the condemned man from behind, and then grimace as he wiped the blood from his hand. It was then that he gripped the timber firmly and thought, I will do it for your sake. In any case, you are a Jew like me.

He walked through the city gates again. His thirst tortured him, and his head throbbed. The timber was heavy. Its sharp edges chafed. Sweat ran down into his eyes when he glanced at the prisoner. It was inconceivable that a man with such a battered back had been able to carry the timber even one step.

As the street grew wider outside, the crowd also became larger. The great crowd filled the entire street behind them and streamed up to the side of the guards. Simon adjusted the cross gnawing into his shoulder and bit his lips together. He cursed these heartless morons who ran about with their cold prying eyes, jostling to have a look. Never before had he known that listless eyes could be so cruel.

There were also sympathetic people in the crowd. There were women who beat their breasts and cried. Their wailing was as shrill and piercing as that of a funeral. When they caught up to him, they turned and spoke to the condemned man. Simon caught a glimpse of the prisoner's face again. It was almost beautiful to watch him speak. He told the women that they should not cry for him but for themselves and their children. He spoke like a prophet about times of plague, when women who had never been mothers would be considered fortunate. He said it with a piercing seriousness. It seemed as if he himself suffered at least as much from knowing that this day would come as he suffered from his wounds.

Suddenly, they heard an unintelligible command in Latin, and the troops halted. The soldiers freed him from the cross and laid it on the condemned man. Simon wanted to stop them, but they pushed him away and pointed to the city walls. He could go packing.

He stretched his aching back and touched his tongue to his numb lips once again. He hesitated for a moment. Then he overcame himself and followed along in the train. He at least had to know what this strange prisoner who spoke like a prophet was all about.

There were many steps remaining. Only now when he was free again could he look around. They were right outside the walls, in the large corner between Herod's palace and the new wall to the north. The towers stood in jagged lines on both sides of them. The great road coming from the north and following along the wall was behind him, and in front of him there was a basin with a quarry, vegetable gardens, and occasional grave openings in the smoothly hewn rock.

The troop had halted on the flat golden stone slab that was called the place of the skull. It was obvious that this would be the place of execution today.

The soldiers formed a human chain and pushed the people away so they wouldn't be hindered in their work. Only now did Simon see that there were also two others to be executed. Apparently, no one was concerned about them. Everyone pushed into the place where the soldiers put the cross that Simon had just carried on his back.

Here amongst the crowd, he learned that he had carried the cross for the prophet from Nazareth. He forgot his thirst for a moment. He stood up front, only a few feet from where they knocked the condemned man down before they stripped him of his clothes. They offered him a ceramic cup with stupefying wine. That was the only mercy in all of this mercilessness. But when he tasted it, he refused to drink it. Then they stretched his arms out, and one of them swung the clumsy hammer with a practiced hand. At first, the blows fell softly, but reverberated harder and harder until the thick spike sat well within the log.

Simon saw how it tore at the condemned man's face as every muscle tightened to a hard knot under his skin. His lips moved, and when the man with the hammer moved over to the other side, Simon heard the condemned man praying to his Father. But Simon couldn't make out the words.

Simon began to suffer more from the spectacle than from thirst. It dragged on forever, until all four of the spikes were driven properly into place. Then the soldiers took the cross and slowly lifted it up so they could drop it into the hole in the mountain where it would stand. Simon turned away. He had heard one of the others scream in pain as the pole hit against the rock with full force and the weight of his body tore into the spike wounds. He wanted to strike out at those who stood there yelling and pushing each other aside so as not to miss a second of the excitement when the torture began in earnest. He heard the heavy thud of wood against stone from behind him and then a low moan. It would almost have been better if he had screamed like the others. These half-muffled moans between clenched teeth were worse than the wild screams of accusation.

The soldiers wedged the cross firmly into place with stone chips and began to play dice for the bloody clothes. Now there was free access to the place of execution, and the crowd rushed forward. Simon swallowed the feeling of nausea and drew closer. He looked up shyly at the crucified man. The holes in his hands had widened, and he bled profusely. There were swarms of flies in the wounds on his shoulders and knees, and the dust blown up by the hot wind stuck to the sweat of his naked body.

Now the haze was even denser. The sun was blood red through the veil of gray haze, but its power seemed to only grow. It was almost at its highest point now, and the whole space was a crucible filled with glowing molten metal.

People walked back and forth across the place of the skull. The great road went right by, and there were constant replacements for those who could no longer hold out in the heat. They went forward to the cross, shook their heads contemptuously, and reviled him as he hung there. It was always the same refrain in their insults: he said that he was the Son of God and the Messiah. Now he could to show it. Even noble priests and scribes went up to the stone slab and looked at him with sharp eyes. They too said the same thing: He was Israel's king. They would believe him, if he came down from the cross.

They looked at one another. They smiled unmistakenly and nodded as if they had attested for each other in a good proposition. They held their hands out to the people and pointed their thumbs at the crucified man, saying, "He has helped others, but he cannot help himself."

Simon felt nauseous again. He had helped others . . . Was it against the law in this land to help others and not yourself?

He thought he might go mad with thirst, but he overcame his misgivings and went forward to the soldiers who had a jar of lousy vinegar wine with them. He tossed them a couple coppers and pointed at the jar. They grinned scornfully and shook their heads. He dug in his girdle and offered his last as. Then they nodded and put the jar to his mouth. Not until they yelled at him did he put it down again. He wiped his hand across his mouth and felt the sting and the salty taste of dried sweat. Then he panted as he went down among the stone blocks and sat there in the cool. He couldn't look up anymore, but he positioned himself so that nothing would escape his notice when it came to the fate of the prophet from Nazareth who said he was God's Son.

*

It was as if his hands had been cut off and a hundred white hot tongs pulled at the bloody stumps. Every nerve and every sinew was a string of quivering pain that ran along the arms and branched out across the chest, so that the agony distributed itself a thousandfold and bored into every fiber of his body like needles.

While the quaking strings of pain wove memories, they tore into the exposed muscles and stretched the tendons to the breaking point. Everything was a single bloody tangle of wretched martyrdom. The fat publican whom they murdered on the slopes of Bethoron stared at him with a cracked skull. His father beat him in wild anger, and the whole of his back was as if it was on fire. Comrades grinned at him and tore money out of his hand, threatening to indict him.

He writhed in pain screaming. And as he writhed, the pain flowed like molten magma down through his arms, making the pain a hundred times more unpleasant.

There was a time when he believed in God and in his people. He had expected a day of liberation. He had taken part in ambushes and butchery. He had lost the taste for work and lived on the profits of raids. Then the desert became his fate. And now nothing remained but burning fire in every inch of his body.

He saw forms move in front of him through a red fog. He heard hissing voices spit scorn. They were like rasps mercilessly dragged over his tortured flesh.

He began to understand that this wasn't happening for his sake. He should let it go. They were not concerned with him. It was the other one, the unknown man. It was him they called the Son of God and scorned as the Messiah, a pitiful and abandoned messiah who could not climb down off the cross. He was seized with loathing and bitterness. These voices were chafing his irritated body all because this man over there had been a jerk and a fraud.

He heard the comrade farther away cry in pain. Wild blasphemous words passed over the man's lips. Even he cursed this impotent Messiah.

Then he forced a cry from his swollen throat. He felt it as if the lips tore away from his teeth where they had dried together and the skin peeled off from the inside. The voice was no longer his own. It cut hoarse and sharp through his parched throat, but it sufficed to give expression to his contempt for this miserable man they called Jesus.

The reviled man turned to him. He had heard the reproach and turned his head. He looked at the man who reviled him. It was one long look, a look that was full of agony, horrifying agony, but free from all fear and misery. It was a look that wanted to belong and share these curses, and was amazed by the reward of ungratefulness. The look was so different that he began to observe the man. He was obviously in boundless pain. They scorned him and spit upon him, but he never responded to it. Like dark shadows, they passed by in the red fog. Their eyes gleamed white. Their lips hissed. Their snakish heads swayed ever higher and higher, and their forked tongues played, and then they slashed. They slashed again and again. The poison ran blackish green over his body. Fangs cut red notches in his flesh, but the blood that ran out washed the poison away. It never penetrated his limbs. It showed in his gaze. It was clear, without a drop of poison . . .

No, now he was certainly raving. There were no snakes. There were only men in long white coats and soldiers in leather jackets. And yet it was true that the poison didn't penetrate the man. More and more, his gaze was filled with agony, but it was pure and unpoisoned, full of righteousness and goodwill.

It grew ever darker around his cross. He hovered in a burning dark-red cloud of anguish, where he was drawn down by lead weights and still held up, pierced through by white-hot iron. In the red darkness, he saw two figures by the other's cross. They did not curse. They sank down in the powerless night, and when the night became the red of day again, they still stood there. The man on the cross looked at them, and the woman looked at him with eyes that held a world of suffering and tenderness. Then a power went out from him on the cross. It was just a few words. But they were words with a peculiar power and authority that created and changed things. They were as soft as a mother's hand and as solid as the rock down on the ground. They carried away mountains of worry and concern. They embraced years and decades, and bent both the wills and futures of the two figures according to the goodwill that could be seen in these eyes of agony. It was just a few words, and then everything was arranged for the woman there. He understood she was the mother of the crucified man.

The red haze began to take on the color of dark congealed blood. With bitter shame, he thought about his own mother. He had not given her a thought today. He knew that he would soon be numb to the painful red fire. Still, he looked one more time at the man over there, the man who thought of his mother and who reigned from his cross and, in the midst of his powerlessness, let power go out to help others. Then clarity suddenly flamed up within him. He sensed, straight through the darkness and pain, that the other had power and that he could climb down from the cross if he wanted. It was only that he did not want to. He had helped others . . . But he did not help himself. This was his secret. He was God's Messiah, and for just that reason, he hung there and shared the burden of the curse with his brothers.

Again, the man way over cried from his cross. His voice was hateful and bitter.

"Are you the Messiah? Then help yourself! And help us!"

Then he was seized by a sorrowful indignation that was different from everything else he had felt in his life. In the red fog, he heard his own voice, strangely distant and strangely powerful:

"Do you not fear God, you who are under the same judgment? That we suffer is only right. We suffer what our deeds are worth. But he has done no evil."

He looked at him again, the one they insulted because he was God's Son, he who helped others but not himself. Would he dare? He did not deserve it. But because the Messiah's secret was this—that he helped his brothers—he still dared. And he, a man who hadn't prayed in many years, knew that it was a real prayer that now passed his parched lips:

"Jesus, remember me when you enter your kingdom."

He, the Messiah, who had the power to help, looked at him again. The agony in his eyes was momentarily weaker than the light in them. It was like an outstretched hand and light from a door that opened in the night.

"Amen," he said. "I tell you, today, you shall be with me in paradise."

The red fog floated before his eyes again, and the darkness came upon him. The red gloss narrowed into a little dancing ball of fire within a great black depth of pain and torment. Again, he was in pain, only pain, nothing but pain. His nerves were like trembling wires in a white-hot furnace of torment. But in the same smelting fire of pain, only a few feet from him, he knew that there stood another cross, a cross with a suffering Messiah. His own miserable misspent life was not forgotten by God.

*

Simon got up.

Half-numb from the heat, with the nauseous feeling of helplessness and repugnance, he sat, leaning against the rock in the quarry. Now he tumbled up and turned toward the place of the skull.

Jesus had cried a terrifying cry, filled with anguish and torment, that ripped through bone and marrow. It still echoed in his ears: "Eli, eli sabachthani." It was a verse from the psalms, the most desperate of all the words of scripture: "My God, my God, why have you forsaken me?"

Simon climbed up the rock. The heavy haze had congealed into black darkness. It was as threatening as the darkest thundercloud, and it brooded so close to them that it seemed to rest directly upon the hot ground. The sun had disappeared long ago. There was an oppressive anguish that laid itself upon all of nature. The leaves drooped limply on the trees, and the blood-red spring flowers between the stones bowed their heads as if they were ready to die.

He stood there again between the three crosses. The throng up there had thinned, and no one insulted the man anymore. Everything had softened and became subdued under the burden of the sweltering-hot haze. A man came with a sponge that he had put on a reed. It dripped with the sour wine he filled it with. He held it up to the crucified man, and said something about whether they should see if Elijah really came and took him down. Apparently, he had not understood the psalm verse.

Simon looked away from the cross. He could not bear it any longer. He had seen men die in this manner before, but he had never seen a face that had been so marked by such frightful anguish. So must the cursed look in the eternal fire of judgment. Or perhaps not even they could look like this? They were all evil. They must in some way be akin to that which they suffered. But this face did not belong with such anguish. There was something unnatural, something flagrantly unreasonable, in seeing this man suffer in this manner.

It was as if divinity itself was cursed, as if the holy was given over to Satan and the righteous suffered the payment for sin. It was as if someone who belonged indissolubly together with God had still been forsaken by God.

Simon couldn't do it any longer. His strong body shook. He felt feverish and forlorn. With heavy dragging steps, he went toward the city. The darkness billowed up above the crenelated towers of the city walls. The hills disappeared in the black haze. The air burned and was full of sharp dust that made the eyes shut. And over there, the evil darkness wrapped itself around the three crosses with near relish. It was like a wind of horror from the abyss.

My God, my God, why, why?

*

They had stood here for a long time, patiently and persistently. In the manner of women, they had bided their time. They had seen the powerful go forth and dish out their scorn. They had seen the enemies stand together like victors on the battlefield. They had known their smallness and helplessness, and they had bided their time.

The heat was frightful, the darkness thick; the wind, the dust, and the flies agonized them, but they held out. It was too much for the powerful. The victors had enough and drew back. The big strong men said that no one could stand here any longer. One after another, they disappeared. But the women held out.

They heard the desperate cry, and they drew closer, inconspicuously and cautiously so that no one would drive them away. They watched the men down there stir and go still again. The soldiers reclined on the ground, exhausted by the heat. They only moved to chase the flies away. Only the officer stood looking at the cross.

Again, the Master cried. His cry pierced through the haze. It was as if all his power had coursed through him and rose up against the heavens. Though one could tell that his lips were already stiff and hard, they could distinguish the words "Father, into your hands I commit my spirit."

Then the men up there rushed. They cried to each other and pointed at the city. It was as if the earth writhed in agony. A quake shook the stone under them, and the hot air rocked. The men yelled in extreme amazement, and the centurion ran to the cross. Very slowly and carefully, he touched the naked skin of the crucified.

Then the women went forward. The other spectators had already dispersed. They drew their coats over their heads as if they wanted to protect themselves from the darkness. They laid hands over their heads as if they feared that something would fall upon them. They beat their breasts and looked about with quick shy glances, like a man does when he thinks he is in danger in the dark.

The soldiers sat up again. They had moved closer to each other, crouched together like scared goats in a storm. Only the centurion stood upright, austere and serious, as if he held vigil for the dead. He looked at the women with a glance that had something of the Roman pride remaining and then said in broken Greek.

"This man was the Son of God."

He Came among the Rich
First When He Was Dead

He bit his teeth together and pried again. The spike remained anchored fast in the timber. It was then that he climbed down from the cross and offered the soldiers a coin to get them to help him. But he had seen how they cut the hands off of criminals when they took them down, and he didn't want them to do that with Jesus.

The spike squeaked and gave after a little tug. He dried the sweat from his forehead and pried again. It was already dusk, but there were no stars this evening, and he did not want to see when the Sabbath started.

Someone stood down there and greeted him. He recognized Nicodemus and stepped down. They looked shyly at each other. They had not spoken much about this before, and they barely knew where the other stood. Now it was clear.

Nicodemus went over to his donkey and lifted the burden gently. He opened one of the bags and looked through the contents.

"You can take as much as you want," he said.

It smelled of aloe and myrrh. Joseph nodded. His first thought was that such a quantity of the expensive oil was completely unnecessary. But he understood Nicodemus. He himself had emptied his coffers when he went to Pilate. He would have paid whatever it took to save this dead body from the landfill fire in the valley of Hinnom.

It was strange that Pilate was so accommodating . . . He had gone there with his heart in his throat. He thought he was risking his life and freedom by showing his ties to the executed insurrectionist. But Pilate didn't even ask for money. Pilate had only been careful to ask if the condemned man was already dead. Then he had sent for the centurion, and when he had spoken with him, he readily gave permission and almost showed a hint of regret.

The best was that Nicodemus had his servant with him. He took over the pliers and attempted to pull the spike. They silently worked as it grew darker.

When the body lay on the ground, the dead man's mother and one of his disciples came. They stood quietly and looked at her distress. There was nothing they could do.

Could he have done anything before? He had been too late for the first trial, and then at the second, the matter had already been decided. What could he have done that Jesus could not have done for himself? Yet Jesus, at least, had given his confession and was killed for it. He himself had been silent. He had more to atone for than he could accomplish this evening.

They helped to carry the body down into the garden. It was with a little shiver that he took hold of the cold arms with the black streaks of clotted blood. Jesus was already hard and stiff. It was inconceivable that this heavy lifeless mass that was sagging down in the linen sheet spread out for him had still been the man that stood straight and tall before his judges at dawn.

Now he was finished. Nothing remained but disappointment and disgrace. And then their helpless affection had nothing to look to but the dead corpse.

They washed the blood away as well as they could. Their unaccustomed hands took hold of his limbs with timid reverence. Then they stretched him out, and again, they looked at his stiff face and broken lips and wrapped him in the linen sheet. Afterward, they took the shroud and began the arduous work of ointment and bundling. It went as well as it could. Perhaps there was opportunity to do it better when the Sabbath was over.

It was almost dark, and they had to finish. Joseph lit his lamp and entered the grave first. It had just been finished, and the stone was light colored and bland. The stone hewer's chisel marks were still visible by the thousands. To the right, the arch bowed over the grave benches that were cut completely into the stone.

He looked down into the elongated niche that was sunk into the bend along the rock wall and filled the whole space under the arch. He had thought his own body would rest there.

The others came in. They carefully lifted the dead man through the low tomb opening. Then they put the white shroud down in the stone niche and eased the limp body onto the stone bed. Like a fallen prince, he lay there in a pure-white shroud. The damp chill of the tomb was filled with the odor of the ointments.

They had done all they could, and yet nothing was done. They left with few words. Laboriously they rolled the large stone slab and managed to keep it on its edge, lifting it with the help of a couple boards over the rim of the door before letting it fall into its hole. It shut with a dull thud. It sounded like the stone had sighed.

They went home just as quietly. The women cried the whole time, a quiet and hidden crying that did not want to be seen by the world.

Joseph wished that he could cry like them. What would he do now? He could not eat the Paschal lamb since he had made himself unclean with the dead body. In the morning was the Sabbath. And then?

It was best to travel to Arimathea and see if the blossoms on the olive trees had fallen victim to the terrible heat. Then he would not have to encounter his peers on the council and answer their derisive questions . . .

And then he might attempt to live even farther away. A prophet was dead, and a great hope was extinguished. But God still lived. Nothing had come of all that they had expected. But the wait still remained. The kingdom had not come; the promise had not been fulfilled. But the promise still remained . . .

I Have Sinned

"I have sinned . . ."

Judas twisted his hands and lifted his head. His eyes showed his distress. Then he continued:

". . . Because I have betrayed innocent blood."

Now it was said. He had tried to avoid saying it, but there was no way for him to escape. He would still go up to the temple, because the high priest and all his aristocratic ilk were gathered up there during the great Passover sacrifice. He had to wait endlessly in the heat. Now he finally stood before them.

They looked at him, scornful and hostile. Their faces became impenetrable, absolute, and closed off to his confession. It seemed as if they refused to let it into their consciousness. They were content to look at him scornfully. Their eyes said that he looked ridiculous, theatrical, and overly emotional.

"How does that concern us?" they said. "Answer for it yourself."

Judas lifted his hands, spread his fingers out, and wove them back together again. Then he tore the leather pouch out from under his robe, ripped it open, and threw the contents at their feet so that the silver shekels slammed against the stone floor and clangs rang out through the wide arches. He left without looking. He didn't notice the men who thronged about him in the forecourts. As if being chased, he ran to the gates. Now he was rid of the money, the cursed blood money. And then that wasn't quite right either. It was just no longer his. The land was already purchased. The down payment had been made. It was the promised purchase price that he had thrown away.

He laughed loudly. That fit perfectly. Laughed at by the high priests, despised by his friends, and now he was the owner of a piece of land that he could never pay for . . .

And guilty of another man's death!

But he had never thought that it would go this way! Jesus himself had said that he was the Messiah. If it was true, this never would have happened. He had only taken him at his word . . .

But did that help? He wasn't the Messiah. He was a zealot and a fanatic, a strange dreamer who lived in his own crazy world . . .

A fanatic, yes, but should he be tormented for that? A dreamer, certainly. But particularly good in his foolishness. Insane, sure, but most crazy in that he trusted in the one who had betrayed him and wished well for his enemies in the end . . .

Judas watched, as if in a dream, how the stone walls passed him by and how oncoming humans stared at him with strange eyes. Did they already know what he had done?

He had rejoiced in this piece of land. He had wanted to have it as a last piece of security, an opportunity for a future here in Jerusalem. Now this dream too was shattered.

Was he not a fanatic and a dreamer too? Why had he allowed himself to be carried away? Was it not the fault of the Master, he who captivated everyone with his word and got them to do the most unreasonable things?

Perhaps it was his fault. And still, he had meant well. He had never been false, never sought his own advantage, but shared everything. Never again would he, Judas, the son of Simon from Kerioth, encounter anyone who took him in as this man had. And he had betrayed this man!

He had seen a glimpse of him when they led him out . . . No, he wouldn't think of that. And still, the picture was burned into his brain. It followed him up one street and down another.

Where would he go? There was no place to go. Who concerned themselves with Judas Iscariot any longer? Who would know a traitor who was guilty of spilling innocent blood?

He noticed that he no longer ran around haphazardly. He walked half-asleep, and still he was hideously aware of why he went to the gates of the city.

*

This was God's judgment. God's wrath rested upon this land. And upon who would it rest heavier than on Simon, the son of Jonas, he who was once called Peter?

The sun shined again today, but still he lived in complete darkness. There was only one thing that stood firm, with hideous clarity: now it was finished.

He had failed as fundamentally as a man could fail. He was a betrayer. He was just as bad as Judas. He was a denier and a perjurer. When the Master went away to die, he bore not only the burden of the Pharisees' evil and the unbelief of the people, but even Peter's own denial and ungratefulness. They were all guilty for his suffering.

And now he was gone! Never would Peter be able to hear a word from his lips that could explain the unexplainable. Everything would remain an unsolved mystery. He would not ever be able to ask him for forgiveness.

Was it strange that Gods wrath was upon them? He had felt the darkness terribly yesterday. As a cursed soul, he had wandered about from hiding place to hiding place. He had dared climb up onto the city walls once, and he saw the three crosses. It had been too much for him. He had been powerless, broken down in body and soul, condemned and forsaken by God himself.

Must not the earth itself heave in bitterness when something such as this happened? When the ground trembled yesterday, he had believed that it was the hour of vengeance. And who would it then affect if not him?

However one explained the unexplainable events of yesterday, it was obvious that something fearful had happened, something that touched the foundations of existence. When he saw the sun go up in the morning after a sleepless night, they had come and told the story of how, at the morning sacrifice, the priest had rushed out of the temple in extreme fear and the high priest was called there. It was whispered that the veil within the Holy of Holies was rent. It bode misfortune and downfall.

Had it not been the Sabbath, Peter would have fled the city. Now he lay prostrate on his mattress waiting for the hours to pass. He had already made up his mind. At dawn, he would go to the harness maker and get the belt repaired. Then he would gather his things in Bethany and walk home. James and Andrew would follow. It was already agreed.

So then it was finished . . .

Was it also finished for the people of Israel? Had they now rejected the last of God's envoys? Had they spit upon God's outstretched hand? Was it a judgment of God that Jesus had died? Had God taken his hand from them forever?

They did not deserve better; neither did he himself. But why had it hit the innocent? Why would the Master suffer? Now the dark powers ruled, he had said. It was a terrifying truth. But had not God then always rescued them from the powers of darkness? Had darkness received power over God's Messiah too?

Was he the Messiah?

If he was not, then the darkness had woven its spell upon them and blinded them for years. In such a case, none of them dared any longer to distinguish between black and white, between truth and lie, between right and wrong.

Or was there something more powerful than God's Messiah? Could the powers of darkness be victorious over God's envoy?

In any case, it was sure and certain that the Master's enemies now had all the power in the land. No one could any longer speak the name of Jesus without being scoffed at. He would be called a false teacher and a deceiver by all the coming generations, if his name was even remembered. And one would feel bad for those who had once had put their trust in him.

Peter could never speak in the Master's name again. He could no longer walk in the glory of God. He had forfeited all right to it. He would walk home and manage his affairs. He would take up the net and try to harden himself against the disgrace. Perhaps it would be best to flee back to Bethsaida? Or farther away?

"Behold, Satan has asked to have you in his hand . . ."

Had God perhaps abandoned them and handed them over for the sake of their unbelief? Were they forsaken for all time, without future and without hope?

A single drop of comfort he had in the darkness was this: the Master had at least not hated him, had not despised him. Dared he interpret his last looks as if there was just as much love as before? This was then the drop of comfort, but it was given him in a cup that was filled to the brim with reproach. It was precisely this inconceivable love that he had so sinned against. It was this good Master who had prepared such sorrow for this unfortunate day. And it could never be made good again.

Was it possible for something like that be forgiven? Should he be able to pray any longer? Dared he even look up toward God after this?

No, he did not dare. And still, there was something within him that cried for mercy the whole time, cried without words and perhaps without hope of the prayer being heard, but he still could not stop crying.

Someone came from down there. He went out onto the roof and then sat behind the wall of the upper room to avoid encountering anyone. By this time the next morning, he would already be far down the road to Jericho.

The Day That the Lord Has Made

The daylight quivered a little as it hovered above them. The city slept. Thestreets were empty. Even the fortress tower seemed to sleep as it leaned against the massive walls. A lone rooster greeted the waking day with a shrill crowing, and another answered outside the wall.

On the other side of the city gates, they encountered a newly awakened wind carrying the scent of rain-soaked ground and fresh greenery. An early bird moved around in the dark behind the leaves, attempting to strike up a warble. No one answered, and again, it became completely quiet.

The women walked in complete silence with their bundles on their head. Their soft feet made almost no sound as they touched upon the stony ground, and their eyes were directed toward the half-invisible steps that slowly brought them down through the valley and into the quarry.

Soon they would be in front of the place where they had seen him laid. They stopped and consulted each other again. They weren't sure if there were enough of them to move the stone away. In the worst case, they would have to get some of the disciples. But they didn't really want to. The men would certainly say that all this was unnecessary. They had already bound him and given him salves and ointments. As if they even understood the matter. The women had to smile. At home, it was always their responsibility to bind up the dead, and now for once, they wanted with all their heart to do this work that they would otherwise like to push away from them. They were not about to leave the matter in the untrained hands of men. They had followed the Master to the last bitter moment up there on the rock. They had earned the right to give his dead body this one last service.

The daylight rapidly grew above their heads. The stars faded and the light rose up above the Mount of Olives in a clear blue that became ever brighter and filled with gold. The birds began to sing, and in the steps before them rose an ever-growing jubilee to the new day as they walked along. Even the blood-red anemones that covered the ground had gotten their color back and looked up to the heavens expectantly.

It was then that Maria Magdalena shrieked. She peaked over the crowns of the olive trees at the mountain before them, took hold of the bundle on her head, and began to run with small short steps.

Again, the grave disappeared before her eyes. She ducked smoothly under the trees and gingerly stepped over the low stone wall. The whole time, her eyes searched the great rock where the grave was, over there to the left of the garden.

She got stuck in the branches of a fig tree. Trying in vain to pull away, she took the bundle from her head and loosened her cloak before running again. Now she saw the grave. She let her glance sweep over the crown of the rock and over the smoothly carved area before the opening to make sure she didn't miss anything. There was no doubt about the matter. There, on the smooth stone floor that formed a small vestibule, they had wrapped him. And now the huge flat stone door lay there, face down, the empty black entrance to the grave gaping at her behind it.

She was ready to burst into tears. Who had done this? The Romans? The high priests? What had they done with him?

She rushed through the opening, ducking in to take a look. She stepped aside to let the light of dawn in. With her cheek against the stone, she searched the dark.

The heavy odor of myrrh wafted against her. There was something white laying there in the dark. It was bundling. Immediately, she saw that it had been removed from his body. And behind it, there was a long dark gaping hole in the rock. That was where they had laid him.

In the deepest distress, she turned around. The others stared at her, their eyes full of fear. She screamed at them, saying he was gone. Then she began to run back. Peter had to come now. He must find them help. He must find out where they had taken him.

Who had done this? Surely they hadn't taken him to where they incinerated garbage, where they had thrown the other two? She stopped. Perhaps she ought to have looked in the garden. No, it was best that she found some help with this.

She was running again, panting as she climbed with soft steps. The clouds in front of her were a faded red, and the blue morning air was permeated by a warm golden-red shimmer. The song birds joined into a blur of trills that drowned out the roosters crowing. The sun would soon be seen behind the mountain. She stopped to pant, took courage, and ran again.

Where had they taken him?

*

Peter tied his girdle. Now there was nothing to do but wait until the bread was finished baking, and then he would go to John Mark's. The others had promised to meet him there with their knapsacks. Then everything would be ready for the departure.

He looked out through the open door. Perhaps they would make it out of the city before the sun rose above the Mount of Olives. Then he would never again return to this city that murdered the prophets and stoned those who were sent to her.

No, he couldn't unravel the whole skein again. What was done was done. He went to the door and picked up his sandals. He was lucky that he'd had them repaired already yesterday.

He tugged at the new belt to test it. It held firm. Then he went to the bed roll and gathered up the last of his possessions.

He heard rushed feet down in the garden. Someone shouted for John.

He got up and stood completely still. There was anguish in the voice and steps. He listened attentively. A door shut.

Then he rushed out onto the roof and down the stairs. It was empty in the garden, but the door was open.

There, in the dim light, he ran straight into the arms of John and Mary Magdalene. Panting and disheveled, she begged them to come with her. She said that the grave was empty, that they took him away, and that the stone was on its face.

They looked at each other with quick glances, half-perplexed and half-determined. Then they ran through the garden's open gates out onto the street.

Out in front of the palace, Peter slowed his pace. He couldn't keep up the hard pace any more. His side ached and his legs refused to follow. He began to pant and continued with long stumbling steps, though he half-ran a bit farther.

John noticed it and slowed his speed. He had gotten a good head start but looked around every once in a while in order to not lose Peter. He, of course was the one who should show the way.

Peter was ashamed that he had almost left the city without taking a look at his dead Master's grave. It tortured him that he hadn't thought about it before. But perhaps it was best that way. There was so much that he hadn't seen and would not see. He looked shyly at the wall, behind which was Gabbatha. He remembered how he had stood there and screamed so that it could be heard all over the city. It didn't help that he had even put his fingers in his ears.

Did that really happen the day before yesterday? It seemed as if a month had passed since then. That was a different time, a different life, a different world. A chasm of darkness and guilt separated now from then.

They had come out on the open field. The steps went down, and it became easier to run. The first rays of sun swept across the Mount of Olives. The soft velvety greenery of fig trees glowed, and golden butterflies fluttered over the steps. The air smelled of morning flowers.

He had to walk a little farther. He was soaked with sweat, and his side felt like he had been stabbed with a knife. John was still out ahead of him, and Mary followed far behind.

There was the grave!

The golden rock shined in the morning sun. The grave's smoothly hewn front was turned to the east, and the stone rose like a golden-brown wall behind the fig trees. The opening was black, like an open mouth.

John had stopped in the little open foyer. He bowed forward, almost shyly, and seemed hesitant to enter.

Again, Peter ran. His head throbbed and his ears were ringing. He looked at John as he panted. Then he ducked down and pushed his broad shoulders through the opening.

At first he didn't see anything, but as soon as he left the opening, a stream of light fell in and flooded the grave. In just a second, he comprehended everything. The chamber was new and neatly carved. It would have grave benches on three sides, but there was only one finished—it lay to the right as one came in. But it was empty. The grave bed was empty and dark, and in the corner along the side, there were binding clothes. The head cloth lay in its own place by itself, neatly folded.

It went dark again and John entered. He stepped to the side and looked around quietly, then shyly touched the bundling. He was very solemn and didn't say a thing.

Peter began to speak. He had gone through all the different possibilities that he could think of but found no reasonable explanation. He began from the beginning again, but it just became all the more mysterious. The other looked quietly and doubtfully at him, as if he wanted to be alone and still didn't want to say what he thought.

They went out into the sunlight again. Mary Magdalene was there crying. They looked around the garden for a bit. But it was improbable that anyone would have left him there.

Where were all the other women? Had they found any clues?

Peter suggested that they should go back into town. He was utterly perplexed. Perhaps it was better to go down to the place of incineration. In any case, they would have to get in touch with the women first. They wouldn't be able to start traveling until this was resolved.

Mary Magdalene stood and watched them disappear in the valley behind Golgotha. She had to smile through her tears. How similar they were in all weather! The one had approached the grave as if he was entering the Holy of Holies. He was quiet and listened as if he expected to hear heavenly songs of praise. The other had entered breathing heavily and sweaty, as if he had found a lost calf. And the whole time, he had spoken without finding a word that could resolve the mystery. And then they left as wise as they had come and left her alone there.

She cried again. Where had they taken him?

*

The road bent sharply around the corner in the wall where the stones were blackened and polished with age. Then it dove under the dark archway between a pair of houses built together and came out again on the crown of a long stairway that glistened in the morning sun. In the midst of these stairs, John Mark had his house.

The gate stood open, and a roaring murmur of voices assailed them. Peter had the presence of mind to shut the door behind him and barricade it with the beam. One couldn't be too careful.

He turned around and chased after John through the archway and into the garden. The shade underneath the pillars still retained the cool of the night. Mosaic tiles and small stones encompassed a washbasin that exuded a damp coolness, and the fruit-bearing bushes stood dark and rigid, as if they hadn't quite woken up yet. But the wall and moldings over the colonnade were already warm and radiant in the morning sun. The heavens were clear blue, and the doves cooed on the roof.

The garden was full of people. Andrew, James, Philip, and many of the others stood between the pillars, and a whole swarm of men and women crowded around them. On the ground lay staffs, knap-sacks, and bundles. One of them had come open, and the trampled spices spread their sharp scent on the stone pavement.

The women interrupted each other as they spoke. They were beside themselves emotionally. They tugged at the coat sleeves of the men; they cried and they laughed alternately.

Some of them turned around when they heard the steps. Their eyes were wide with excitement. Their hands shook. Their words were choked. Was it confusion, delight, or fear?

"Have you seen him?" they yelled. And before Peter could shake his head in response, they had begun to tell all at once, interrupting each other. They had seen him. But first, they had seen an angel. No, there had been two. The second one sat on the other side. But he came to them by the corner in the wall. They could not believe their eyes. They had thrown themselves at his feet. And now they should go to Galilee as the angel had said. No, first the angels had asked why they were seeking the living among the dead; they had said he had risen. And the Lord had also said that they would see him in Galilee. They shook with fear, but he told them not to be afraid. And the angel had pointed to . . .

Peter saw how Andrew shook his head thoughtfully and looked at Philip, who gave a quiet, wistful smile. Peter threw the palms of his hands up to the women, as if he was trying to silence a crowd of screaming children. Then he tried to ask them more. He received ten answers for every question, and none of them made him any wiser. The women were like twelve-year-olds who were wild with joy and could no longer curb their excitement. It was hopeless to try to get any clear answers from them. They said they saw the Master, but they didn't know where he came from nor where he went. They said that they saw angels, but they could not describe them. There were only a few—one or two men clothed in white—in the grave. They said that the angels had a particular greeting for Peter, but it was only that he should go to Galilee, and that was just what he meant to do.

The women were crying with zeal and excitement. They assailed the men with their protestations, they constantly began to tell the story over again, but it was impossible to get them to calm down and say an intelligible word.

There was banging on the door.

John Mark went and looked through the peephole. Then he removed the brace. It was a bunch of Galilean pilgrims and some disciples from the tracks around Jerusalem.

The women's excitement returned to them in a second. Peter looked at Andrew. The others came and gathered around, forming a ring. All eleven of them were there.

"Loose talk," James said harshly.

They nodded thoughtfully.

But where was he? The grave was in fact empty.

"It will be best if we stay," Peter decided. Then he looked around and asked, "Who will get us something to eat this evening?"

*

That such beauty could inhabit a world that was so grim!

Cleopas glanced over the powerful heights. Their crests were flat and wide, but they bowed toward the valley in slopes that were ever steeper the closer they came to the white ravine at the bottom of the valley. Each slope stepped down in stair-like ledges. They were all covered in verdant vegetation and lined with blue shadows that grew ever longer in the evening sun.

The path followed along one side of the valley. One after another terebinth stood wide and leafy between the low stone walls. Thousands upon thousands of blood-red anemones could be seen on the slopes, and there, between stone slabs peeked out brown and blue. Swallows swept by, the skies were clear blue, and it was completely quiet among the desert mountains. Only far away in the village on the horizon did the children laugh while they played, and their shrill voices sounded like the songs of birds in the tranquility.

He looked at the other man who walked with his head hanging and hadn't said a word in a long time. He surely felt the same. Of what concern was the beauty of spring to them? For them, the time of miracles had passed, and the sun they had thought would dispel the darkness over Israel forever had been extinguished.

Jesus had still been a prophet powerful in word and deed before God and all people. They had heard him over again, every time he came to Jerusalem. They had been convinced that he was the one who would redeem Israel. They had believed that this Passover would be a time of miracles as memorable as the Passover when the Lord brought his people up out of Egypt. They had heard him every day in the temple; they had prepared themselves with prayer and repentance to be worthy. They had become more and more confident that God's time was near.

And then for it to end as it did! They had seen the high priest sneer on the way from the place of execution. They had heard the temple guard mingle among the pilgrims in preparation, and jeer at this pitiable braggart who tore down the temple and drove the clouds of heaven and still did not know that one of his own had gone and fetched the police!

There was a wall of contempt and hatred that would surround the name of Jesus for all future generations, if it was even remembered. There was nothing to do about the matter. God's ways were inconceivable, and all one could do was bow to them. So they had turned back to tend to their vineyards and their ripening wheat fields.

It was a relief when they were able to take up company with one of the thousands of Passover observers returning from the holiday. He caught up with them where the valley turned and the path went up to the wide flat ridge. He asked them what it was that bothered them as they walked so that they talked about it the whole way. They stopped and looked at him almost reproachfully. Was he a stranger in Jerusalem who he did not know what had happened there?

"What then?" he asked, and they opened their hearts and let all their bitterness and disappointment flood out. They did not hide that they regarded Jesus as a great prophet and that they had hoped that he would be the one to redeem Israel. And when the stranger didn't contradict them or sneer at them, they also told him what had happened today: how the women found the grave empty, how they spoke of seeing angels and said that he lived, that a few of their own went and confirmed that the grave was empty as the women had said, but that there was no trace of him.

Then the man began to rebuke them, not because they had been gullible and followed an imposter, but because they were so skeptical and had too little faith to believe in all that the prophets had said. Had they never understood that the Messiah must suffer all this in order to enter into his glory? Had they never read that this was what would happen when the Holy One of God came to earth?

Then he began to instruct them. He went through Moses and the prophets and all the scriptures and showed how they all were filled with talk about the Messiah, how he was modeled and heralded, and how it was written of him that he must suffer and be rejected to fulfil God's will and redeem all people. Was it not written that he would be a guilt offering and that the Lord's will would then have success through him?

The sun had begun to sink before them, the colors on the mountain became deeper, and the odor of the ground became stronger. While they walked, the past began to shine with new splendor, and their eyes were amazed to see the ways of God with a clarity they had never before known. They saw that the Lord's chosen servant would be rejected and betrayed by men, so despised that his own would regard him as nothing and be offended for his sake. But he bore their infirmities, and he took their pain upon himself. Yes, it was written that he would be wounded for their transgressions and would be beaten for the sake of their misdeeds.

Like a gray strand of pearls sewn into the blue-velvet hem of the shadow, the long stone wall made its way over the back of the mountain. The sun was so low that it strewed splashes of gold through the grass. It was completely still, and one heard the hum of the swallows that chased by. They saw everything with dreamy eyes. The veil had been lifted, and they had seen the image of God's own Messiah: the king who came to his people, humble and riding on a donkey to bear the sins of many and to intercede for the transgressors; he who had been tormented though he humbled himself and opened not his mouth but stood quietly when he was reviled.

It was completely still and silent even in the village streets. An old man sat still by the wall and looked out over the meadows, as if he wanted to preserve this lovely moment when the sun did not burn but sank color and life into everything, when even the dry earth in front of the rocks was covered with fragrant flowers.

The stranger took his farewell to continue to the west. Then they both asked at once if he would not be their guest. And when he hesitated, they asked again, compellingly coaxing him. They didn't want to let him go. So he gave in and went in with them.

They were expected, and the table was already set. They washed and reclined at the table in the dim room where just a flicker of the golden-yellow evening sunlight illuminated the wall. The sun was now so low that the beam of light drew an almost horizontal line across the room.

Cleopas rested on his left elbow and reached for the bread to give the blessing. Then the stranger stopped him. With a smiling face, he took the bread out of the house father's hand and lifted it. Then he began to give thanks and bless it. Dust danced in the light as it reflected on his face while he praised God.

Both of them stared at the intercessor's face. Who was this? Who was he who thanked his heavenly Father who he hid this from the wise but revealed it to the simple? Who was it who praised the Lord of heaven and earth for all of his gifts and most of all for the day that he crowned all of his promises with fulfillment and all his words with completion. Who was this who blessed the fruit of the earth and bid them to eat of the bread that came down from heaven to give life to the world?

He broke the bread and offered it to them. Then they knew that it was he who had broken the bread with them before and made them guests at the heavenly banquet.

The sunlight on the wall went dark; all the yellow dust disappeared. A blue and melancholy twilight filled the room. And he disappeared in the same moment, just as quietly, just as calmly and irrevocably as the sun.

They looked at one another. Neither of them dared to say anything. They feared they were dreaming. But they still held the bread in their hands, the bread he had offered them, and on the table lay the crumbs that had fallen from their hands. But his place was empty.

Slowly and reverently, Cleopas brought the bread to his lips. Only when he had consumed it did he begin to speak shyly in a whisper, as if he feared to chase something away that still lived in the room or break asunder the last echo of the Lord's voice.

Then they got up. They didn't need to speak to each other. What the one left unsaid, the other filled in, and what neither of them said was said by both without words. They put on their sandals. They quenched their thirst with wine and water and put the bread, olives, and a piece of cheese in their bundles. Then they walked out again into the blue twilight.

On the way, they went through everything again from the beginning. They were increasingly overwhelmed by their joy, but there was still a trembling reverence for the unfathomable that softened their cheer.

Why had they not recognized him from the beginning? Had he intentionally hidden it from them? It was as if he went through the Holy Scriptures and hid himself there. When he had first come to meet them there, their hearts had begun to burn; everything began to shine with new splendor. Already at that point, they had seen his glory, and he had awakened their faith. But it was when he broke the bread and offered it to them that they understood that he who had been broken for their sake was now living among them.

The moon came up and made it easier to walk on the stones in the path. They had a silver shine to them against the black grass. Cleopas threw out the strange question: if they had not believed the scriptures as he had interpreted them, what would have happened then?

They were unified in their answer: then he would have gone away, and they would never have recognized him. And they praised God, who had opened their eyes and ensured that they believed what had been interpreted for them.

The night began to get cool, and the way was long, but the longer they walked, the happier they felt. They were agreed that they should go to John Mark's. There they would find the eleven, this they knew, and perhaps some of the other disciples too.

They remembered how tired and despondent the disciples had looked that morning and how strangely lifeless their faces had appeared among the women who could not contain their joy. What would they do now with our joy?

Cleopas smiled.

"If they don't believe us, then they must still believe the scriptures," he said. Then he was pensive before adding, "If we could only interpret them like him."

*

The one row of houses was white like marble, the other lay in deep darkness, and even the street was shrouded in blue shadows. They half-ran down the stairway. Their feet hurt and their shoulders ached of exhaustion and cold, but they couldn't keep from running the last few steps.

Their almost deafening knock on the gate echoed down the quiet street. A moment passed before they heard the careful steps within. They had the feeling of eyes watching them somewhere out in the dark. They knocked carefully and gave their names. Then the gates opened and they caught a glimpse of the old hunchbacked servant. He greeted them and then put the brace back behind them. Then he followed them over the moonlit garden toward the stairs to the upper room.

Cleopas realized that he had been right when he heard songs of praise in the street. They sang up there. They sang robustly and resoundingly.

He stood a moment on the stairs and listened. This was the Hallel of Passover! He heard the words clearly:

I thank you because you answered me
And became my salvation.

Peter was the lead singer this evening. His voice was full and clear:

The stone the builders rejected . . .

Cleopas continued up the stairs. He was almost in tears when the answer roared up there from all the others:

It has become the cornerstone.

Did they understand what they were singing? Did they understand that they touched upon the holiest of all that was holy, the most wonderful of all the wonderful things that God had done?

One would be able to believe it if one would judge according to the faithful song of joy. Cleopas sang half-audibly. Now he had tears in his eyes:

The Lord has done this,
It is wonderful in our eyes.
This is the day the Lord has made,
Let us rejoice and be glad in it . . .

They had come to the door that led into the great upper room. Although it wasn't barred shut, they were not let in until they gave their names. The door was immediately shut behind them.

Cleopas rubbed his eyes in order to see clearly. It was just like a Passover from his childhood. The whole hall was illuminated by lamps. As many as could find a place laid on the sofas around the table, others sat on the floor with their legs crossed, and, in the deep window niches, they had curled together and made themselves comfortable with blankets and quilts. The table was littered with the best of what the house had to offer. There was wine and honeycombs, Jericho dates, and salted fish from Magdalene. There was festal joy on all their faces, and they all sat together like one big family. The song of praise roared with the peculiar joy of the Paschal night, and the last word of it rose to a jubilee that lived on all their faces and lifted the hands of the women to the heavens.

Thank the Lord, for he is good,
For his mercy endures forever.

In the same moment, as the last line of the verse was sung and the long series of syllables that flowed forth in the same tone had broken in the little final melody, they were welcomed with a shout. Hands reached out, places were made for them, and shouts and questions echoed from all corners of the hall.

The Lord is arisen! He is risen indeed! He has shown himself to Peter! Mary Magdalene has seen him!

Again, the shouts washed over them, and an unintelligible tangle of voices tried to tell the story. He had stood outside the grave. Mary had thought he was the Master of the garden. But then he had called her by name, and then she recognized him. And the two angels had asked why she cried. And Peter had . . .

Cleopas had to smile. Now they were all like the women in the morning. And he himself was just the same. He motioned with both hands; he yelled that they should let him speak. He began to tell the story about the peculiar pilgrim, about all that they heard on the way, and about how they recognized him when he broke the bread. He noticed that he was telling the story incoherently and confusedly. He could not remember all the words from the scriptures, he was not able to frame the proper picture of God's Messiah, who according to God's council, would suffer for his brothers, and he could not describe the ineffable thing that happened when the Lord broke the bread. But he saw how they listened. He saw how their eyes were huge and amazed. He saw the young nod to each other and the old smile through tears of joy.

Suddenly he had a feeling that someone was looking at him from behind. Something was happening behind his back. He turned around. In the same moment, he broke midsentence and went silent, as if something blew out his voice like a flame.

On the floor between James and the old woman with the girl in her arms stood someone who had not stood there a moment ago. He stood in the midst of the others who sat shoulder to shoulder on the floor. He stretched out his hands and turned to them as if cautiously urging them to come forward. When he moved toward them, they looked up and all went quiet, staring at him as if petrified.

It was the Lord.

Cleopas knew it immediately. There was nothing about his clothing he recognized, neither in the face. It was instead everything that was the Lord: every movement, every little expression of his being that lived in his limbs and in his face. It was he who was the Lord himself behind every outer form and every temporary garment.

"Peace be with you," he said.

His voice was like his figure. All that was him lived in it. There was harmony with all the merciful and powerful words with which he had healed the sick and unburdened those laden with sin. It was the normal everyday greeting, and yet it was like a greeting from heaven. When he held out his hands and wished them peace, it was as if he swept away everything that was broken and gave them new peace with God, where all the past was forgiven and all their betrayal was forgotten.

They who sat on the floor rose up. They crowded around him, some moved back, and others leaned forward to see. Some hid their faces in their hands, others yelled in the greatest confusion; some fell on their knees and grabbed hold of his clothing.

The ring around him widened. It was obvious that they were more afraid than they were delighted. Did they think that he was a ghost?

His voice was heard again, loud and clear, full of mild laughter and good stringency. He seemed to smile at them and asked why they were so afraid. He seemed to rebuke them and asked them why they doubted.

They no longer turned away, but they stood immovable and dead quiet. Cleopas bowed to the side and saw a glimpse of the Lord, who smiled and held out his hands. He pointed to his feet. He asked them to see that it was him. He moved closer and stretched out his arms. He asked them to touch them. A ghost does not have flesh and blood, as they could see he had.

All at once they froze. It was as if no one dared to reach out with a finger and touch him. Did they all fear that this was a dream and that they would wake up as soon as they moved from where they stood?

The Lord looked around.

"Do you have anything to eat?" he asked.

It was some of the women who began to move. They took what was closest to them on the table and offered it to him: a bite of honeycomb and a piece of the broiled fish. He held it up, smiled at them, and ate it in their sight. Cleopas could see his hands again. They had been pierced through but still not disfigured. They were not like other hands and still they were in every stage and every movement the hands of the Lord, a reflection of everything he had done and worked. These red marks were no longer wounds. They were adornments and signs of glory, seals of the Messiah's suffering and seals of the New Testament that was executed in his blood.

While the Lord ate, the others lost their petrification. They bowed to him. They touched his clothing. They fell down and grabbed hold of his arms. They laughed and cried. They kissed his hands and ran their own through his hair. He pushed them to the side and went over to the others, greeted them and offered them peace. Then he sat at the table, motioned the disciples to him, and invited them to sit around him. They moved to the sofas together, and the others moved closer and made a ring around the ring around him.

He began to speak to them about what he had said when they journeyed together in Galilee and on the roads around Jerusalem. The peculiar words brought forth new clarity. What they had never understood became wondrously simple, and they felt in his hand the key to all the mysteries of the past.

Cleopas sat and looked at the ring of faces that closed in around the Lord. Now they experienced the same thing that he had wanted to relate to them but could not describe. Now their hearts had also been opened so that they understood that the Messiah must suffer this, that he must give his life as a ransom for many, but that God could not abandon his Anointed to the kingdom of death and neither let his Holy One see the grave.

The Lord began to speak about that which would happen. Now repentance would be preached in his name for the forgiveness of sins. It would begin in Jerusalem, and it would go out to all people. They would be his witnesses. But first, they must be clothed with power.

In the midst of his joy, Cleopas felt a nagging uneasiness that the Lord would now immediately disappear from their sight, as when they recognized him earlier. Cleopas knew that the Lord would not remain. There was something new about him, something free and changing but that could not be noticed with the eye or grabbed ahold of with hands nor described with words. When the gaze went from the Lord's face to the apostles', it was as if it came from a great spring flower to the stones among which it grew. And yet their faces were livelier than they had ever been before.

The eleven were the innermost ring around the Lord. Behind them came the new faces in new rings. They were Galileans and Jerusalemites, strangers from Alexandria, from Asia and Cyrene. There were old men with bald heads and gray beards, and children who slept in their mother's arms.

And this was just the beginning! Just as he had here forgiven everything and established everything anew, so also the circle would widen and the great news would constantly find new eyes to widen at this amazing joy.

The Lord continued to speak. He gave them the power and authority to forgive sins. The new covenant had now been executed in his blood. Now forgiveness would be shared freely and for nothing, just as they themselves had received it for nothing. Everyone who believed and received would be children of the kingdom. If they forgave anyone his sins, then they would be forgiven.

Cleopas felt how his heart pounded. Now they would not be able to keep him for much longer. Then they would be left alone again in the midst of this hostile city that lay out there in the darkness. He thought about the men who lived outside the boarded-up gates. He was seized by a great doubt. They were just as contemptuous and scornful as they had been in the morning. To them, all this would be complete foolishness.

But the Lord spoke again, and Cleopas was comforted. There was a resolution to all the mysteries, an answer to every question, a possibility in the midst of all the absurdity—he who had died for their sake but who God had awakened and made to be the Messiah and Lord. God had done this. Now nothing could be impossible any longer. If God had conquered death, destroyed their sins, and given them back their Lord, then it was not to abandon them again. The Lord would surely disappear from their eyes, but they would never be alone. This was only the beginning.

While He Blessed Them

"Lord, is it now that you shall restore the kingdom to Israel?"

It was Simon the Zealot who asked. James looked at him with a furtive smile. He still talked with the old words, as if he expected that the Lord would become Caesar and that they would receive provinces to govern. James knew very well that the kingdom would be something completely different. What, none of them could say, yet they still thought about it every time the Lord stood among them. He himself possessed the new. He was the same as before and yet completely different. He was unbound from the length of the journey and the hours of the day. He was not shut out by any door, and no stone wall could keep him. They had spoken of what this meant: This must be eternal life. This was the power of the resurrection that made all things new. And this was the power that would again give birth to the new form the kingdom would have.

But when would it come? Simon had asked for them all, and even James looked at his Lord questioningly.

But the Lord gave the imperceptible smile that always appeared on his face when they questioned him childishly, and he didn't answer their questions but instead told them about that which they should have asked.

"It is not yours to know the time or the hour that the Father has ordained in his power. But when the Holy Spirit comes upon you, then you will have authority to be my witnesses both in Jerusalem and all of Judah and Samaria and to the ends of the earth."

In all of Judah . . .

How huge the land looked from up here! They had climbed the Mount of Olives. There was no wind, and the air was perfectly clear. A few individual clouds floated over the mountain tops to the north, and the evening's shadows began to grow long in the desert. The horizon was endlessly distant. Here lay all of Judah and Perea; over there lay the mountains of Samaria and the cities of the Decapolis. And over there began the great wide world.

And where would they be his witnesses?

He would not even show the power of his resurrection before men. James wanted that. He would have begrudged the high priests to stand there with their mouths open and fear in their eyes. But he had understood that this was not the meaning. He who didn't want to believe would not see anything. There was no way around repentance and faith, even now. The power of the word would open hearts and eyes. Otherwise, they would remain shut. That the Lord would finally triumph over their despisers was obvious. But he would never shame them into obedience. His kingdom was not of the same type as Herod's or Pilate's, where a man showed his power and forced respect. It was as he himself had said when they asked why he did not reveal himself to the world: If anyone loved him and kept his word, then he would share in the new kingdom that would now come. But he who did not believe these words or that God himself spoke to him, he would not be convinced even if someone rose from the dead.

Suddenly, James took his gaze off the horizon and looked at the Lord. He had lifted his hands, just like the high priest lifted them when he blessed the congregation in the temple. James fell down because these hands were not the same as other men's. And even when they were not lifted in blessing, they encompassed all that which lived in them when Jesus walked among men. There was the miraculous power of faith that had lifted the dead girl from her bed. There was the authority that had stifled the cry of the possessed man in the dark. There was the royal power that could calm the waves and the compassionate healing judgment that threw off fever and disease. There was the almost caressing tenderness that had touched the heads of children to give them a share in the kingdom, and there was the devotion with which he broke bread during the thanksgiving and set it before him, full of the same divine life that was hidden within himself.

Ever higher did these hands of blessing raise themselves. Now they were over the eleven. Now they seemed to lift themselves over the city that lay down there, and over the whole land.

Only then did James realize what was happening. The Lord vanished from their sight. He was taken from their view, but not in the same manner as so often before. This time, he was taken up. He went into the heavens. How it happened, James could hardly fathom. When he looked up, there were only white clouds that blinded him. Then he heard someone ask why they stood there looking up to the heavens. This Jesus who had been taken up should come again in the same way.

It was two strangers who came there. They spoke with the self-evident familiarity that normally characterized those who were disciples.

The eleven looked at one another. At first, they said nothing. James thought about the morning when they left the mountain and only dared to whisper. Even now, their voices were shy when they finally began to ask each other if they all had seen it. Some asked if it was all over now. But Peter answered, "No, now it begins." Then it was quiet.

Then Peter lifted his hands and prayed. He prayed to his heavenly Lord, and while he prayed, they understood that it was Jesus whom he meant. They all lifted their hands and looked upwards. Peter thanked him for the years of pilgrimage and for the discipleship, for being permitted to be his envoy, and for how, in the future, they would enter into his glory though they did not deserve it. He thanked him for salting them with the fire that had burnt everything they trusted in and they themselves, because they fell so short with all that they tried to do on their own. He thanked him for how they now must expect everything from above, and that the work was not their own.

They all said amen. The strangers disappeared. They looked after them in wonder. Then they nodded to each other meaningfully. The only thing left to do was return to Jerusalem and wait for the Spirit that had been promised to them.

On the slopes, they encountered a pair of noble Jerusalemites who were obviously on the way to their suburban houses. Though the route was shorter than a Sabbath's journey, they rode on their donkeys. They sat on ornate leather saddles. Their hair was styled according to the latest fashions, and they had a servant behind them. James stepped to the side and felt a condescending look fall upon him, half-indifferently and half-pityingly. He looked down at his feet. His clothing was frayed at the hem. Rags and threads hung

around his brown legs, and his sandals were so worn out that his big
toe touched bare ground.

He laughed. This was more insane than any children's story. To
these fine lords, he would also preach that Jesus was the Messiah.
And to the whole city down there!

He hugged John hard.

"Have we ever seen anything crazier?" he said and smiled
broadly at his brother's wonderment.

"Look," he said. "Do you see the soldiers up there on the tower?
They were probably those that spit on him . . . and do you see the
rabbis walking on the rooftops, there to the left by the Water Gate?
They are learned men who can do something more than you, more
than all eleven of us together . . ."

John looked at him in complete bewilderment. Again, James
laughed and continued: It was really splendid. They couldn't do anything; they had never received even a hint of anything that could
be called formal education. They had no money, no rich friends,
and no influence. And now they would go out and preach that the
despised Jesus was the Savior of the world. They would make disciples of all nations, baptize them and teach them to observe what he
commanded, he who had been executed. It was really precious!

He laughed like a boy.

"What would you give me for it? And do you know what is the
most splendid of all?"

Then John also laughed.

"Yes, I know," he said. "It is this: that it will be a success for us."

James nodded, then he added in correction, "Not for us. But for
him."

When the Day of Pentecost Had Come

The old man lifted his head over the stone edge of the bath. The water ran over his bald head, wetted the tufts of his hair, and washed down his face. He caught it with his hands and scrubbed his thin limbs. He kept his eyes shut, his toothless mouth smiled, and he blessed the God of heaven that he was able to experience this day.

James kissed him on both cheeks and bid him to go in peace. He didn't have much time for each and every one of them. They stood in a long line waiting in the garden.

The next man was a little silversmith from the lower city. He stammered as he confessed his sins: false witness, adultery, witchcraft, and irreverence toward his contemporaries. And then the worst—he had been present and screamed "crucify" at the Passover. Could such a thing be forgiven?

James nodded. All could be forgiven. In the name of Jesus.

The other picked up his robe so that it hung on the belt over his hips. Then he bowed deeply over the washbasin. James poured water over him. He was not the first to confess that he had taken part in the killing of God's Messiah. It was precisely those people who Peter reproached because they gave Jesus over to those who despised the law and let him be nailed to the cross.

It was strange with Peter's preaching. At first, James admired it. The words came so clearly, as powerful as hammer blows, decisively and challenging. But then he had quit admiring. This was not the work of man. It was another who spoke through Peter, and one ought not admire him but pray. What had just happened was impossible for men.

James said amen to the silversmith's confession and asked him to come in the morning to a prayer that would be held in the temple at the ninth hour. Then he turned to the next man.

A young woman came forward. She was from Lydda and had come up for the feast of Pentecost. She cried, and it was not easy to hear what she said. James didn't bother questioning it. The Lord heard her in any case.

While he poured water over her long hair that fell into the basin like black ribbons, he got to thinking that never during his Lord's life had something happened such as happened today. Why had there been so many today that no one could count them? Why had it not happened while Jesus lived?

He had hardly thought about the matter before, he was ashamed to realize. This was the work of the living Messiah! He was the Lord who had walked with them on the mountains of Galilee, who spoke today and made it possible for all these men to have their sins forgiven. First, he had died in order to escape judging them, and then he had come back to offer them a share in his kingdom, where all was forgiveness and new grace. And now he had clothed his servants with power and poured out his Spirit because what happened was impossible for men.

The woman sobbed more slowly while she thanked God. He left her to her mother and looked at the young farmer who stepped forward.

What number was he? James had lost count. There were over fifty now, and it was still only a portion of them who he had received as his share. They had taken portions of them in groups. They had had a great quandary with the water. In all of Jerusalem, there were only twelve places where one could baptize as John had baptized in the Jordan. And they could not think of using the ponds for the sake of the high priests. They decided to use the washbasins in the house where they lived and pour water over those who wanted to be baptized.

There was in this young farmer's confession one thing that made James thoughtful: He confessed that he had commanded his wife to get water on the Sabbath. Was this really breaking the Sabbath? And had he nothing worse to reproach himself for when it came to his wife? Did the man feel his sins?

James thought for a moment about what he should do. But then he thought about how infinitely ignorant he had been himself when the Lord called him and even when they had gone up to Jerusalem. But he was still permitted to be a disciple, and Jesus had been patient with him. Now he was sent out to make disciples of others by baptizing them and teaching them to observe all that the Lord commanded.

The farmer had finished his confession. James motioned to him to bow over the stone edge. Jesus had died even for him. The call to the kingdom applied even to him. If he did not now understand what it really meant, then he would surely comprehend it when he had been a disciple long enough. Then he would also understand the truth, and the truth would set him free.

James stopped for a moment. It hit him that this must be the incredible work that remained before these people learned to observe all that the Lord had commanded. It had taken the Lord years of work and patience to open their eyes. He would be a good enough disciple if it happened for him the same way. Years of patience and work . . .

Slowly and solemnly, he sunk his hands down into the water and began to say the words the Lord had put on his lips.

*

His lips quivered when he gave thanks. He held the bread in his hands to break it as the Lord did. But he could not express the fullness of his heart in words.

Through the open windows in the wall, he could see the blue night and stars of the early summer night shining over the mountains. There weren't many lamps burning in the hall. Under each of them were seen tightly packed figures and brown hands lifted in prayer. He was reminded of dark summer nights around Galilee with a tired band of disciples sitting around the Master. He was reminded of summer evenings in the bold-colored sunshine with the Lord standing on a stone block in the midst of the thousand heads in the crowd, blessing five barley loaves. And he thought about the night when the Lord Jesus was betrayed . . .

Then it broke loose from his lips. Yes, it was meet, right, and salutary that they praised God at this hour and that they always and everywhere sang his praise. What they never thought possible, he had allowed them to see, and what was impossible for men, that he had done. Where there was always guilt and failure, where there always ought to have been wrath and judgment, there he had given them a new birth to a living hope. In boundless mercy, he had pushed aside his people's sins and restored them to the Messiah that they betrayed and rejected. He had given his people the Paschal lamb, whose blood took away the sin of the world, and instituted a covenant where all was forgiveness and undeserved mercy. Therefore, the company of heaven rejoiced, and on earth, his people joined in the praise that would never end.

Peter took the bread. He blessed the bread and repeated the words that the Lord said that night when he was betrayed: "This is my body, this is my blood. Broken for you, shed for many for the forgiveness of sins." Now he understood it. It was really for them that the Lord had died. It was not just the Pharisees who took him to the cross. It was all their sins that he bore in his body up on the wood of the cross. Therefore, they also all had a share in the grace that was now offered to them in lavish and undeserved richness.

James and Andrew took the broken bread out of his hand and offered it to others. It was all like before, and yet everything was new. Their Lord was gone, and yet he was with them in a new way. The world out there was the same as in the Passover, and still a new era had dawned. They lived on the border between two worlds, on the threshold of new age. The power of the resurrection was already revealed. The first fruits had entered the kingdom, and they would soon follow after. Now there was struggle and hardship. Already the high priests and the Pharisees threatened and gave them to understand that if they did not quit preaching boldly, there were means of silencing them. And then they triumphed and knew that they could never be defeated. They would continue until the return of their Lord.

How long would he tarry? Perhaps until the next Passover?

Or perhaps even longer? The gospel would first be preached to all people. Grace would be offered to all before the judgment came. That which happened now had happened for all and would be preached to all. Until the Lord was finished with his work.

He could tarry a long time. Perhaps Peter would be old and gray before the day came . . . No, he would not think of that. God alone knew the day. For Peter, it was enough to know that the time was precious, that the task was immense, and that there was grace and blessing without limit.

He offered the last piece of bread to Andrew, happily conscious that it was no longer him but the Lord himself who acted here. Therefore, he did not worry himself about the future. It was so comforting to know that the task that lay before them was absolutely ridiculous. For just this reason, they had only one thing to do: to obey that which was commanded of them, to speak that which had been given them, and to blindly trust in help from him who had defeated death. And he was with them. Every day. Until the end of the age.